W9-BHB-431

THE GREAT GAME

Foreign Policy Issues
A Foreign Policy Research Institute Series

Series Editor
NILS H. WESSELL

Managing Editor
CHARLES B. PURRENHAGE

The Great Game

Rivalry in the Persian Gulf and South Asia

Edited by
Alvin Z. Rubinstein

PRAEGER SPECIAL STUDIES • PRAEGER SCIENTIFIC

Library of Congress Cataloging in Publication Data
Main entry under title:

The Great game.

(Foreign policy issues)
Includes index.
1. Persian Gulf Region--Politics and government--Congresses. 2. Indian Ocean Region--Politics and government--Congresses. I. Rubinstein, Alvin Z. II. Series.
DS326.G66 1983 320.953 83-13831
ISBN 0-03-064016-4 (alk. paper)

Published in 1983 by Praeger Publishers
CBS Educational and Professional Publishing
A Division of CBS, Inc.
521 Fifth Avenue, New York, New York 10175 U.S.A.

23456789 052 987654321

Printed in the United States of America on acid-free paper.

Foreword

The Great Game is another volume in the Foreign Policy Research Institute's book series, *Foreign Policy Issues.* The series, including both collectively and individually authored works on contemporary international relations, provides a publications outlet for work by researchers at the Foreign Policy Research Institute (FPRI) and by other authors in the academic and policy communities.

The Foreign Policy Research Institute is particularly pleased to be associated with this volume, which was conceived by Alvin Z. Rubinstein and took shape as the result of the Conference on Security in Southwest and South Asia, sponsored by FPRI with the generous assistance of the Rockefeller Foundation, that took place at the Villa Serbelloni in Bellagio, Italy in June 1982. Dr. Rubinstein, a Senior Fellow at the Institute, organized the conference.

In recent years, the Institute has sponsored several national and international conferences, including the European Seminar on Critical Defense and Foreign Policy Issues, the Seventh International Arms Control Symposium, the Conference on Military Intervention in the Third World, and the Executive Conference on the Strategic Dimensions of Economic Behavior. Moreover, the Institute has conducted annual meetings with the Institute for the Study of the USA and Canada, USSR Academy of Sciences.

In sponsoring these meetings, the Institute has sought to act as a catalyst in the policymaking process, bringing new ideas to the attention of government officials, and developing an appreciation among the public and in the academic community for the pressing concerns of policymakers. By publishing the papers from such conferences, we seek to expand their impact in both the public and private sectors.

Of related interest to readers of this volume is *The Iran-Iraq War: New Weapons, Old Conflicts,* edited by Shirin Tahir-Kheli and Shaheen Ayubi, published by Praeger as the first volume in the FPRI book series.

Nils H. Wessell
Series Editor
Foreign Policy Issues
A Foreign Policy Research
Institute Series

Preface

Change in the Third World usually comes about through cataclysm rather than cooperation. In 1978, 1979, and 1980 three developments brought major upheavals in the regional and international politics of South and Southwest Asia—the communist coup in Afghanistan and subsequent Soviet occupation, the fall of the shah and the emergence of a militant theocracy in Iran, and the Iraqi-Iranian war. Each of these developments is a watershed of sorts, marking a radical departure from the past and ushering in an era of enormous uncertainty and endemic tension.

In the years ahead significant threats to international peace are likely to come from the tensions and conflicts that develop in the geostrategic quadrant that is the Persian Gulf-Indian Ocean region. This area has acquired a centrality in world affairs far different from the position it had in the recent past. The reasons are not difficult to identify: Economically, the oil of the Persian Gulf is a crucial and coveted resource; politically, Khomeini's revolution in Iran and the USSR's military takeover of Afghanistan have transformed the geopolitics and outlooks of all regional actors and further aggravated U.S.-Soviet rivalry; strategically, as the superpowers sustain their military buildups, one purpose of which is to project power in this vital region, so the various regional actors intensify their acquisition of modern weaponry; and militarily, the Arab-Iranian hostility and the Soviet campaign to crush the Afghan freedom fighters' movement will continue for a long time to embitter the general atmosphere and sow seeds for future unrest and insecurity.

An international conference on Security and Stability in South and Southwest Asia, sponsored by the Foreign Policy Research Institute, was held at the Rockefeller Foundation's Study and Conference Center in Bellagio, Italy, from June 14 to 18, 1982, with the following purposes in mind: to examine developments in these regions since the late 1970s and their implications for the area as a whole and for the future of the superpower rivalry; to evaluate the continuities and changes in the policies and perceptions of various regional actors; to assess the dynamics of U.S. and Soviet policies toward the region; and to speculate on the prospects for security and stability in the region. The focus was on the political and strategic dimensions of the different but interrelated issues and on providing as accurate an assessment of the situation as possible.

A number of individuals and institutions made the conference possible, and it is with great pleasure and a sense of gratitude that I acknowledge their assistance and generous support. The Foreign Policy Research Institute provided the funding without which the conference could not have been held; the Rockefeller Foundation made available its facilities in Bellagio, Italy, an environment conducive to serious, sustained, and candid discussions; Professor Aswini K. Ray, of Jawaharlal Nehru University, helped to make possible the participation of colleagues from India; and Lynn Smith of the Foreign Policy Research Institute provided essential administrative assistance. Those of us who presented formal papers benefited greatly from the comments of the discussants, who played an active role throughout. A list of all conference participants is to be found in the appendix. Working with the contributors has been a professional delight, and I would like to express my appreciation for their cooperation and courtesy.

June, 1983
Bryn Mawr, Pennsylvania

Contents

Part IV Functionalism

Part V Looking Ahead

Part I

REGIONAL DYNAMICS

1

The Stability of the Gulf: Domestic Sources and External Threats

Adeed Dawisha

Times, and indeed fortunes, change. For some, the change is deliberate and gradual; for others, it is rapid and dramatic. For the countries and peoples of the Persian Gulf area, the social and economic changes that have swept their once remote and insignificant region have certainly been rapid and dramatic. The great explorers of the nineteenth and early twentieth centuries, fired by the spirit of adventurism and seduced by romantic imagery, braved the inhospitable terrain in order to sip tea with the "noble bedouin." These early Orientalists would be hard put to find more than a handful of true bedouins in today's Gulf, dominated as it is by modern concrete buildings and large, air-conditioned automobiles.

Wealth, especially the accelerated momentum by which it descended on the Gulf in the wake of the October 1973 war, has been a mixed blessing. It has obviously improved the quality of life in a number of important social contexts: It has made universal education possible; it has facilitated a better health service; it has led to improved communications and housing schemes; it has allowed for the rapid imports of Western industrial know-how; and it has generally given the peoples of the Gulf the means to try and bridge the immense intellectual and technological gap that has existed between their region and the developed world.

Yet, it is possible that these social and economic changes have occurred too quickly and have, as a result, caused traumatic upheavals that have reverberated throughout the region. The impact of rapid economic and social modernization on a traditional, even primitive, society might very well lead to crises of personal identities and values that almost inevitably would be transformed into societal confusion and dislocation. It has been argued that this is what actually happened in Iran and what is gradually happening in the Arab countries of the Gulf. Yet time and time again, the pessimists have been confounded. The systems seem to persist, and there are very few indications that they have reached the beginning of the end. They seem to have successfully survived domestic, religious, and social dislocations, the Iranian revolution, the Iraqi-Iranian war, the takeover of the Grand Mosque in Mecca, and the perennial Arab-Israeli conflict. How have these states been able to survive and withstand all these powerful internal and external pressures?

This chapter will address itself to these complex issues. Could it be that the West has exaggerated the potency of these pressures; could it be that we have underestimated the ability of people to adapt to a rapidly changing environment; could it be that we have concentrated our intellectual efforts on the divisive tensions within Gulf society without bothering to examine the inner unifying forces in these communities and the ability of rulers to emphasize and manipulate the latter at the expense of the former? Or perhaps what we see now is simply a conglomerate of hollow political structures resting precariously on decaying social foundations. This chapter will not solve the puzzle; rather, it will attempt to identify and analyze some of the myriad complex internal and external factors that affect Gulf politics and political behavior.

INTERNAL FACTORS

The three traditional pillars of society in the Arabian Peninsula have been and continue to be Islam, the tribal heritage, and the family. Islam is a most powerful and pervasive force in the peninsula. Almost the entire population inhabiting the region is Muslim, whose devotion to religion probably surpasses that of their more urbane coreligionists to the north. This is probably because, although other Muslim countries can boast thriving civilizations that predate the advent of Islam—pharaonic Egypt, Babylonian Iraq, Phoenician Syria and Lebanon, and Achaemenid Iran—the cultural heritage and historical legacy of the countries of the Arabian Peninsula is traceable to the Islamic civilization alone. This unbroken Islamic continuity is at the heart of social and political activity in the peninsula. Moreover, unlike Christianity, Islam is a social, political, legal, and cultural system. In the Sharia the Muslims have a law that deals with all constitutional and legal matters and as such is treated, in orthodox

Islamic theory, as the only legally acceptable code. Consequently, to the devout Muslim, there can be only one legitimate system of government and that is derived from Islam.

The normative imperatives of Islam tend to bestow legitimacy on the centralized structure of political authority that characterizes all the political systems of the peninsula. The first major decision that the Muslim community had to make was the election of the first khalifa (caliph; successor) on the death of the Prophet Muhammad. The khalifa was given religious and political authority, a decision based on the Sunna (the traditions based on the sayings of the Prophet) that "religious and temporal power are twins." Moreover, obedience to the ruler is embodied in Islamic political heritage through the pronouncements of a number of renowned Muslim jurists, theologians, and philosophers in the centuries following the death of the Prophet, who "fostered the belief that rebellion was the most heinous of crimes, and its doctrine came to be consecrated in the juristic maxim, 'sixty years of tyranny are better than one hour of civil strife.'"[1] Such a doctrine, based on theological prescriptions, would tend to reinforce the authority and stability of the centralized and authoritarian regimes of the Arabian Peninsula.

The sectarian division within Islam between Sunnis and Shiites has constituted a problem for the Gulf rulers. All of the states of the Arabian Peninsula have substantial Shiite communities, ranging from 10 percent of the population in Saudi Arabia to more than 50 percent in the United Arab Emirates. In all cases, the economic and social status of the Shiites has lagged behind the rest of the population. The consequent disaffection was fueled by the revolution in Iran, which brought radical and expansionist Shiite clergy to power in Tehran. This, however, only meant that the Gulf rulers began to concentrate on improving the Shiites' standard of living to counteract the attraction of the Iranian clergy. This, plus the general disillusionment of the Gulf Shiites with the Iranian revolution, seems to have dampened any rebellious inclinations the Shiites may have had.

Tribal heritage is another important pillar of the social and political structure,[2] in which the roots of the modern Gulf states lie in the deeply ingrained traditions of tribal society. The structure of the modern political systems in the peninsula is an outgrowth of the distribution of political power as it had traditionally existed in and among the many tribes that inhabited the area. Indeed, even with the impact of wholesale Western modernization, which is rapidly changing the physical features of the bedouin's life, societal attitudes and mentality in general continue to draw heavily on the old and trusted tribal values.

Tribal attitudes, by their very nature, have contributed to the stability of the political systems in the Gulf. For centuries, the pattern of political loyalty in the tribal community was hierarchical, with authority focused on the sheikh, or tribal chieftain. Assisted by a number of tribal elders and religious personages, the sheikh acted as the central authority, the final arbiter of power, and the ultimate dispenser of justice. However, he could not operate outside tribal laws and customs and was as bound by them as any member of his tribe. In the process of transferring the loyalty of the bedouin from the tribe to the nation, the kings, sultans, and emirs of the Gulf states have tended to act, and be perceived, simply as tribal overlords. They have consistently endeavored to create a perception among their populations of "ruler accessibility," which itself was a hallmark of tribal political authority. Monarchical and princely adherence to tribal custom induces loyalty from a population that, while increasingly urbanized, still is influenced considerably by inveterate bedouin custom and tradition.

No less important is the role of family in Arab society generally and in the communities of the Arabian Peninsula in particular. The extended family is probably the core societal unit in the Gulf, the relationships within which have had, for centuries, a major determining influence on social and political attitudes in the Gulf. The traditional bedouin maxim of "my brother and I against my cousin, and my cousin and I against the outsider" can obviously be utilized by the ruling elite to foster national unity against a real or manufactured external enemy. The extended family, moreover, has traditionally been hierarchically structured with authority resting securely in the hands of the oldest member. Deference to, and respect for, family elders creates a far greater conformity within an Arab family than is usually the case in a Western family, where intrafamily relationships are less hierarchical. Transferred to the national milieu, the respectful acceptance, in a family context, of a hierarchical structure with a clearly identifiable authoritative personage at the top tends obviously to lessen rebellious tendencies among the populations against authoritarian regimes.

Political systems built on these three traditional pillars of societal coherence are basically stable. It was only through exposing these traditional systems to the process of modernization that cracks in the hitherto stable polities began to appear. The first problem was that of economic development. The sudden injection of massive wealth was naturally going to create inequalities that could lead to social disintegration. This has not happened because, unlike in Pahlavi Iran, where the rich became obscenely rich and the poor remained pathetically poor, the populations of the Gulf were so small and the oil bonanza was so great that everybody was able to benefit, and the various regimes were able easily to satisfy the minimum economic aspirations of the mass of the people.

Lack of indigenous manpower, however, meant that with the sudden rise of economic opportunities, the small populations of the Gulf could not on their own sustain the wide-ranging industrial and agricultural growth. Economic expansion, therefore, began to depend more and more on the importation of foreign labor. In 1979, the percentage of foreigners in the population was 13.9 in Bahrain, 21.0 in Saudi Arabia, 25.0 in Oman, 52.5 in Kuwait, 61.8 in Qatar, and a staggering 70.0 in the United Arab Emirates.[3] Many of these foreign workers feel themselves still as outsiders and second-class citizens; and with their numbers rising, yet their social position relatively deteriorating, they have come to represent a source of concern for the various Gulf regimes.

Even more ominous for the political order is the change in the nature of Gulf society that was bound to occur as a result of rapid economic development. With increasing urbanization, accelerated education, and creeping Westernization, traditional values and attitudes, which had underpinned the stability of the Gulf regimes, were bound to be questioned. Religion was confronted by Western secularism, tribal values were being gradually eroded by the necessities of urban living, and the expansion of economic life began to dissipate the physical unity and inner coherence of the family. Thus confrontation between traditionalism and modernization would, as a logical conclusion, create a social crisis if not controlled. But here again, it would be difficult for the ruling elite to determine the parameters of possible control. The vexing question has always been how to balance the amount of imported modernization that is necessary for the advancement of society against the social and political shocks that might follow on rapid economic development. It is naturally a precarious balancing act, an indeterminate art rather than an exact science, where risks are many and outcomes unpredictable. But once bitten by the modernization bug, there is no turning back; the risks of unfulfilled rising expectations are even greater. So the ship of state has to move with the tide, and the rulers have to cut sail intermittently, often haphazardly, hoping that their strategy is the right one. In this, the various Gulf regimes have acted differently; the Kuwaitis and Bahrainis have gone farther down the risky road of social modernization than the more puritanical Saudis and Qataris. Whatever the pace, however, the fear of what may happen is universally felt, and as yet, there is no sure way of indeed knowing what may happen.

The problem for the rulers is to predict how much more pressure from the impact of modernization the old legitimizing values would be able to withstand. Some of these rulers believe that while rapid change is certain to produce tension, it would nevertheless take at least another generation for the present material revolution to bring about substantial social change. And in any case, there is much confidence in the traditional values of religion, the tribe, and the family to see the people through this transformation. Thus, Saudi Arabia's minister of planning, Hisham Nazer, insisted that the institution of the family was "the arsenal of Islam which will defend the Saudis against the corruptions of the modern world."[4] Other rulers would probably concur; concern is mounting, but there is no atmosphere of an impending disaster.

The present concern is directed less at possible social upheavals than at the near certainty of increasing political demands following in the wake of rapid economic and social development. The exposure of the Gulf's traditional societies to Western liberal democratic values would almost certainly lead to increasing demands for greater political participation. This first stage of political development need not be perceived as a threat to the existing political orders; indeed, the old ruling elites have shown themselves capable of adjusting to the new situation by successfully absorbing the emergent technocratic class into the various government structures. The problem lies with the second stage of political development that would manifest itself in further popular demands for the decentralization of the authoritarian systems. It is in this regard that "political modernization lags far behind social and economic development. The former would be likely to shake the very core of the power structure, and no regime proposes to bring about its own demise by political reform detrimental to its hold on power. The notion that without a strong center the whole society may fall apart is no figment of the imagination—no mere rationalization on the part of the rulers."[5] Here is the basic dilemma: Once the Gulf rulers decided to proceed with economic development, they knew there would be no turning back. Yet the process of development was bound to lead eventually to fundamental questioning of the political order itself. But it was no longer a matter of choice; they had committed themselves to the process of modernization, and the most they could do was to safeguard and emphasize the traditional values in the hope that these would continue to sustain them. That these values have done so thus far shows how firmly they are embodied in the political and social cultures of Gulf societies, and one should not be surprised if at the end of the decade these values, the traditional pillars of society, continue to prop up the existing authoritarian regimes.

EXTERNAL FACTORS

By far the greatest danger to Gulf stability over the last decade has been the Islamic revolution in Iran. The immediate appeal of the first truly grass-roots revolution that succeeded in overthrowing a secularist and Westernized "tyrant" was immense within the Muslim population of the Arab world. The Islamic revolution in Iran was accepted by Arab and non-Arab Muslims as a proof and a lesson of what Muslims could do if they clung doggedly to their faith. Many Muslims saw the Iranian revolution and other related activities, such as the takeover of the American Embassy, as the first Muslim victory over non-Muslims since the sixteenth and seventeenth centuries, when the Ottoman Empire was at its zenith. To the mass Muslim public, the victories of the ayatollahs during 1979 and 1980 over the "enemies of Islam," manifested by the West and its "enfeebled lackeys" in the Muslim world, represented the advent of a new heroic age of Islamic assertion and power. For Muslims suffering for centuries under Western intellectual, technological, and military superiority, the eclipse of the shah's, and by definition the West's, might in Iran simply emphasized that it is through Islam, rather than nationalism, Westernization, and other such modern concepts, that the Muslim world could defeat the Western "imperialists."

In this, the Gulf rulers, as indeed the Muslim rulers in the rest of the region, were at a disadvantage. Unlike the Iranian clergy, they were neither able nor prepared to confront the enemies of the Muslim world; on the contrary, many were allied closely to the very people who had "humiliated" Islam for so long. When, therefore, Tehran called on the faithful to rejoice with Iran over its defeat of the "American Satan," the people went to the streets in Dhahran, in Dubai, and in Bahrain and rejoiced. No one questioned the substance of the message; the masses were seduced by the imagery and the symbolism. The other Muslim rulers could do little more than wait and hope that the crisis would pass. To the rulers of the small Gulf states particularly, the power of the ayatollahs seemed overwhelming and at times even unstoppable. At the height of the love affair between the mullahs and the masses, on the first anniversary of Khomeini's triumphant return to Iran from exile, major riots occurred in Kuwait; in Bahrain, which took two whole days to quell; and in Qatif, in Saudi Arabia, which led to the near demolition of two banks, the burning of more than 50 buses and cars and the local electricity office, and the death of at least four people.[6]

But, like most tempestuous love affairs, when the initial intoxication soon begins to wane, and the act of seduction itself soon becomes more labored as frailties that had not been noticed in the earlier thrill of passion begin to appear with increasingly monotonous regularity, the Iranian revolution is beginning gradually to lose its virility. There can be no doubt that the internal Iranian situation is worsening all the time: Political power is diffuse; there is hardly a central decision making focus or an overarching moral authority; Ayatollah Khomeini no longer possesses the charismatic hold on the population that seemed so secure during the early days of the revolution; various political interests and centers of power seem to be in constant bloody conflict; assassinations and political murders are rampant; and the economy is in a state of virtual structural collapse. In February 1982, Khomeini himself admitted that all was not well with the revolution. In a message marking the third anniversary of the Iranian revolution, the Imam conceded that

> The Iranian nation is facing difficulties and problems which are unavoidable consequences of any revolution. They should know that as this revolution is a popular and an Islamic revolution, it has been more fruitful and has had fewer calamities than any other revolution in the world. Our revolutionary people should know that in order to protect Islam and the revolution and in order to safeguard the gains of the revolution and honour the blood of the martyrs, they should exhibit revolutionary patience and forbearance. They should not listen to the hostile propaganda of the enemies of the revolution and of Islam, who with all their might try to make people lose hope and despair of the Islamic Republic. They should know that most of those who are spreading poison against the revolution are those whose illegitimate interests have been harmed and who have been prevented from indulging in corruption and prostitution. Otherwise, the deprived classes who constitute the vast majority of people are faithful to Islam and to the Islamic Republic. Of course . . . the deprived and afflicted classes of the revolution have not endured as much hardship and difficulty as the great prophets and the illustrious Prophet of Islam throughout his life.[7]

As Iran stumbles from one economic crisis to another, as cracks and divisions begin to bedevil the unity of the revolution, and as the post-shah promised land recedes farther into the distant horizon, the early euphoria of the Muslim masses is quickly turning into nauseating disillusion—not so much in Iran itself, since as makers of the revolution, Iranians are likely to cling to the last vestiges of hope that the revolution will be redeemed, that it will soon deliver, that it will come good in the end. Meanwhile, they are still prepared to fight for and die for the ideals of the revolution. But those on the other side of the Gulf have not physically lived through the revolutionary experience; they have neither suffered the pain nor experienced the ecstacy, and as such, they are more fickle, more impatient, and less committed.

More damaging to the mullahs' prestige outside Iran has been their war with Iraq. True, Iran has survived the conflict and, through a fusion of patriotism, religious orthodoxy, and military pragmatism, Iran turned what appeared to be a runaway Iraqi victory at the beginning of the conflict into a ruinous war of attrition that gradually, yet surely, turned Iran's way. But the non-Iranian Muslim remembers well how, at the outset of the war, the Iranian clergy had confidently predicted that the Iraqi Muslim soldiers would soon revolt against the "worthless infidel who opposes Islam." The message to Saddam Hussein from Tehran was clear and confident:

> God will defeat your devices. In the coming days you will learn how the Muslim people and army of beloved Iraq will respond to you, and how the Muslim Iranian army and people will respond to you. You will know how you have dug your own grave—the grave of shame and humiliation in this world, and the grave of hellfire in the hereafter.[8]

The ensuing bloody stalemate in the war was, by definition, damaging to Khomeini's prestige. For it must be remembered that in the minds of Muslims, there existed a crucial difference between the secularist Hussein of Iraq and the spiritual, to some even divine, ayatollah. While Hussein fought the war with mechanical devices, such as airplanes and tanks, Khomeini's devices were mystical, employing the power of God and his angels. Hussein, therefore, unleashed a power against Iran whose failures and frailties were recognized and understood; Khomeini's power, on the other hand, by its very mystical definition, could not have any frailties.

Nor were the ayatollahs capable of achieving the one thing that they and their followers and admirers had so confidently anticipated—

the overthrow of Hussein by the Shiites of Iraq. The Muslims, even the Shiites, of Kuwait, Bahrain, Qatar, and Dhahran must have wondered frequently throughout this senseless war why it was taking the "divine" ayatollah such a long time to dispose of the "worthless infidel." Surely Iraq should have been the ayatollahs' most fertile ground: the only other Muslim country where the Shiites actually formed a majority, a country that neighbored on Iran and in which Khomeini himself spent 16 years in exile from the shah.

At the beginning of the revolution, at the height of Khomeini's prestige, the Iraqi regime worried about the effect the ayatollah's victory in Iran and his conscious effort to export the revolution to the rest of the Islamic world would have on its Shiite population. And, indeed, this was the immediate cause of the war. In a speech in September 1980, abrogating the 1975 Iran-Iraq treaty, Hussein declared:

> The ruling clique in Iran persists in using the face of religion to foment sedition and division among the ranks of the Arab nation. . . . The face of religion is only a mask to cover Persian racism and a buried resentment for the Arabs. The clique in Iran is trying to instigate fanaticism, resentment and division among the peoples of this area.[9]

After six months of war, it had become obvious that the Shiites were not going to revolt against the Baghdad government. Maybe it was because the ethnic division between Arabs and Persians proved a more potent force than the religious affinity between Iraqi and Iranian Shiites; maybe because the intelligent social policies of the Iraqi regime had succeeded in transcending sectarian divisions; maybe because the ayatollahs' power was simply exaggerated by friend and foe alike; maybe because the simple, semiliterate masses of southern Iraq and the Gulf could reach beyond the mist of Tehran's propaganda and see an Iranian reality that did not correspond to the clergy's sterling claims. For whatever reason, the Iranians, vigorously using religious symbolism, were not able to induce the dislocation of Iraq. And this time a clearly relieved Hussein confidently declared:

> There are Sunnis, Shii[te]s and other religions and sects in Iraq. All of them have been fighting obstinately for six months. Why this obstinacy and all these sacrifices, especially as we keep telling them that the land they are fighting on and dying on is not their land. It is very easy to tell the Iranians: "This is your land, the Iraqis are on it, so you have to fight to retain it." But it is difficult to tell the Iraqis to fight on a land which is not theirs. The Iranians have to understand, therefore, that it is not

> Saddam Hussein who is fighting them; it is the whole unified Iraqi people who are fighting to safeguard their values and their new spirit.[10]

Khomeinism, as a symbol of Islamic rejuvenation, as a standard by which devout Muslims, particularly Shiites, evaluated their own political leaderships, is no longer the threat to Gulf stability it was in the heyday of the Iranian revolution. The loss of potency is evident in Iran's own behavior. Whereas, in the past, the clergy's influence emanated from the virility of their mystical and religious symbolism, they now increasingly resort to war and to physical acts of subversion in order to assert their power. During their days of glory, it was the impact of the spoken and written word that shook the very foundations of the neighboring countries. Now the ayatollahs are reduced to behaving like mortals: They send troops and train guerrillas and still cannot induce the required changes in the neighboring countries. In the Iraq-Iran war, it was the Iraqis, battered, humiliated, and demoralized, who sued for peace almost at any price. On the other hand, the ayatollahs, less sure than before of their domestic support and conscious of their declining prestige abroad, found the war a convenient vehicle for bolstering internal morale and "revolutionary unity."

The change in Iranian fortunes is also evident from events in neighboring Bahrain. In February 1980, the mere anniversary of Khomeini's return to Iran created disturbances of such proportions that internal security forces, behaving with a brutality unseen before, needed two days to restore order. Almost two years later, Tehran needed to train more than 70 guerrillas and plant them in Bahrain with promises of support from the Iranian navy in order to destabilize the Bahranian regime.[11] This increasing resort to force as an instrument of foreign policy is a clear indication of the rapidly dwindling potency of Khomeinism as a revolutionary symbol that might destabilize the Gulf states.

Unlike 1979 and 1980, therefore, when Islamic revolutionary ideology constituted the main threat to Gulf security, now it is the actual manifestation of interstate conflict that poses the greatest danger to the stability of the various Gulf regimes. At the local level, there is, as has been discussed above, the Iraq-Iran war. Although the first year of the war probably served the interests of the Gulf regimes, as it highlighted to their own populations the ayatollahs' "human fallibilities," the persistence of the military conflict itself began to constitute an ever-increasing external threat to the Gulf states. Most of the major oil terminals in Kuwait, Saudi Arabia, Qatar, and the

United Arab Emirates are situated just across the Gulf from Iran, and as such were very vulnerable to the Iranian Phantoms, which had already proved their effectiveness in Iraq. If the Iranians were able to penetrate Iraqi air defenses and bomb targets inside Iraq, almost at will, they obviously could devastate the oil installations of the Gulf if they so wished. This was why Saudi Arabia very quickly took the politically risky decision to request five AWAC planes from the United States to protect its skies against any possible Iranian incursion. And, as though to prove a point, a Kuwaiti border town was bombed by the Iranian air force in the spring of 1981. Then, in October 1981, presumably to punish Kuwait for supplying Iraq with financial aid and oil products, the Iranian air force bombed Kuwaiti oil installations at Um Aish, 25 miles from the border with Iraq.

Shaken by this evident weakness to defend themselves or to retaliate in kind, the Gulf states proceeded to emphasize and give priority to defense and security rather than mere cooperation in the economic and cultural fields. On March 10, 1982, Saudi Arabia and the other five Gulf states formed the Gulf Cooperation Council (GCC) in order to enhance intra-Gulf economic cooperation and to strengthen internal security. The similarity of their social and political systems and a common identity of views over possible domestic instabilities naturally excluded Iraq and the two Yemens. The increase in Iran's military power, however, forced the GCC to add another dimension to the original rationale of the council. In February 1982, the interior ministers of the members of the GCC, aware of their vulnerability to Iranian power, and spurred by the Iranian-backed abortive coup in Bahrain, signed a comprehensive security accord. With Iran and the Iraq-Iran war in mind, the assembled ministers declared:

> Gulf security is indivisible. An attack on any one Gulf state is considered an attack on the other states. The responsibility for confronting an attack on any Gulf state falls on all member states of the Gulf Cooperation Council. And an interference in the internal affairs of any Gulf state from whichever source will constitute an interference in the internal affairs of all Gulf states.[12]

Particularly worrying to the Gulf rulers was Iran's mounting military power and its increasing ability to inflict a series of heavy defeats on the Iraqis. What if the Iraqi military effort were to collapse completely? What if the Iranian clergy, exhilarated by their victory and intent on keeping the army's attention away from the internal political and economic chaos, decided to claim a further bounty by moving into Iraq, or Kuwait, or Bahrain, or . . .? These might be morbid calculations, but Gulf neurosis could only be heightened by oblique Iranian threats such as the statement made by the Foreign Ministry in Tehran in May 1982, which reminded the countries of the "*Persian* Gulf Cooperation Council" that

> The thundering victories achieved by the combatants of Islam and disgraceful defeat and surrender of Saddam's mercenaries are clear signs of the superiority of faith over equipment and indicate the great power of the Islamic revolution. It is appropriate for the countries of the region to go through historical examples of disgraceful defeats inflicted upon the massive machine of world arrogance by the Islamic and popular movements and realize that it would not be possible to guarantee a real stability for the region without taking this power into account.[13]

No wonder, therefore, that the Gulf countries, at the helm of which stood Saudi Arabia, actively sought ways to resolve the Iraq-Iran impasses. As early as January 1981, the Islamic summit in Taif, in Saudi Arabia, placed a very high priority on trying to end the conflict. An Islamic mediation team was formed and tried vigorously, but without much success, to narrow the positions of the two conflicting parties sufficiently for a cease-fire to take place.[14] The search for peace, however, continued to be a high Saudi and Gulf priority, for having succeeded in underpinning the ayatollahs' moral authority after the first year, the war by mid-1981 had obviously served its purpose for the Gulf rulers and had begun to create new dangers the Gulf Arabs could well do without.

In complete contrast, the danger for the Gulf inherent in the Soviets' intervention in Afghanistan seemed to create greater ripples of alarm in Washington than in the states themselves. Objectively, of course, America's paranoia, real or manufactured, was as usual hugely exaggerated. The anguished cry that the Soviet takeover in Afghanistan meant that the Russian bear was but a few miles away from the strait of Hormuz either conveniently disregarded or was not aware of the fact that these few miles happened to consist of two mountain ranges and a particularly inhospitable desert. True, Afghanistan allows Soviet air power to be brought closer to the Gulf, thus increasing Soviet airlift capacity for a possible rapid interventionary capability. But all this depends on a stable and supportive environment in Afghanistan itself, and at present, as well as in the foreseeable future, this seems to be a forlorn hope. Anyone who knew anything about Afghan history and geography would have realized the enormity of the task facing the intervening Soviet troops. Nearly three years after the initial Soviet military thrust, almost 100,000 Soviet troops, backed by the most sophisticated and modern weaponry, are no closer to pacifying the rebellious country than they were when Soviet tanks first began to rumble their way through the streets of Kabul.

This in itself must have been a sobering experience for the Kremlin. Would they now dare contemplate a push through Iran, a much larger country with a terrain no less hostile than that of Afghanistan, inhabited by 40 million Muslims, the majority of whom have little affection for their northern neighbors? And even if they were to reach the Gulf, would the Arabs on the other side of the narrow waterway be any friendlier to the invading forces than the Iranians, and what costs would the Soviets incur having to control more than 1,000 miles of coastline against a much more powerful American amphibious capability,[15] helped vigorously by a universally antagonistic indigenous population?

These considerations might have escaped Washington's comprehension, but in the Gulf they tended to reflect the attitudes of the people and leaders alike. There was certainly a great outcry at the time of the Soviet invasion of Afghanistan, but this was due more to Afghanistan's Muslim status and its affiliation to the nonaligned group of nations than to any real fear of impending Soviet aggression against the Gulf. The feeling was, and still remains, that in terms of their economic and strategic importance, Afghanistan and the Gulf could not be equated or compared, and that the Soviet Union must be aware that the West's reaction to Soviet interference in the Gulf would be markedly different from its response to the invasion of Afghanistan. This sentiment was epitomized by Prince Fahd's assertion that the cardinal importance of this area to the West is not lost on the Kremlin.[16] In a typically more outspoken fashion Kuwait's foreign minister, Sheikh Sabah Jaber al-Sabah, insisted: "Nobody in the Gulf believes that there is a Soviet danger; this is being used by America in order to establish bases in the area."[17]

Indeed, it is this American persistence to establish a physical presence in the Gulf that might prove far more destabilizing than the Soviet threat. Constrained by powerful indigenous ideological forces, particularly Islam and Arabism, which preach strict independence from any global power, the moderate, conservative leaders of the Arab Gulf must guard against actions that may be perceived by their populations, and the wider Arab and Islamic world, as infringing on their sovereignty and independence. Thus, even if in their innermost thoughts the Gulf princes and sheikhs would like some kind of protective American presence, they realize only too well that such a presence would create immense popular antagonisms that would lead to the destabilization of their own regimes.

Within this context, Prince Fahd, whose country bore the major brunt of American pressure for some U.S. military presence, stated unequivocally: "We have emphasized that our land will not be used as bases for any foreign power, and we are working to distance our country from superpower rivalry, conflict and interference, since it is in the interests of the region and the world as a whole to keep the area free from great power rivalry."[18] Similarly, referring to an American coercive presence, the information minister of Bahrain said: "You cannot sell this sort of thing to the people of this area. If there is going to be war here, no one is going to win it—the destruction will be too great. We want to be kept out of the international see-saw. Countries like America can really have a deterrent aspect without physically being here."[19] It is time that Washington understands that the imposition of the rapid deployment force (RDF) on the area and its highly skeptical indigenous population could lead to the destabilization of the very regimes the RDF is meant to protect.

Rather than expend energy trying to protect the Gulf states from the imaginary Russian military menace, Washington would be better advised to try and help resolve the Arab-Israeli conflict, thereby neutralizing a major destabilizing force in the area. Yousif Shirawi, Bahrain's minister of development and industry, insisted: "Of course there is a great threat coming from Iran, but we think that the greatest danger to our security is still the non-resolution of the Arab-Israeli conflict."[20] This should not be seen as mere Arab rhetoric devoid of any truth or substance. The reasons for this kind of thinking were fully articulated by Prince Abdulla bin Abd al-Aziz, the crown prince and the head of the national guard. With the disarming bluntness of a true bedouin, the prince scolded his American interviewers:

> We hear constantly that the Soviet Union and Communism constitute the greatest danger to the Middle East. But as a friend, I tell you that you Americans constitute the greatest danger. The reason is your total alliance with Israel. The Arab masses feel abandoned by the U.S. and find it convenient to look to the Soviet Union instead. The policies of the U.S. often make it difficult for your friends to maintain that friendship. It is approaching the point where we will be helpless, where we can no longer stand up and defend that friendship. If the U.S. persists in a pro-Israel policy, the only beneficiary will be the Soviet Union.[21]

The reasons for identifying the Arab-Israel conflict, and particularly the perceived American all-out support for Israel, as the main destabilizing force in the area are all too clear. In the first place, perceived American support for Israel embarrasses the pro-American, moderate Arab regimes, such as those that inhabit the Gulf, and in the long run might affect the credibility of those political leaderships that continue to cling to U.S. friendship and support. The issues of Palestine and Jerusalem transcend inter-Arab discords, almost constituting the standard by which the merits and demerits of the various Arab leaders are judged. Inhabited by conservative Muslim populations and lacking the capabilities to withstand an onslaught from other Arab states, the regimes of the Gulf, with the exception of Oman, but particularly that of Saudi Arabia, which vigorously uses the country's Islamic status as the guardian of the Kaaba as a crucial legitimizing agent, can act only in unison with the majority opinion of the Arab world. And as Arab opinion turns increasingly against the United States for its "blind support of the Zionists," the position of the Gulf regimes correspondingly becomes less tenable.

Also, a major fear of the Gulf rulers is the Soviet Union's increasing influence in the area, and this influence is nurtured by the Arab belief that the Soviet Union has been a consistent supporter of the Palestinian cause. In this regard, the position of the pro-American Gulf rulers is weakened not only because an increase in Soviet influence constitutes a domestic and regional threat to their own stability but also because their position vis-a-vis competitive Arab leaders who are oriented toward the Soviet Union is weakened. Pro-American Arab leaders, such as the Gulf rulers, find themselves having to be extremely circumspect in their public hostility to the Soviet Union and its activities in the area. Because the issues of Palestinian rights and Zionist expansionism continue to dominate the Arab psyche, pro-Western leaders are invariably liable to leave themselves open to the kind of powerful arguments employed, for instance, by Syrian President Asad in a speech he made in March 1981. Responding to King Hussein's accusations that Syria's treaty with the USSR has made Syria a Soviet satellite, Asad retorted with much relish, reminding his listeners:

> What harm has the USSR done us? Why should we be displeased with the USSR? The USSR supports us in the face of the Zionists, who are backed by U.S. arms, ammunition and other means of power. Should we reward the USSR for all this by putting it on a par with the United States, which is giving Israel everything—arms and ammunition? Were it

> not for the United States, Israel would not have been able to occupy a single inch of our territory in Palestine or elsewhere. . . . What does the treaty say? It says that we and the Soviet Union stand, struggle and work against imperialist and racist Zionists. What is there in the treaty that harms the Arabs? Is it in the interests of the Arabs or in the interests of their enemies, that the Soviet Union will support Syria and the Arabs in their struggle against racist Zionism? I am not asking any Arab brother to conclude a similar treaty with the Soviet Union. I am saying that I would support any Arab who concludes a similar treaty with the United States, or any Western state, so long that the treaty stipulates that they will side with us against the Zionist invasion. Let King Hussein conclude a treaty with the United States stipulating that America would adopt total neutrality towards the Arab-Israeli conflict. I would relentlessly support and hail such a treaty.[22]

In the struggle for the hearts and minds of the Arab people, those who are pro-West can muster very few arguments to counter Asad's powerful appeal for the Arab soul. And as long as the Palestinian-Israeli issue remains the most potent political factor in Arab politics, the moderate Arab leaders, particularly the Gulf rulers, will continue to be on the defensive.

Gulf stability, as has been shown, is dependent on a variety of internal and external issues, factors, and events. These are not static, but are liable to change, sometimes abruptly, bringing with them unforeseen changes that may shake the very foundations of the Gulf's political and social systems. Witness the impact the revolution in Iran has had on the states of the Gulf. And who can tell what the repercussions will be of a new Arab-Israeli military confrontation? And what if the ayatollahs, in a moment of mystical madness, decide to bomb the oil installations in Saudi Arabia's eastern province? These and other unforeseen, yet possible, contingencies might very well lead to such turmoil in the Gulf that the reverberations would be felt throughout the world.

Of all the dangers facing the Gulf regimes, it has become almost a cliche to single out the so-called Islamic revival, aided by the Islamic republic of Iran, as the one force which inevitably would lead to the disintegration of the present political orders in the Gulf. It is, however, sobering to think back 15 to 20 years, when Saudi Arabia and the Gulf sheikhdoms were reeling under the seemingly unstoppable tide of revolutionary nationalism. Then, it was not the Islamic revival but Arab socialism that shook the foundations of the Gulf political systems; it was not the prospect of the Islamic community but the vision of the pan-Arab republic that dominated the psyche of the Arab masses; it was not Khomeini of Islamic Iran but Nasser of nationalist Egypt who embodied the essence of the revolutionary march. And if the rulers of the weak Gulf states endured many sleepless nights during the 1950s and 1960s, it was because they were repeatedly told that their archaic political orders were doomed in the face of pan-Arab nationalism.

But they survived. Indeed, they survived the "nationalist crisis" so well that by the 1970s the Saudis and their Gulf allies had emerged as pivotal members of the Arab world. And there is no reason why they will not survive the "Islamic crisis." As was pointed out earlier in this chapter, after the heyday of Khomeini's return to Tehran, the Islamic experiment is foundering. Islam in Iran, like the nationalism of the 1950s and 1960s in the Arab world, has not delivered. The rulers in the Gulf states can sit tight and wait for the Islamic bubble to burst and consume itself. In such an eventuality, they should survive the 1980s and 1990s as well as they have survived the previous decades.

NOTES

1. Hamilton Gibb, "Constitutional Organization: The Muslim Community and the State," in *Law in the Middle East*, ed. Majid Khadduri and Herbert J. Liebesny (Washington, D.C.: Middle East Institute, 1955), p. 15.

2. See in this regard Arnold Hottinger, "Political Institutions in Saudi Arabia, Kuwait and Bahrain," in *Security in the Persian Gulf: Domestic Political Factors*, ed. Shahram Chubin (London: Gower, 1981).

3. Ibid., p. 60.

4. *New York Times*, March 15, 1978.

5. R. K. Ramazani, *Beyond the Arab-Israeli Settlement: New Direction for U.S. Policy in the Middle East* (Cambridge, Mass.: Institute for Foreign Policy Analysis, 1977), p. 42.

6. *Times* (London), March 12, 1980.

7. British Broadcasting Corporation, *Summary of World Broadcasts*, Part 4, The Middle East and Africa [hereafter cited as *SWB*], ME/6953/A/2, February 13, 1982.

8. *SWB*, ME/6531/A/7, September 24, 1980.

9. *Al-Thawra* (Baghdad), September 18, 1980.

10. *Al-Thawra* (Baghdad), March 3, 1981.

11. In this regard, see *al-Mostakbal* (Paris), January 23, 1982, pp. 10–12; see also the accounts of the attempted coup by David Ignatius in *Wall Street Journal*, February 10, 1982, and Robert Fisk in *Times* (London), March 28, 1982.

12. *Al-Sharq al-Awsat* (London), February 25, 1982.

13. *SWB*, ME/7028/A/1, May 17, 1982.

14. In this regard, see the secret memorandum prepared by President Sekou Toure of Guinea, published in *al-Mostakbal* (Paris), February 27, 1982, pp. 10–12.

15. Jonathan Alford, "Soviet-American Rivalry in the Middle East: The Military Dimension," in *The Soviet Union in the Middle East: Policies and Perspectives*, ed. Adeed Dawisha and Karen Dawisha (London: Heinemann, 1982), p. 140.

16. *Sunday Times* (London), February 3, 1980.

17. *Al-Seyassa* (Kuwait), June 15, 1980.

18. *Al-Majalla* (London), January 24–30, 1981.

19. *Times* (London), April 2, 1982.

20. Lecture at the Royal Institute of International Affairs, London, February 3, 1982.

21. *Time*, November 9, 1981, p. 11.

22. *Al-Thawra* (Damascus), March 25, 1981.

2

Perceptions and Policies of the Gulf States Toward Regional Security and the Superpower Rivalry

Michael Sterner

Compared with the decade that preceded it, the 1970s was a period of internal growth and reduced external threat for most of the Gulf states. Threats from radical Arab movements abated, a reasonably stable understanding about the balance of power in the area emerged among the larger regional states, and, no less important, the traditional forms of rulership in the Gulf states proved remarkably hardy in the face of both external dangers and the difficult internal problems of postindependence nationbuilding. It was a decade of seeming vindication for the traditional societies and governments of the Arabian Peninsula and of repudiation of the principles of pan-Arab radicalism. Moreover, from the point of view of the smaller Gulf states, this more secure environment had been achieved without having had to submerge their independence or freedom of maneuver by seeking the protection of more powerful neighbors or by joining a joint regional defense effort.

By the end of the decade, however, the situation had begun to change for the worse. New dangers had arisen with the Soviet invasion of Afghanistan, the collapse of the shah's rule in Iran, and the outbreak of the Iran-Iraq war. This sudden deterioration in the immediate environment was compounded by new strains in intra-Arab relations because of Camp David and a souring of Arab relations with the United States as American diplomacy on the Arab-Israeli problem began to flag. On the Iraq-Iran war, the position of the Gulf Arabs was made more difficult by their miscalculation in backing Iraq and in assuming that the war would bring about the early demise of the Khomeini regime. The Soviet invasion of Afghanistan had shown the USSR capable of occupying a Muslim country in spite of the displeasure of the Arab and Islamic world. And, in response to the Soviet invasion, the United States was stimulated to new efforts to project its own power into the Gulf.

Thus, as the 1980s began, the Gulf states had much to be concerned about. In addition to a sharp increase in the level of threats from within the region, they found themselves the focal point of an intensified rivalry between the superpowers, a situation that added to their discomfort. Security–how to push these various genies back into the bottle and consolidate the gains of the 1970s–has once again become an overriding preoccupation for the Gulf rulers and their advisers.

This chapter attempts to identify the various considerations that shape the perceptions and policies of the Gulf states toward the problem of creating a secure environment. For obvious reasons, Iran poses a special problem in any current analysis. Iran is the major power in the Gulf, and under almost any kind of regime one must assume it will remain so. As such, it will have a decisive voice in the evolution of Gulf security arrangements, for the blunt fact is that the weaker states on the Arab side of the Gulf cannot afford policies that seriously alienate their powerful neighbor. Yet it is clear that the Iranian revolution is still in a state of flux, making any discussion of Iranian perceptions and policies, especially as we might try to project them into the future, largely guesswork. The focus of this chapter, therefore, is on the Arab Gulf states, where the continuity of regimes and the policies they have adopted over the past two decades offer some basis for drawing conclusions.

THE HISTORICAL EXPERIENCE

The perception of the Gulf states toward security has been heavily conditioned by historical experience. It is worth noting that, on the Arab side of the Gulf, all of the ruling houses that have been governing the affairs of these states since well before independence are still in power in 1982.

For 150 years British power dominated the Gulf. Britain's entry into the area in the early nineteenth century came about not because of any inherent attractiveness of the area itself but in order to protect Britain's sea lanes to India. For a century or more, pirates based in the estuaries of the Gulf had preyed on the lucrative merchant trade between Britain and India. By the beginning of the nineteenth century, the British had had enough; in 1819 the government of India sent an expeditionary force to the Gulf that burned the pirate boats, knocked down the mud forts of the local sheikhs, and chased the inhabitants into the hills. Shortly afterward, British representatives signed the first treaties with the rulers of these areas for "the Cessation of Plunder and Piracy."

For the next century, Britain's policy in the Gulf was, as one writer put it, "based on the principle of economy of force to achieve her objectives."[1] The protection of trade and sea lanes was the primary goal. Britain saw no point in involving itself in the internal affairs of the Gulf sheikhdoms.[2] Not until the end of the century, with the discovery of oil and a growing realization that the Gulf was becoming of interest to its great power rivals did Britain feel the need to formalize its role in the area by concluding agreements by which the Gulf rulers undertook not to enter into relations or agreements with any power other than Britain. In return, Britain, in effect, undertook the protection of these principalities from external threat.

Saudi Arabia was not part of the British sphere of influence. Far from the sea lanes, an underpopulated wasteland inhabited by nomadic tribes that paid loose fealty to the Sublime Porte, the Arabian hinterland evolved in a vacuum of great power interest. It was only in the twentieth century, when Abdul Aziz ibn Saud began to establish hegemony over central Arabia and to expand to the sea, that British and Saudi interests clashed. Even these clashes were limited in scope; in general, the Saudis recognized that they did not have the power to contest the British position along the Gulf littoral.

The discovery of oil raised the stakes for the British in the Gulf and brought about a more intensive involvement in the internal affairs of the area. The internal stability of the sheikhdoms, and indeed the character of the regimes themselves, now became important for the protection of favorable oil concession terms and the increasingly lucrative commercial contracts that resulted from oil wealth. The British presence in these states—political, military, and commercial—grew dramatically in the post-World War II years.

BRITISH WITHDRAWAL AND THE FIRST DECADE OF SELF-DEPENDENCE

In 1902, Lord Curzon, the viceroy of India, paid a formal visit to Britain's Gulf dependencies. It was the first time that a British representative of such illustrious rank had favored the sheikhdoms with a visit. To the assemblage of Gulf rulers who gathered at Sharjah to hear his address, Curzon said:

> We were here before any other Power. . . . We found strife and we have created order. . . . We saved you from extinction at the hands of your neighbors. . . . We have not seized or held your territory. We have not destroyed your independence, but have preserved it. We are not now going to throw away this century of costly and triumphant enterprise; we shall not wipe out the most unselfish page in history.

The Gulf rulers would have been permitted a smile at the last phrase, but otherwise they would have found little in the viceroy's remarks with which to disagree. Life *was* undeniably better under British protection. The combination of protection from external threat and noninterference in internal affairs was close to an ideal system from the local rulers' point of view; and in a sense their search in modern times has been to find the twentieth-century equivalent of this eminently satisfactory arrangement. They have reluctantly come to accept the fact that the world is now a far more complicated place and that their own search for security will in turn involve much greater complexities.

Half a century after Curzon's speech, the perceptive among the Gulf rulers might have foreseen that the process of decolonization, a postwar flagging British economy, and a resultant cutback in the British military establishment would inevitably lead to British relinquishment of its nineteenth-century responsibilities in the Gulf. Yet, when the announcement was made in 1968, it came as a shock throughout the area. Several of the Gulf rulers, particularly the ones who thought they stood a good chance of being swallowed up by more powerful neighbors, pleaded with Whitehall not to carry through with the decision.[3] But for London the step was not one of choosing among policy options but the inevitable consequence of Britain's declining role as a world power.

The British worked hard, and with some success, to prepare their protected states for independence. They succeeded in getting the shah's agreement to allow Iran's claim to Bahrain to be determined by a plebiscite of the Bahrainis, which eventually resulted in an overwhelming vote for independent statehood. The British attempted to stitch together a federation of the nine sheikhdoms of the central Gulf, but in the end managed a grouping of only the seven Trucial coast sheikhdoms, with Qatar and Bahrain opting for independence.

The first reaction of the newly independent mini-states was heavily conditioned by the specific threats they believed they faced, as well as by their internal makeup. Kuwait, which had severed its formal links with Britain a decade earlier, had established relations with the Soviet Union in the early days of its independence. It did this as a counter against Iraqi claims to Kuwait, but the decision also reflected the influence of the many Palestinians and other Arabs who had come to Kuwait, bringing with them concepts of Arab nationalism and nonalignment. Kuwait saw its security as best strengthened through making sure its policies and external relations were not dramatically at odds with the Arab radicals. In contrast, British withdrawal meant relatively little change in Oman. Already an independent state, isolated from the currents of Arab politics, Oman kept its British advisers and later did not hesitate to accept military assistance from a non-Arab state, Iran, to help suppress the rebellion in its Dhofar Province.

Some of the smaller Gulf Arab states looked to the United States in these early days to replace the British, but they soon realized that Washington did not wish to assume these responsibilities. Instead, the United States proclaimed its intention to rely on the "twin pillars" of Iran and Saudi Arabia to protect Western interests in the Gulf.

In fact, the "twin-pillars" formulation was a euphemism directed at Arab sensitivities for a policy based on building up Iran as the dominant military power in the region and main bulwark against encroachments by the Soviets. For the former British dependencies on the Arab side of the Gulf, it was hardly reassuring to be now informed that their security rested in the hands of Iran, for most of them had long-standing territorial disputes with their more powerful eastern neighbor. The shah, in fact, immediately moved to assert Iran's title to the British role of overall protector in the Gulf. Iranian forces occupied the two Tunb islands, claimed by Ras al-Khaimah, and the island of Abu Musa, off Sharjah.

At the time, Iranian aggressiveness was at least partly attributable to fear that Iraq, which had been actively extending its influence in the area, would try to establish a dominant position at the lower end of the Gulf, possibly with Saudi and other Arab support. As time went on, however, Iranian concerns eased. The Iraqi threat receded, and Tehran saw that it was not the purpose of the smaller Gulf states to support Arabization of the Gulf or to deny Iran its "proper" role in the region. As the 1970s progressed, Iranian policy gradually shifted toward support for the stability and independence of the smaller Gulf states. The shah accepted the outcome of a plebiscite on Bahrain, worked out an arrangement with Sharjah that allowed oil production to begin on Abu Musa, sent two brigades to help Oman quell the Dhofar rebellion, and ceased to be receptive to overtures from some of the constituent rulers of the United Arab Emirates

(UAE), who saw secret dealings with Iran as a counterweight to Abu Dhabi's growing influence within the federation.

The Saudis reacted more sluggishly to British withdrawal from the Gulf. Saudi ruling councils were divided, with some seeing British withdrawal as an opportunity to settle scores with some of the Gulf rulers who had earlier sheltered under British power. In the end, wiser and more moderate counsel prevailed. The Saudis slowly began to settle some of the outstanding border disputes with their Gulf neighbors (an agreement with Abu Dhabi in 1974 went a long way toward resolving the sensitive Buraimi issue). The Saudis, like the Iranians, eventually decided not to respond to attempts by individual rulers within the UAE to enlist Saudi support against central authority.

But if each of the "twin pillars" acted constructively, it was on an individual basis, not through coordination between them. Through most of this period, Tehran and Riyadh regarded each other with mutual suspicion. An inherent lack of cultural affinity between these two powers was part of the problem. The Iranians regarded the Saudis as unwashed tribesmen whose credentials on the international scene could not compare with the 3,000-year history of Persia. The Saudis found the imperial pretensions of the shah and his court distasteful and the attitude of most Iranians toward the Arabs condescending.

The growth of stability—one might even say of a regional security system—in the 1970s also owed much to the skillful diplomacy of the smaller Gulf states during this period. Imbued with a realistic sense of their own relative weakness compared with Saudi Arabia and Iran, they worked hard, and in the end successfully, to cultivate good relations with both of their powerful neighbors. After some initial missteps, they were careful to avoid policy statements or associations that suggested an attempt to exclude Iran from Gulf affairs. At the same time, they worked to establish close ties with the Saudis and rarely took a foreign policy position without first ascertaining, through careful consultations, what the Saudi reaction was likely to be.

The record of the 1970s is particularly impressive if one remembers how uncertain the prospects for stability were at the beginning of the decade. Few in 1970 would have been certain that the seven Trucial rulers could learn to live together, and that the UAE's future as a unitary state, a decade later, would no longer be questioned. A decade ago, it also seemed moot as to whether the sultan's rule in

Oman could survive the challenges posed by Imam Ghaleb and the Soviet-supported rebellion in its southern province. Yet, today, both of these threats have been overcome, and the sultan's rule is more secure than ever. The record is impressive, not only from the standpoint of these states' abilities to stand up to external dangers but from the strengthened position of their ruling houses to deal with internal problems as well.

GULF STATES' PERCEPTION OF SECURITY THREATS

Preoccupation with Internal Security

It is important to keep in mind that, with the exception of Iran and Oman, all of the states under consideration in this discussion are new national entities and are still heavily preoccupied with the task of nationbuilding. They are basically inward-looking and inclined to see much of the problem of security in terms of what affects their own internal stability. When the writer arrived as the U.S. ambassador to the United Arab Emirates in 1974, he was amused (and somewhat deflated) by the candor of one of the palace counsellors, who confided that the main reason Sheikh Zayed wanted an American ambassador in Abu Dhabi was to provide visible proof to his fellow rulers and neighbors that Washington thought the UAE was here to stay. The self-confidence of the Gulf regimes has improved since that time, but we still tend to forget the modesty of these rulers' objectives and the extent to which external relations are ordered to help cope with pressing internal problems. Vast quantities of oil have helped to obscure the point, leaving the impression that these states have greater strength than in fact they themselves believe they have.

A failure to recognize this has often caused gaps in perception between the United States and the Gulf states: Washington wonders why (again, excluding Oman) they are not more concerned by the Soviet threat, while the Gulf states still see Afghanistan as far away and are more concerned by external threats closer at hand that have a greater likelihood of creating internal pressures.

For the Arab Gulf ruler, a crucial consideration is the extent to which such an external threat has the potential to strike responsive chords within their own societies, for Gulf rulers rate much lower the probability of being taken over by overt military aggression than the threat of being undermined from within. Their judgment has always been that, in this sense, the Soviets have few direct assets in their countries.

Revolutionary Iran and the Arabs

The Gulf Arab states had accommodated themselves to a powerful Iran under the shah's leadership. They did not much like the shah's personal style, but they recognized that his policies were compatible with and even supportive of their own interests. The shah had done his best to weaken the Arab nationalist states that had attempted to destroy the established ruling houses in the Arabian Peninsula. He detested Nasser, a sentiment shared (if not openly expressed) by most of the Gulf rulers. His activities against the Baathi regime in Baghdad had helped to get Iraq to pull back from its efforts to promote revolution in the lower Gulf. The shah was also staunchly anti-Soviet. His support for the Omanis in suppressing the Dhofar rebellion, although causing initial discomfort in some quarters of the Gulf, was generally applauded when it succeeded in its purpose.

The collapse of the shah's regime, therefore, came as an unpleasant shock, particularly as it brought to power a leader who had proclaimed the incompatibility of Islam with monarchical forms of rule. Two dangers immediately presented themselves. The first was that an Iran under hostile leadership, either in the name of Iranian nationalism or a fundamentalist Islamic jihad, might attempt to bring the small Gulf states under Iranian domination. The second was that the idea of an "Islamic revolution," whether or not actively promoted by Tehran, might spread to the Arab side of the Gulf.

Incidents occurring in Saudi Arabia shortly after the revolution in Iran—the takeover of the Grand Mosque in Mecca and disturbances on two occasions among the Shiites in the eastern province of al-Hasa—seemed to be troubling manifestations of either or both of these possibilities. As it turned out, however, none of these incidents could be traced to active Iranian machinations (although certainly events in Iran touched off the Shiite disturbances and may have helped to inspire the Grand Mosque insurrectionists to action as well). Nor have there been any recurrences of such incidents within the past year, a fact that has helped to reassure the Saudis, at least as far as any immediate threat is concerned.

Yet the Saudis know the danger is still present. The increasing likelihood that the Iranian revolution will consolidate its hold on the country, and the impressive showing of Iranian military forces in the spring of 1982 in expelling Iraqi forces from Iranian territory, will serve to increase the luster of the Islamic revolution in the eyes of many Arabs. Even if they escape a more violent fate, the Saudis and other Gulf Arabs now see the unpleasant prospect of having to live with an Iran that is still the major force in the Gulf but under management that will probably be more hostile to their interests.

The problems of adjusting to the new regime in Tehran have been compounded by Arab policy in the Iraq-Iran war. The Gulf states shared Baghdad's miscalculation that Iranian defeats, coming on top of internal problems, would bring about Khomeini's downfall. Kuwait may face the most acute problem in this respect, for it not only contributed sizable sums to Iraq's war coffers but became the transshipment point for most of the arms being sent to resupply Iraq. Iranian aircraft have twice bombed Kuwait, but from the limited amount of damage done, Tehran's motivation appears to have been to convey a warning rather than to carry full-scale hostilities to Kuwait.

Once the tide of the war turned, however, and particularly in the aftermath of the sweeping Iranian military successes of the spring of 1982, some of the Gulf states began to trim their sails back toward Tehran. As the war drags on, the Gulf states, committed to financing any shortfall in Iraq's war effort, find themselves in an increasingly uncomfortable position. They are exasperated by Baghdad's insistence on a guns and butter policy, but their only form of leverage would be to withhold assistance, which might cause Iraq's collapse and pose a far greater security threat to themselves.

With respect to the smaller Gulf states, there is probably still a basis for some kind of postwar modus vivendi, if Tehran is willing to let it evolve. The incident in Bahrain of December 1981, when some 70 armed Bahraini Shiites who had received training in Iran were apprehended by Bahraini security forces, is not a particularly auspicious omen. But the connection between the central Iranian authority and these insurrectionists is not altogether clear, and it is too early to conclude that Iran is committed to a policy of implacable hostility toward the existing Gulf Arab regimes. Tehran might decide to accept them, provided they adjust their policies to accept Iran's "rightful" status as paramount power in the Gulf and make sure Iran is consulted about their foreign policy actions and statements. This will be a difficult adjustment for the Gulf Arabs to make (it raises some serious questions, for example, about the future of the Gulf Cooperation Council, which excludes Iran), but the Arab Gulf states have shown remarkable pliancy in the past and may well manage the trick again. In the long term, the Gulf states will see maintaining Iraq as a counterweight to Iran to be in their interest.

Islamic Fundamentalism

Many experienced Gulf officials and business people tend to discount the threat from Iran in any direct or immediate sense. They consider the possibility of overt Iranian military action against the Gulf states to be remote, and they do not believe that Tehran has sufficient assets on its side of the Gulf (with the possible exception of Bahrain, where the Shiite community numbers one-half of the population) to foment internal insurrection, even with the help of organizers smuggled in from Iran.

Instead, they are more concerned over the danger that at some point in the future the Islamic revolution could become an attractive alternative to existing social and government systems in the Gulf. The experience of the 1970s is seen by many as a narrow victory for the traditional forms of rule over the dangers of external threat and the challenges of internal development. In the course of the decade, these regimes gradually acquired greater respectability and legitimacy in the eyes of their peoples as a reasonable vehicle to manage the transition from primitive tribalism to the complexities of modern life.

Yet there is a pervasive sense among many in the Gulf that the process of adapting the system of tribal rule to the requirements of modern life has not moved fast enough. They are not worried so much by the lack of democratic institutions in the Western sense as by the increasingly inadequate responsiveness and efficiency of government to public needs, and by the failure, thus far, to alter either the reality or the image that these states are governed as family fiefs with a disproportionate share of political power and wealth accruing to members of the ruling family and associated merchant families. Unchallenged by viable alternatives, these traditional systems might fare relatively well in spite of their inadequacies, but it is feared that the *idea* of an Islamic republic (as opposed to the practice in Iran, which few Arabs would wish to emulate) may call new attention to the weaknesses of the existing political systems.

Some of these observers are probably more alarmist than the facts warrant—there are few signs of organized disaffection in any of the Gulf states at present. But they are also on the right track. Inherently weak, possessing neither the efficient internal security forces of a totalitarian system nor strong armed forces to repel outside predators, the Gulf states have as one of their few recourses to defense the adoption of systems of rule that command the overwhelming respect and support of their population. Although oil wealth has bought time for the rulers of these states to manage the evolution of their political systems, it has also so accelerated the progress of education, of material expectations, and of political consciousness that rulers can ill afford to rely on political institutions and practices that were suitable a generation ago but may no longer be so.

The Arab Context

The Arab world is the primary interstate framework within which the Arab Gulf states see their future evolving. Ties of language, of culture, and of a shared history make their intra-Arab connections a tighter psychological framework than does Islam or ties based on purely geographical or political considerations. The influx of large numbers of Arabs from other countries (with the exception of Oman) has served to strengthen the sense of linkage with the Arab world. It is within the Arab arena that much of the Gulf Arabs' search for security is directed, but it is also from within this arena that some of the most serious threats to their security have emerged.

The experience of the 1950s and early 1960s is still vivid in the minds of the peninsula Arabs, particularly the Saudis. As revolutions swept monarchies away in Egypt and Iraq, "Nasserism" and "Baathism" became doctrines of widespread appeal through much of the Arab world. The new secular ideologies backed by the power of these northern Arab states proclaimed their hostility to monarchical and traditional forms of government elsewhere in the Arab world and actively sought to undermine them.

The period was particularly traumatic for the Saudis, but Kuwait and Oman as well have faced serious threats from Arab neighbors. Upon Kuwait's independence in 1961, Iraq immediately asserted a claim to Kuwait. Baghdad was forced to back off when British troops, subsequently replaced by an Arab League force, supported Kuwait's independence. A decade later the fragile beginnings of statehood for the middle Gulf principalities were made more difficult by Iraq's efforts to establish influence throughout the Gulf. At about the same time, Oman was subjected to an insurgency promoted by its pro-Soviet neighbor, the People's Democratic Republic of Yemen.

In the end, however, it was the revolutionary regimes that declined in their power to influence events beyond their borders, and the established regimes built on traditional forms of rule that showed surprising powers of survival. Nasserism was dealt a mortal blow by the Egyptian defeat in 1967, and Nasser's death three years later brought to power in Egypt a new leader who repudiated Nasser's policies of trying to undermine the conservative Arab states. The Baathi movement split into two wings based in Baghdad and Damascus, and in each of these capitals the Baath ideology was soon overshadowed by traditional Arab military authoritarianism and sectarian rivalry, a transformation that destroyed whatever original appeal Baathism had as an idealistic pan-Arab movement. In contrast, the monarchies, although experiencing some close calls, survived in Morocco, Jordan, and Saudi Arabia, as did traditional forms of rule in the principalities and sheikhdoms of the Gulf.

No Arab ruler is so naive as to entrust the security of his country to Arab League action; collective defense is rendered impossible by the many and serious political differences that divide the Arab world. But, like other Arabs, the Gulf states have long relied on building temporary alliances with other Arab states as one way of offsetting external threats and defusing internal pressures. Feeling the lash of radical Arab disapproval in the 1950s and 1960s, the Saudis moved to repair relations with their fellow monarch King Hussein, a difficult step because of the long history of bitter animosity between the Hashemite and Saudi houses. Nasser's short-lived attempt to form a union with Syria in 1958 generated an immediate announcement of an offsetting union between Jordan and Iraq. Kuwait's fears of being swallowed up by its predatory northern neighbor Iraq in the early 1960s pushed it to resolve long-standing border disputes with Saudi Arabia.

For the most part, Arab rulers recognize that their alliances with individual Arab states are more important in political and psychological terms than military. Kuwaitis know that it was the British that saved them from an Iraqi invasion in 1961, not their fellow Arabs. Sultan Qabus knows he could not have afforded to rely entirely on Arab help against the People's Democratic Republic of Yemen.

But the Saudis and the smaller Gulf states will continue to see managing their Arab environment—to the extent they can do it—as crucially important to their security. There is another important reason for this that has already been touched upon. Political movements within the Arab world have the potential to create internal divisions for a given Arab state, whereas movements outside the Arab context are far less dangerous in this sense. The peninsula Arabs in particular want no return to the nightmarish days of the 1950s and 1960s, when polarization of Arab politics along radical/conservative lines generated not only serious external threats but severe internal pressures as well.

Within the Arab context, therefore, the Gulf Arab states will pursue two main lines of policy as a way of buttressing their security. They will seek to maintain flexibility in their relations with other Arab states so as to maintain a balance of power and be in a position to form temporary alliances that strengthen their security. And they will work to build an atmosphere of consensus among Arab states and seek to blur differences over such divisive issues as the Arab-Israeli problem, for they see this as far preferable to polarization, which would expose them to both external threats and internal pressures.

The Arab-Israeli Conflict

During the 1950s and early 1960s, the Gulf Arabs paid little attention to the Arab-Israeli problem. As they saw it then, the issue was far away, and although they had a general sense that the Palestinians had suffered an injustice, they considered it the result of corrupt Arab leadership for which they bore no responsibility. A sharp change in perception occurred in 1967, when the catastrophic defeat of Arab arms brought a new sense of menace from Israeli "expansionism." The Palestinians, for the first time, began to organize themselves as a political and paramilitary force. Palestinians already living in the Gulf states did much to arouse the emotions of their hosts. In Kuwait, an estimated 25 percent of the population is Palestinian. In Saudi Arabia and the United Arab Emirates, the proportion is lower but the number of Palestinians are still significant, as are the influential positions they occupy within these societies.

To the Gulf Arabs, the Arab-Israeli issue presents a host of worrisome and frustrating problems. Their deepest concern is that a continued impasse in the negotiations will, over time, increasingly radicalize the Palestinians. They fear this element of grievance could reinforce other currents of disaffection—for example, that Palestinians could at some point make common cause with the Islamic fundamentalists (Khomeini's early espousal of the Palestinian cause provides sufficient evidence that this is not far-fetched). Also, these rulers see the Arab-Israeli conflict as the main vehicle for the expansion of Soviet influence in the area. Conversely, they see the issue as the principal obstacle to better relations with the United States and in particular to cooperation with the United States on bilateral and regional security matters.

It does little good for American policymakers and diplomats to argue that an accurate reading of security threats in the area does not support the single-minded preoccupation that some Arabs accord the Arab-Israeli problem. The issue is no longer susceptible to entirely rational discussion. The Arabs have built up a head of emotionalism over it out of frustration that they have not been able to make Washington see their point of view. The more Washington points to the Soviets as the real threat to the area, the more the Arabs are driven to hyperbole about the Arab-Israeli problem.

PERCEPTIONS OF THE SUPERPOWERS

The Soviet Union

The traditional societies of the Gulf, based on adherence to Islam, a strong property sense, little historical experience of exploited urban classes, and their own unique form of tribal leadership, offer a fundamentally inhospitable ground for the doctrines of communism. The Gulf states were untouched by the antimonarchist and anticolonial political ferment that swept through the major Arab capitals in the 1940s and 1950s, providing the conditions for the growth of leftist political ideologies. Virtually without exception, the rulers of the Gulf and their key advisers see communism as an inimical and distasteful doctrine. Their antagonism was reinforced when the Soviets allied themselves with the new authoritarian regimes of the left in Cairo, Damascus, and Baghdad and gave open support to these regimes' efforts to promote the downfall of the Saudi and other Gulf governments.

Relations between the USSR and the various Gulf states cover a wide range, reflecting differing historical experience and internal political makeup. Kuwait is the only Arab Gulf state that has diplomatic relations with the Soviet Union. This step was taken in 1962, soon after Kuwait became fully independent, when relations with the Soviets appeared to provide an additional insurance policy against an Iraqi takeover. At the opposite end of the spectrum is Oman, which has experienced a Soviet-supported insurgency firsthand and which sees its policy interests best met by a declared pro-United States, anti-Soviet stand.[4] In between are Saudi Arabia, the United Arab Emirates, and Bahrain. The UAE and Bahrain would probably like to follow the Kuwaiti model of nonalignment, but have been deterred from doing so by an unwillingness to get out of step with the Saudis. The Saudi attitude reflects a historical experience of very close relations with the United States, but also an increasing receptivity to the idea of establishing a more balanced relationship with the two superpowers.

The Arab Gulf states' perceptions of the Soviet threat and the superpower rivalry have gone through several phases since the 1950s:

- The period of 1954–67, when the Soviets were expanding their presence in key Arab states, was a period of U.S.-Soviet competition, with the Soviets making very definite gains in reducing the Western position in the Middle East.
- The decade 1967–76 marked a period of decline for Soviet clients in the area, of rising U.S. prestige because of its role in the Arab-Israeli negotiations, and of increasing confidence on the part of conservative Arab regimes in their ability to survive. It was a period of détente in U.S.-Soviet relations.
- The years from 1976 to the present have been marked by resurgent Soviet activity and gains, with Soviet intrusions into Angola and the Horn of Africa, the Soviet occupation of Afghanistan, the collapse of the shah's rule in Iran, and the outbreak of the Iraq-Iran war. This has been a period first of a declining U.S. confidence in its world role during the post-Vietnam period and then of renewed U.S.-Soviet confrontation as the United States awakened to the increased threat.

The events of the last three years in particular have increased the Arab perception of the Soviet threat and their own sense of vulnerability to it. Afghanistan showed that the Soviets were prepared not merely to work through proxies but to occupy a Muslim country with its own forces. The Arabs must also have found it disquieting that Arab interests as a whole did not weigh more heavily in the Soviet decision to adopt a neutral stance in the Iraq-Iran war. Clearly, the Soviets considered Iran the strategic prize.

The Saudis, as well as the other Gulf governments, have condemned the Soviets for their action in Afghanistan, yet interestingly, the renewed sense of threat has not brought about any fundamental shift in the Gulf states' posture toward the superpowers. Instead, it has sharpened the debate within the Gulf governments as to whether the best way to deal with the Soviets is to continue to have nothing to do with them or to begin dealing with them in a limited way.

Adherents of the latter view appear slowly to be gaining ground. Statements by Saudi leaders since the Soviet invasion of Afghanistan indicate continued receptivity to the idea of improved relations with the Soviets. In fact, some of the Saudi statements suggest that the only remaining obstacle to the establishment of relations with Moscow is the Soviet occupation of Afghanistan.[5]

The logic supporting a more normal relationship with the Soviets seems to flow partly from the argument that if the Soviets are given a greater stake in relations with the conservative Arab states, it will help to moderate their behavior, as they would then have to take into account the interests of those states in their calculations. There may also be a feeling that relations with the Soviets could give the moderate Arabs leverage in certain situations where they are now in a position to influence only one side, such as in the continuing dispute between North Yemen and the People's Democratic Republic of Yemen. But the main impulse appears to stem from a changed perception of the superpower balance of power—a perception that the Soviets are a force to be reckoned with in the area and that some trimming of sails in Moscow's direction is now prudent.

Yet the arguments are not all in one direction, and clearly, if the Saudis are moving in this direction, they are doing so with great caution. Access to the most advanced U.S. military equipment is still seen by the Saudis as an important objective, and they would have to reckon the costs that a move toward the Soviets might have in making U.S. congressional approval for future arms even more difficult. Moreover, as long as the Soviets are in Afghanistan, the Saudis clearly do not want to give them any free rides. With the exception of Kuwait, the Gulf Arabs did not respond positively to the Brezhnev proposal in December 1980 for "neutralization" of the Gulf. They recognized it for the ploy it was to divert attention from the continued Soviet presence in Afghanistan.

Can the Saudi response to post-Afghanistan overtures—what William Quandt calls Saudi recognition of the reality of Soviet power—be read as appeasement of the Soviets? Or more importantly, are the Soviets likely to read it that way? Moscow must certainly be gratified that its invasion of Afghanistan has not done more to alter Arab positions. Yet the Soviet action, together with the collapse of the shah, has also produced a more vigorous U.S. policy. The Soviets must be concerned by the resultant increased capability of the United States to deploy military force into the area.

The United States

Unlike Saudi Arabia, the smaller states of the Gulf had no historical experience of close association with the United States. Moreover, with the exception of Oman, they emerged from British tutelage as independent states with already sizable communities of Palestinians,

Egyptians, Syrians, and other Arabs who had brought with them concepts of Arab nationalism and nonalignment. The rulers of these states wanted U.S. recognition and access to U.S. arms and technology, but they avoided any closer association, fearing the internal and external pressures that such a policy would bring.

The Saudi experience was fundamentally different. Saudi Arabia's emergence into nationhood was in close partnership with the United States, beginning with the oil concessions granted to American companies in the 1930s and the U.S. government's willingness, during World War II, to advance Saudi Arabia money against future oil revenue. The close links forged between the United States and Saudi Arabia in those trouble-free early days still exert a strong hold in certain quarters of the Saudi royal family.

But a number of factors have brought about a fundamental shift of attitude over the past 30 years:

- The Saudi government found, in the 1950s and 1960s, that its close identification with the United States was adding a further dimension of political disability in its already difficult battle of securing the Saudi dynasty against attacks from the Arab nationalist movement. Saudi unwillingness in 1962 to extend its agreement to allow American SAC bases on Saudi soil was the first step toward a modified relationship.
- The Saudis also discovered during this period that although their security link with the United States could be useful as protection against external threat, it could do very little to help Saudi Arabia protect itself against internal threats.
- The Arab-Israeli problem injected an issue of increasing difficulty and intensity between the United States and Saudi Arabia. U.S.-Saudi differences culminated in the early 1970s, when King Faisal felt that the United States had done too little to support Sadat and had not heeded his warnings about the imminence of a new Arab-Israeli conflict. Although U.S.-Saudi differences eased in the 1973–77 period, they worsened again, leaving this issue one of the major sources of strain in present-day U.S.-Saudi relations.

In the last decade, other troubling elements have added to the trend toward Saudi reappraisal of the U.S.-Saudi security relationship:

- Compared with Soviet policy, U.S. policy over the past decade has struck the Saudis and the Gulf Arabs as unsteady and undependable. As a result of Vietnam, they witnessed U.S. withdrawal into a period of self-doubt about its role as a world power. Much as they have welcomed the recent reassertion of U.S. purposefulness, Gulf

Arabs wonder whether it can be considered a permanent feature of U.S. policy.

• Gulf Arabs see a disturbing trend in Washington to rely on rhetoric rather than meaningful action—a kind of speak-loudly-and-carry-a-small-stick policy. They welcomed the Carter Doctrine, but noted that the United States did nothing, in fact, to save its friend the shah. They wonder how seriously to take a superpower that reacts noisily to the USSR's invasion of Afghanistan but then rescinds one of the only effective means of leverage it had on the Soviets because of domestic pressures. They wonder in particular what the Reagan extension of the Carter Doctrine means in practical terms ("We will not allow Saudi Arabia to become another Iran"). What precisely would the United States do, or could it do, if internal pressures similarly built up against the Saudi regime?

The trend is not all one-sided. Saudis are keenly aware that when they have faced crunches in the past, the United States has responded rapidly with military assistance and support that would have been unavailable elsewhere. The United States sent a squadron of fighter aircraft to Saudi Arabia in the early 1960s and deployed them along the Yemeni border to warn Nasser to keep hands off Saudi Arabia. Two decades later U.S. willingness to send AWACs to Saudi Arabia in the wake of Iranian air attacks on the Gulf was seen by the Saudis as a vitally important reinforcement of their defense capability at a critical time.

The Saudis do not discount the value of this support, but they see it as applicable almost exclusively to overt military threat, and in the meantime they are frustrated and angry that the United States is either unwilling or unable to be equally supportive of Saudi needs in the political sphere. Few Saudis would recommend a dismantling of the U.S.-Saudi relationship. But Saudis are becoming, in the words of one observer,[6] "less sentimental" about their relationship with the United States. They are weighing the limitations and liabilities—as well as the assets—of close association with the United States in a more hardheaded way.

If one could eavesdrop on the typical Gulf Arab ruler or foreign minister as he was thinking aloud about the superpower rivalry and its effect on Gulf security, something along the following lines might be heard:[7]

> No U.S. presence in the Middle East can protect us from a really concerted attempt by the Soviets to take over the area. Only the U.S. strategic deterrent can do this, and we certainly want the United States to

> maintain that deterrent. To the extent that local arrangements can help to enhance it, we will try to be discreetly helpful.
>
> But we do not want any U.S. bases on our territory. Such bases would not make a critical difference in deterring the Soviets, nor would they protect us from the threats we are most likely to face. To the contrary, they would expose us to serious internal and external political problems. Therefore, if there has to be a U.S. military presence in the area, we want it over the horizon, not on our shores.
>
> There is another reason to keep U.S. bases out of the area. One of the main objectives of Soviet policy is to keep the United States from achieving a privileged position in the area that might be used against the Soviets strategically. If we grant the West such positions, doesn't it merely have the effect of stirring the Soviets to greater efforts to undermine us?
>
> Along those same lines, aren't we more likely to defuse the Soviet threat by having normal relations with the Soviets than by trying to exclude them completely from the area? Besides, if the balance of power between the superpowers—at least as far as being able to project it into the Middle East is concerned—is slipping from U.S. superiority to greater equality, is it wise for us to adopt a posture of one-sided alliance with the West?

There is, moreover, a lingering suspicion among Gulf rulers and their advisers that granting bases to the United States in the area could facilitate a U.S. takeover of the oil fields at some point in the future. Henry Kissinger's comment that the United States might have to use force to secure the oil fields if necessary made a deep and lasting impression in the Gulf states.

Iranian Perceptions

The shah's policy was to build Iran as a regional power and to maintain a military alliance with the United States as a counterweight to the ever-present threat from its powerful neighbor to the north. In the last decade of his rule, the shah entered into some commercial deals and purchases of arms of limited scope with the Soviets, motivated mainly, probably, by the belief that this would increase his leverage with the United States.

In one blow, the Iranian revolution deprived the United States of its position in Iran, conferring upon the Soviets a significant strategic gain. Moscow is undoubtedly as uncertain as all of us about how the Iranian revolution will evolve; presumably, the immediate Soviet objective is to make certain nothing happens that would give the

United States an opportunity to regain its former position in Iran. We must assume this was the major consideration in Moscow's decision to adopt a carefully neutral stance in the Iraq-Iran war and to make Soviet arms available to the new regime through its satellites.

In spite of Tehran's anti-U.S. animus and Moscow's care to position itself favorably with the new regime, there is no solid evidence that Tehran has moved significantly closer to Moscow since the revolution. From all accounts, the Soviet Union runs a close second to the United States in terms of unpopularity with the Iranian people. Tehran needs to maintain tolerable relations with the Soviets for the time being so as not to become totally isolated and to keep open the supply line for arms from North Korea, Libya, and other sources. But there is clearly no ideological compatibility between Iran's present regime and the USSR, and it seems not unreasonable to suppose that over a longer period, the basic strategic concerns that have motivated Iranians in the past, to seek a counterweight against pressures from the north, may again assert themselves. It will presumably be a long time before Tehran turns to the United States to play this role, but there does appear to be greater scope for a rebuilding of European-Iranian ties, both in terms of economic development and reequipment of the Iranian armed forces.

REGIONAL SECURITY

Since the early 1970s, following Britain's decision to relinquish responsibility for protection of the area, the Gulf Arab states have been actively interested in proposals for greater cooperation among themselves to enhance their mutual security. They have seen such schemes as conferring a number of benefits: making it clear to outside powers that the security of the Gulf is first and foremost the responsibility of the Gulf states themselves; strengthening the capability of the weakest among them to resist threats from more powerful neighbors; and ameliorating rivalries among themselves by requiring them to think cooperatively about their mutual security. In particular, the Saudis in recent years have seen such a collective grouping to be in their interest as a way of reducing the vulnerability of the smaller Gulf states to outside attack or subversion.

Early proposals for Gulf regional security groupings tended to founder for two reasons. The first was the difficulty of finding a collective framework that could encompass states representing great discrepancies in power and political policies. In the early 1970s, for example, it appeared quixotic at the very least to be trying to include Iraq in a security framework when most of the smaller Gulf states felt this was the quarter from which their greatest security threat stemmed. Yet Baghdad would have blocked any arrangement that excluded Iraq, whether or not Iran was involved.

The second problem was the difficulty the small states themselves had in reconciling their differing approaches to regional security. At one end of the spectrum was Kuwait, which followed nonaligned policies vis-a-vis the superpowers and saw its security largely in terms of maintaining good relations with the Arabs—and, in particular, with Iraq. At the other end was Oman, which sought U.S. protection as a replacement for British power and which had a close security relationship with Iran in its immediate problem of suppressing the Dhofar insurgency. Through the 1970s, the Saudis and remaining small states of the Gulf attempted to bridge this gap, but without success. For one thing, the security arrangements that the individual states had entered into seemed to be working. At no point during this period did any threat appear so serious to all as to provide sufficient motivation to overcome differences over the approach to regional defense. The concept remained attractive, but no way was found to give it practical expression.

The Soviet invasion of Afghanistan and the Iranian revolution, particularly the latter, changed the political topography of the Gulf and opened the way for a regional grouping of the Gulf states. The events in Iran greatly increased the sense of danger in the Arab side of the Gulf and at the same time removed the main impediment to a grouping that was based frankly on Gulf Arab interest.

The formal vehicle for this closer relationship on security matters has been the Gulf Cooperation Council (GCC), established in 1981 among Saudi Arabia, Oman, the United Arab Emirates, Qatar, Bahrain, and Kuwait. Much of the GCC's achievement is still in the planning and study stage, but even at this level the accomplishment to date has been notable. A Gulf Economic Community, modeled on the European Community, has been agreed to, which apparently gives Gulf citizens rights of free movement of goods and capital and ownership of land and businesses in all member states. In the area of defense, although the six have not yet reached the point of concluding any formal defense arrangements, their defense ministers have met frequently and initiated several studies of defense cooperation.

The abortive coup in Bahrain in December 1981 stimulated greater cooperation in internal security as well. Following the incident, each of the smaller Gulf states except Kuwait moved quickly to conclude bilateral security pacts with Saudi Arabia. Whether the six intend to attempt to formalize these bilateral arrangements under the council imprimatur is not yet clear. Saudi Arabia's ability to come to the assistance of its smaller brethren in an effective military sense is extremely limited, a fact about which the leaders of the smaller Gulf states have few illusions. But the pacts are far from meaningless on a political plane, and arrangements for the sharing of security information, which should be relatively easy to implement, should in themselves be of considerable value.[8]

The Saudi role will remain central to the GCC's development, particularly with respect to the organization's increasing focus on security matters. The Saudis are the sole cohesive influence capable of mitigating Omani-Kuwaiti tensions over the strong anti-Soviet and pro-U.S. stand of the former and the generally nonaligned position of the latter. Much also will depend on the emerging attitude of Iran toward the GCC. If the regime in Tehran sees the council as somehow conflicting with its own primacy in the Gulf and makes an issue of it, the six may have to go slow, or in any case make sure the council's evolution moves in a direction that Tehran can live with.

Beyond the immediate orbit of collective self-defense, the Gulf states have tended to avoid formal military alliances with other regional powers, seeing such ties as creating internal vulnerabilities that outweigh any advantages. Saudi Arabia did, however, quietly work out a deal with Pakistan several years ago for the stationing of a brigade of Pakistani troops in Saudi Arabia in return for significant economic assistance.[9]

Pakistan seems the best possible candidate for this role: It is Muslim, has a good fighting tradition, and is politically neutral in terms of intra-Arab rivalries. The presence of a significant force of Pakistani troops should serve as an incremental deterrent against external aggression or an internal coup, although this asset must be balanced against the political liability for the ruling house of appearing to be propped up by "foreign mercenaries." Moreover, Saudi leaders would be foolhardy to count too heavily on a force that would be committed to combat on their behalf only on orders from a foreign capital: In the event of an internal coup, for example, Pakistani action could well be neutralized, if it appeared the insurrectionists had a reasonable chance of gaining power, by unwillingness to take any action that would make it more difficult for Islamabad to establish good relations with a new regime.

CONCLUSION

An analysis of this kind tends to confirm the superficial but accurate conclusion that defining security, and deciding on the best means to strengthen it, is a highly subjective business. The perceptions of the Gulf Arabs toward this problem stem from a deeply rooted conviction of their own weakness and a conclusion derived from this that the best means of defense is to get along with everybody and to avoid alliances that might provoke hostile intentions in some other quarter. Although there have been some narrow escapes, this policy has worked well for them in the Arab context, and there is now an increasing disposition to apply it in the broader context of relations with the superpowers as well.

Several conclusions about the nature of the superpower rivalry and about U.S. and Soviet intentions and capabilities appear to be ingredients of this evolving policy. The first is that since World War II there has been a gradual shift in the balance of power from one of preponderant U.S. strength to one of greater equality between the superpowers. The second is a growing doubt about the capability of the United States to respond effectively to the threats that seem most probable. Third, although by no means unanimous, there appears to be a shift among Gulf elites toward the thesis that, in spite of a more evenly balanced U.S.-Soviet power equation, the objectives of the Soviets in the Middle East are essentially defensive; that they do not intend to try to take over the area by physical force and that short of this, the governments of the area can establish a modus vivendi that need not be to the latter's disadvantage.

The first two conclusions are supportable by an objective examination of the events of the past 20 years; the third is more debatable, although it is, of course, no less the subject of continuing and unresolved debate within Western circles as it is among the councils of the Gulf Arabs. Taken together, however, these subjective conclusions have combined to give greater weight to the argument within Arab councils that military alliances should be shunned and that reliance should instead be placed on a diplomacy that makes enemies of neither superpower and preserves freedom of action between both.

Yet the attachment of the Gulf Arabs to Western culture, institutions, technology, and commerce runs very deep, and any movement at a political level toward greater nonalignment will be taken cautiously and with a view to preserving these advantages. If American diplomacy on the Arab-Israel issue can begin to make progress toward a negotiated settlement, it would remove at least some of the emotionalism and political strain that presently impede Washington's efforts to reach a meeting of minds with the Gulf Arabs on security issues.

There is also scope on both sides for greater sensitivity to the concerns of the other in the dialogue about security. If the Arabs are justifiably frustrated by Washington's clumsy emphasis on formal alliances and military arrangements as an assurance of security, Washington would be justified in complaining about an attitude on the part of the Gulf Arabs that is too often parochial about the global superpower rivalry. Their intense preoccupation with local affairs does not often allow them to understand that Soviet victories in a contest in Latin America, or Africa, can embolden Moscow to take greater risks for gains closer to their doorstep. While complaining about U.S. insensitivity to their own political concerns, the Arabs has been too casual about offering political support to the United States on global issues that should be of common concern.

In turn, Washington needs to be more sensitive to the fact that the Gulf rulers are still heavily preoccupied with the problems of internal development and to listen more closely to their concerns about political considerations that either strengthen or weaken their hand in promoting this process. In one respect at least the Arabs are right on target: They see the experience of the last 30 years in the Middle East as demonstrating conclusively that more Western positions have been lost, and more pro-Western governments destroyed, through internal upheaval than as the result of external aggression.

NOTES

1. Donald Hawley, *The Trucial States* (London: Allen and Unwin, 1970), p. 164.

2. British efforts to put a stop to the slave trade, a humanitarian rather than strategic interest, did inevitably draw Britain into the internal affairs of these principalities to a certain extent.

3. The U.S. government, also, was taken aback by the British decision and asked London to reconsider.

4. Interestingly, Oman is the only Arab Gulf state that has established diplomatic relations with the People's Republic of China, a step it undoubtedly saw as a further counterweight to Soviet influence.

5. These statements are detailed in William B. Quandt, *Saudi Arabia in the 1980s* (Washington, D.C.: Brookings Institution, 1981), pp. 69-71.

6. William B. Quandt, in comments on the television series "Saudi Arabia," produced by the Public Broadcasting Service and shown in April and May, 1982.

7. Good candidates for a soliloquy along these lines would be the present foreign ministers of Kuwait, Saudi Arabia, Bahrain, and the UAE. The foreign minister of Oman would presumably have something different to say.

8. It was reportedly a tipoff from Dubai that helped the Bahrain authorities to round up the Shiite conspirators in a timely manner.

9. Implementation of the arrangement has in fact been stalled over Saudi Arabia's request that Pakistan assign only Sunni officers and troops to this detachment.

Part II

U.S.-SOVIET RIVALRY

3

The Evolution of U.S. Strategy Toward the Indian Ocean and Persian Gulf Regions

Gary Sick

Until recently, the Indian Ocean was of little significance in American strategy. The first sustained encounter with the region was in the nineteenth century, in the days of the great clipper ships. These early contacts led to a treaty with the sultanate of Muscat and Oman in 1833, which is duly recalled on occasions of state with Oman to this day. However, U.S. diplomatic and military involvement was meager. In 1908, President Theodore Roosevelt sent his "Great White Fleet" around the world, necessarily traversing the Indian Ocean. That brief passage may have represented the first introduction of U.S. naval forces into the area.

During World War II, the Indian Ocean assumed considerable importance as a supply route to Russia for delivery of lend-lease military equipment and other supplies. A U.S. Middle East Command was established in the Persian Gulf at that time. The approximately

---

This historical essay is drawn from more than 20 years of involvement with U.S. policy in the Indian Ocean region. In preparing this chapter, I have relied heavily on my own experiences and my personal notes, as well as discussions with other participants. With very few exceptions, the actual material in this paper can be gleaned from a careful reading of the public record—the press, numerous congressional hearings, and scholarly accounts. I have not, however, undertaken the laborious and time-consuming task of winnowing 30 years of documents to provide citations. Thus, this discussion lacks an elaborate scholarly apparatus of footnotes and extensive bibliography. Whatever contribution this study may have to offer is on its own terms as a retrospective memoir by one who was deeply engaged in many of the events described. The responsibility for factual accuracy, as well as interpretation, is strictly my own.

40,000 U.S. troops in that command still represent the largest sustained deployment of American military forces into the region.

Nevertheless, those initial contacts were temporary and exceptional. For more than 150 years, the United States regarded the Indian Ocean as a British preserve, and American strategy deferred to British military and political leadership in the region. Even those few naval forces that the United States retained after World War II—the flagship and two destroyers of the Middle East Command—were hosted by the British navy at Jufair on Bahrain Island.

This discussion will attempt to trace the changes in U.S. perceptions in the region of the Indian Ocean and Persian Gulf from World War II to the present. As we shall see, American attitudes have altered drastically as a result of three developments: the withdrawal of the British military presence, the increased U.S. demand for the oil resources of the Persian Gulf, and the evolving Soviet political and military role in the region. In turn, the U.S. response to changes in the strategic environment involved a mix of several different policy instruments: the direct application of U.S. military presence, political and military arrangements with friendly regional states, diplomatic and economic association, and some efforts at regional arms control. The interplay between these various elements will provide the analytical underpinnings for the historical account.

The evolution of American perceptions and policy will be traced through seven successive periods over 35 years. Based on that review, some observations will be made about U.S. performance and some thoughts offered about what lessons may be drawn for future policymaking in a region that has emerged as a vital component of U.S. global security policy.

COMPETITION UNDER THE BRITISH UMBRELLA: WORLD WAR II TO 1960

During the 15-year period after World War II, the Indian Ocean region was regarded almost exclusively by American policymakers as an arena for the extension of U.S. containment policy. Because the British were considered to have unquestioned military superiority in the region, competition with the USSR was largely of a diplomatic and psychological nature.

There was, of course, concern about the possible extension of Soviet military power. The Soviet failure to withdraw its military forces from northern Iran in 1946 triggered the first direct clash of the postwar era, and it is properly regarded as one of the opening salvos of the cold war. The issue was successfully resolved through U.S. and British diplomatic pressure in the United Nations, backed by predominant U.S. global military power plus some clever diplomatic maneuvering on the part of the Iranian government. Nevertheless, this episode remained a vivid memory for American leaders of the day, and Iran continued to be regarded as the "front line" in any possible U.S.-Soviet confrontation in the region. It did not, however, entail the deployment of any U.S. ground forces in the region.

The Indian Ocean was the region where the fingers of U.S. Secretary of State John Foster Dulles's regional defense pacts stretched to meet—never quite successfully. The ANZUS Pact (1951), SEATO (1954), the Baghdad Pact (1955), and its successor CENTO (1959) each involved one or more Indian Ocean states, with Pakistan as the occasionally uncertain linchpin. Associated bilateral agreements between the United States and Iran, Turkey, and Pakistan led to the first formal U.S. security commitments in the region. In each case these agreements provided that the United States would "take such action, including the use of military forces, as may be mutually agreed 'subject to U.S. constitutional limitations' to oppose aggression from any country controlled by international communism." These commitments were given some substance militarily by a network of air bases in Turkey, Saudi Arabia, and Pakistan.

American concerns during this period centered on the competition with the Soviet Union and China for influence in what later came to be called the Third World. In some respects, the Indian Ocean could be considered the "Third World Ocean." One-third of the world's population lives on its shores, and the nations surrounding it are economically underdeveloped, many sharing the experience of colonial occupation. This region was the seedbed of the nonaligned movement, born in 1955 at the Afro-Asian Conference in Bandung, Indonesia, where many of the Indian Ocean states were prominently represented.

The United States regarded this nascent movement with great suspicion. The sharp ideological polarization of the cold war did not, in Dulles's view, allow for a middle ground. The efforts of many of the Indian Ocean states, and others, to develop an independent doctrine not aligned with either superpower tended to be viewed as an opening for communist influence and ideology to replace the Western colonial legacy. This concern was sharpened by the considerable success enjoyed by Chou En-lai at Bandung, at a time when the United States did not distinguish between Soviet and Chinese objectives.

Still, U.S. strategy was almost exclusively diplomatic, economic, and political, rather than military, in nature. Even the mutual defense pacts relied on global U.S. military strength rather than the local presence of any U.S. forces. The three ships of the Middle East Command were acknowledged to be a symbolic presence with no significant military potential. The string of air bases stretching across the region offered the most tangible manifestation of U.S. military power in the region; however, these sites did not play a central role in U.S. strategy. Moreover, the strategic air base constructed in Dhahran, Saudi Arabia, in 1946 was under almost constant negotiation from 1956. The U.S. presence was terminated by mutual agreement in 1962. The use of Peshawar in Pakistan was seriously compromised by its association with the shootdown of the U-2 spy plane over the Soviet Union in 1960. Much more important was the scattering of communications and intelligence-gathering sites throughout the region that tied the area into a global U.S. military communications network and provided invaluable information about Soviet and Chinese strategic weapons development and testing.

Otherwise, U.S. policies concentrated on competition for influence through the traditional instrumentalities of aid, trade, and diplomatic maneuver, supported by military assistance to certain states, such as Saudi Arabia, Pakistan, and Iran.

The pattern of Soviet activities was not dissimilar. The Soviets leapfrogged the U.S. circle of containment to build a structure of political relationships, beginning in earnest in the post-Stalin period. This included the start of a long campaign in the mid-1950s to woo India, the opening to Iraq after the anti-Western coup of 1958, and the initiation of local projects such as the building of port facilities in Hodeidah, now in North Yemen, near the mouth of the Red Sea. A Soviet oceanographic ship appeared in the Indian Ocean for the first time in 1957, probably signaling Soviet intentions eventually to conduct submarine and anti-submarine operations in the region.

INCREASED AMERICAN ACTIVISM: 1960–68

Under Presidents John Kennedy and Lyndon Johnson, the United States demonstrated a greater willingness to consider unilateral intervention and active U.S. involvement in areas of regional dispute throughout the world. The possibility of projection of U.S. military power in distant areas led to a greater awareness of the need for an infrastructure capable of supporting such operations. The most dramatic outcome of this activist surge was, of course, the growing involvement of the United States in Southeast Asia. However, the new climate in Washington also led to new initiatives in the Indian Ocean. The most visible and enduring result was the acquisition of military access rights on the island of Diego Garcia in the Chagos Archipelago.

As early as 1960, there were voices within the U.S. Navy calling attention to the need for military facilities in the Indian Ocean. In that year, a U.S. carrier, the U.S.S. *Bonhomme Richard*, visited the Indian Ocean for the first time. The navy was intensely aware of the vulnerability of shore-based facilities to the nationalist currents then flowing so powerfully in the Indian Ocean and elsewhere. There was also the beginning of a concern that the British presence might at some point be withdrawn, leaving a power vacuum that, it was feared, the Soviets or Chinese might fill at the expense of Western security interests.

It was argued that future U.S. interests might require the direct extension of U.S. power into the region, and to wait until the need for support facilities was unmistakable might be too late. Thus, some navy strategists proposed "stockpiling" some facilities for possible future use. Specifically, they identified a string of lightly populated islands in the Indian Ocean and elsewhere that were strategically located and that might be expected to remain relatively immune to the nationalist pressures being felt on overseas bases around the world.

This concept struck a responsive chord within the top echelons of the Kennedy administration. In 1962, the Joint Chiefs of Staff conducted a study of the "strategic islands" proposal, and private discussions were initiated with the British, who proved receptive to the idea of joint facilities in which they, in effect, would provide the real estate while the United States assumed primary responsibility for base construction.

The strategic circumstances that might make such support facilities necessary were not spelled out in great detail. However, in the Indian Ocean, the focus of strategic attention was the future defense of the Persian Gulf, where Soviet intentions were suspect. The Soviet postwar military penetration of Iran was well remembered, and a new Soviet thrust through Iran was widely regarded as the most probable scenario for a future crisis. However, the most immediate requirements were quite modest, relating primarily to the need for communications support. The U.S. Navy favored Diego Garcia from the start, largely because of its location, virtually in the center of the Indian Ocean.

Ironically, the government of India may have encouraged this trend when it asked for emergency U.S. air defense assistance during its war with China in 1962. A review of U.S. resources at the time revealed serious weaknesses in the ability to respond even to limited contingencies, thus bolstering the arguments of those pressing for a new strategy. Furthermore, partly as a result of the Indian experience, the Department of State became convinced of the need to have a U.S. military presence to lend muscle to American diplomacy in the region and to underline, for our friends in the region, U.S. ability to meet its commitments.

As a consequence, during the Johnson administration, it was the State Department and the White House that were pressing a reluctant Department of Defense (especially Secretary Robert McNamara) for a more active military and naval posture in the Indian Ocean. Talks with the British were pursued throughout 1963, and a survey of Diego Garcia and several other islands was proposed. However, the Department of Defense resisted pressures to establish a major naval presence, such as the permanent deployment of a carrier task force, in light of competing military requirements in the Pacific and Mediterranean.

In the fall of 1963, the carrier U.S.S. *Essex* and a naval task group participated in the annual Midlink exercise of CENTO. In early 1964, President Johnson approved a symbolic cruise by a carrier task force into the Indian Ocean to signal the beginning of what was to be a policy of introducing U.S. military power into the region on an intermittent but regular basis. This so-called Concord Squadron entered the Indian Ocean via the Malacca Strait on April 4, 1964, and visited Madagascar, Kenya, Aden, and the Gulf of Oman, where the shah of Iran observed flight operations from the bridge.

Although plans for detaching a number of Indian Ocean islands proceeded simultaneously, this effort was consciously disassociated from the policy of periodic naval presence. The Department of Defense maintained (somewhat disingenuously) that carrier forces were self-contained and required no independent regional base support. The islands were viewed strictly as potential communications sites and as a prudent investment in the event of future contingencies.

In May 1964, the British cabinet approved the detachment of the Chagos Archipelago and several other small islands from Mauritius and the Seychelles. The following month, U.S. Secretary of the Navy Paul Nitze made a speech that referred to the "power vacuum" in the Indian Ocean and mentioned the possible U.S. acquisition of base rights. A survey of the islands was carried out preparatory to the repatriation of the inhabitants, primarily to Mauritius, and the termination of copra production. The British government changed in October 1964, but the new Labour Government fully supported the program worked out by its predecessors.

Initially, consideration was given to the development of a military airfield on Aldabra Island, off the east coast of Africa. That plan was abandoned, however, in the face of intense opposition by British naturalists who feared disruption of the delicate ecology of the island and its surrounding waters.

As the final negotiations were proceeding, the British discovered that the costs of land acquisition and resettlement would be considerably higher than originally anticipated, and they requested U.S. financial assistance. After some resistance, the United States agreed to set aside up to $14 million in research and development costs associated with the Polaris missile system (which the British were purchasing from the United States) to cover approximately one-half of the total costs. In November 1965, the British Indian Ocean Territory (BIOT) was established by a British Order-in-Council. In December 1966, an Executive Agreement was signed between the United States and Great Britain providing for the availability of these islands for joint defense purposes.

The strategic rationale for the establishment of BIOT was in fact the perceived need for future support facilities in the context of long-term contingency planning. However, the potential value of BIOT as a long-term strategic investment was not sufficient to overcome political opposition in a skeptical Congress, so the executive branch was led to inflate the nature of the immediate threat (hence the talk of a "power vacuum") and to search for a persuasive tactical justification. This problem was compounded by new developments. By the late 1960s, the original requirement for communications support was largely transcended by the advent of communications satellites and by the development of alternative sites in Australia. Linkage of BIOT to support increased naval operations (originally planned as a presence two months out of every six) was resisted by the navy itself and was further obviated as U.S. involvement in Southeast Asia diverted attention and resources from the Indian Ocean. (In fact, the policy of intermittent deployments was never implemented.) Even support for ships in transit to Vietnam was not required after the Suez Canal closed in 1967. Furthermore, there was little evidence of an immediate Soviet threat, as the Soviet naval presence in the region was limited to annual participation in Ethiopian Naval Day celebrations and (starting in 1967) periodic deployments in support of Soviet space operations.

The combination of congressional pressures, British interest in seeing construction started, and the need to respond to critics—including some within the administration itself—demanded a rationale that went beyond an ill-defined long-term contingency. Consequently, the military found itself—not for the first time nor probably the last—being urged for political reasons to develop a more compelling strategic rationale and to earmark funds for early development of military facilities on Diego Garcia.

As a result, U.S. interest in, and strategic plans for, the Indian Ocean were widely perceived as more expansive and more urgent than they were in fact. That perception had consequences within the region and elsewhere that became evident during the subsequent period.

NIXON DOCTRINE: BRITISH WITHDRAWAL TO THE OCTOBER 1973 WAR

Between 1968 and 1973, the strategic environment in the Indian Ocean was altered in several significant ways. The most important of these was the announcement by the British government in 1968 that it intended to withdraw from its historic position east of Suez, a process that was completed by the end of 1971. Almost simultaneously with the British announcement, the USSR began to deploy military forces to the region on a regular basis. That process began very slowly. In 1968, 2–4 combat vessels were maintained in the area, together with supporting auxiliaries, for a total of about 1,900 ship-days for the year. (A ship-day represents one ship present for one day.) By 1969, this level had more than doubled, with a total of 4,100 ship-days; and there were 5,000 ship-days by Soviet units in 1970. By 1973, this figure had increased to 9,000 ship-days, although that was somewhat misleading because it included a detachment of Soviet minesweepers helping to clear the harbor at Chittagong following the Indo-Pakistani war.

The first Soviet submarine appeared in October 1968, and in August of the same year, the first long-range reconnaissance flights by Soviet Bear D aircraft occurred. These bomber aircraft, equipped for ocean surveillance, originated from Soviet airfields, overflew Iran, conducted surveillance in the northwest Indian Ocean, and then returned to Soviet bases without landing in the region. The mission of these aircraft was declared to be "support for Soviet space operations"; however, they were assumed from the start to be associated with Soviet naval activities, as they are in other Soviet naval operating areas such as the North Atlantic or Pacific.

During the same period, Brezhnev launched a political campaign to squeeze Western presence out of Asia. His call for an Asian collective security arrangement attracted no support in the region, but it was generally interpreted by the Western powers as a rather transparent effort to play on the nationalist sentiments of the regional states and to add a political dimension to the increased Soviet military presence.

When the Nixon administration took office in 1969, it immediately initiated a major review of U.S. policy in the region, focusing first on the Persian Gulf. In that same year, President Richard Nixon announced in Guam the Nixon Doctrine. It was understood that the policy review was to consider how this doctrine of U.S. support for, and increased reliance on, regional powers could best be applied to the situation in the Gulf and Indian Ocean.

At the same time, pressure was mounting in the region and in the UN General Assembly to halt the perceived growth of superpower military competition in the Indian Ocean and to transform the Indian Ocean into a "zone of peace." Ceylon (later Sri Lanka) was the leader in this movement, with strong support from India, which had been extremely critical of the plans for Diego Garcia from the moment of their announcement. The "zone of peace" concept was first formally proposed at a Non-Aligned Conference in Lusaka in September 1970. A resolution was introduced into the General Assembly the following year which called for "elimination of any manifestation of great power military presence in the Indian Ocean, conceived in the context of great power rivalry." The resolution passed in December 1971, 61–0, and became an annual fixture on the General Assembly's calendar. The controversial nature of the resolution was demonstrated by the unusually large number of abstentions (55 nations), including the United States, the Soviet Union, and most of the major maritime nations of the world.

The review of Persian Gulf policy was completed by the Nixon administration in late 1970. Based on this study, the White House concluded that the British intent to retain much of their political presence in the Gulf meant that there was not so much a power vacuum as a realignment of the power balance. There was great potential, it was felt, for instability in the Gulf, but the situation was unlikely to be responsive to U.S. power. In short, it was viewed as a political problem rather than a military problem. Furthermore, because the principal concern was oil, and because the United States imported relatively little Persian Gulf oil at that time, U.S. interests were seen as largely derivative of the interests of America's allies, who were much more dependent than the United States on oil sources.

Based on this appreciation of the situation in the Gulf, the Nixon administration adopted a low-profile policy that placed primary reliance on security cooperation with regional states. Because it relied so heavily on the two key states of Iran and Saudi Arabia, it quickly became known as the "two-pillar policy." It had four key elements: first, to promote cooperation between Iran and Saudi Arabia as a desirable basis for maintaining stability in the Gulf, while recognizing Iran as the preponderant power; second, it was decided to maintain the tiny U.S. naval presence (the three ships of the Middle East Command) without change, although there was great sensitivity to the growing opposition in the Gulf, particularly on the part of the shah of Iran; third, it was decided to expand the U.S. diplomatic representation in the Gulf and to promote U.S. technical assistance; and fourth, to encourage the lower Gulf states to look primarily to the United Kingdom for their security needs by restraining U.S. sales of arms in that area.

This policy was perhaps the clearest translation of the Nixon Doctrine into concrete practice anywhere in the world. The United States was heavily committed in Southeast Asia, and the American public was increasingly opposed to any expansion of U.S. commitments abroad. Consequently, the U.S. government would look primarily to Iran (and to a lesser extent to Saudi Arabia) to protect American interests in the region. In lieu of a military presence, the United States would assist regional states to develop their own security forces through arms sales and advisers, while providing technical assistance for development purposes. This policy was fully implemented and served as the basis of U.S. policy toward the Gulf, with only minor refinements, for nearly a decade.

Because the two-pillar policy concerned itself exclusively with the Gulf, it left unaddressed a number of questions about U.S. interests and military strategy in the broader area of the Indian Ocean. Further studies were initiated to examine those questions, particularly the issues of naval presence and bases. This was the first such review of regional military policy in nearly a decade and the first attempt by the U.S. government to examine systematically the elements of an integrated Indian Ocean strategy. The underlying assumptions that emerged within the policy community are both interesting and instructive in the light of later developments.

First of all, it was felt that the Indian Ocean could not be regarded as a political unit. There was simply too much diversity to consider it as a whole. The region was on the other side of the world and had been of little military interest in the past. The United States had few political commitments in the region and did not even make heavy use of maritime or air transit lanes there. No state or group of states in the region, it was felt, had the same importance to the United States as was the case in Europe, the Far East, and Latin America.

It was recognized, however, that U.S. interests would be harmed if the region fell under the domination of forces hostile to the United States and the West, particularly the oil resources of the Persian Gulf. These were of great importance to the economic well-being of the West, although not directly to the United States itself. Consequently, great emphasis was placed on military cooperation with friends and allies in the region, who were expected to shoulder a major portion of the requirement for a military presence.

It was also recognized that the United States had a number of residual interests in the region because of the area's position as the "backyard" of conflicts in the Arab-Israeli sphere on the one side and Southeast Asia on the other. It encompassed 30 members of the United Nations and, as a major ocean basin, could not be separated from certain global interests involving the use of the high seas. Furthermore, in time it might come to have increased importance as a strategic region stretching along the southern borders of the USSR and China. But all these were essentially subsidiary concerns.

The Soviet naval presence was seen as a cautious probing exercise that, over time, would probably result in a gradually increasing Soviet naval presence. However, the major Soviet threat to U.S. interests was seen as more likely to occur elsewhere in the world, closer to Soviet support facilities in their own homeland.

In sum, the administration concluded that the United States had a relatively low level of interest in the region, and what interest there was could be satisfied by normal commercial and political access at a fairly low level.

This remarkably benign view was not universally shared. A small but vocal group—centered primarily in the Pentagon but with significant support at the State Department and the White House—took a much less sanguine view of the situation. These individuals felt that the United States had substantial interests in the area—investments, oil, and other primary resources—and that the increased Soviet political and military presence constituted a critical challenge in view of anticipated political instability. From their perspective, the United States and the USSR were in global competition in the Third World, and Soviet gains would come only at the expense of U.S. and Western interests. Consequently, it was argued, the United States must make a major effort to exert itself in the Indian Ocean as part of a global effort to preserve its security interests.

These competing ideological perspectives were never reconciled. The issue was ultimately decided by the absence of available U.S. military resources that might be used in the Indian Ocean. At a time when American forces were stretched thin in Vietnam, a forward posture in the Indian Ocean was simply not feasible.

Funding was sought and approved for construction of an austere communications station on Diego Garcia, notably including an 8,000-foot supporting runway. Work began in early 1971, and the facility became operational in March 1973. This was essentially a continuation of plans inherited from the previous administration, and proposals for an upgraded facility were defeated in Congress.

Otherwise, no new military deployments or strategy were initiated. In fact, even routine deployments and exercises were rendered marginally more difficult by the official designation of the Indian Ocean as a "sensitive region" where military deployments and exercises had to be coordinated in advance with the Department of State. The Middle East Command was upgraded slightly by the assignment of a more capable flagship and the rotation of more modern destroyers to the Gulf. However, it was still regarded as a symbolic rather than a fighting force.

Various proposals for possible arms-control initiatives were also examined during this period, including the earliest efforts to identify the technical problems that would have to be resolved in any effort to limit naval presence or competition. In practice, however, the concept was short-lived. In March 1971, Soviet Ambassador Anatoly Dobrynin raised with U.S. Secretary of State William Rogers the issue of mutual restraint in the Indian Ocean. Three months later, in a policy speech, Leonid Brezhnev mentioned the problem of "ships sailing far from their own shores" and indicated that the USSR would be prepared to deal with this problem on an "equal basis." In July 1971, U.S. Ambassador Jacob Beam in Moscow, during a meeting with Foreign Minister Andrei Gromyko, referred to Dobrynin's informal approach and told him that the United States agreed in principle that it would be in the mutual interests of the United States and the Soviet Union to avoid military competition in the area and that the United States would find it useful to know more about what the Soviets had in mind. Gromyko responded that he was not briefed and suggested that he would look into it. The matter was never again raised by the Soviets.

A new element of U.S. Indian Ocean policy was introduced in December 1971, when the carrier U.S.S. *Enterprise* and a Seventh Fleet task force were sent into the Bay of Bengal during the Indo-Pakistani war over Bangladesh. This was the first quasi-operational deployment of a major U.S. naval force to the area. The precise role of this force was left ambiguous, probably intentionally, although it was clearly intended as a gesture of reassurance to Pakistan (and possibly to the Chinese), as well as a veiled warning to India to restrict its war aims with respect to Pakistan.

It is doubtful that the force had any significant effect on the outcome of the war; however, it did sensitize regional states to the possible use of U.S. power in the region. It undoubtedly added new impetus to the zone of peace movement, and the first annual UN General Assembly resolution on the zone of peace was passed the same month. It also prompted a major Soviet response, in the form of a surge deployment of a considerable naval force, including cruise missile submarines for the first time. This force, which remained in the Indian Ocean even after the U.S. force departed, marked a watershed in the size and sophistication of Soviet naval deployments to the region. Also, the Soviets contributed a mine-clearing force, which spent more than a year clearing the harbor of Chittagong after the war, thus introducing a sizable new increment in the routine levels of Soviet naval deployments in the region.

Within the U.S. government, the deployment of the *Enterprise* was regarded as a unique exception to the policy of extremely low profile naval presence that had previously been adopted. Once the crisis settled down, the United States returned to its previous pattern, and the basic policy remained unaltered. There were no new initiatives or policy reexaminations until the 1973 Arab-Israeli war. However, within the region and elsewhere, this distinction was probably lost. The deliberately low level of U.S. military presence in the region tended to be obscured in the publicity surrounding the dramatic exception to the rule.

In looking at this initial period of the Nixon administration, it is also instructive to remind ourselves of some of the prevailing attitudes on oil, as the oil of the Persian Gulf was explicitly recognized as the one area of interest underlying a U.S. strategic concern with the region. It is important to recall that, when the Nixon administration took office, crude oil was selling for less than $1.50 per barrel and that as late as mid-1973, the price was only $2 a barrel. In fact, the price of oil had remained virtually unchanged for a quarter of a century ($1.53 in 1929), although it had dipped and then recovered. Even the most pessimistic cassandras, who were beginning to warn of an energy crisis, risked ridicule to suggest that we might face oil prices of $10 per barrel within the next generation.

By mid-1973, only 10 percent of U.S. oil imports came from the Gulf, accounting for only 3 percent of total U.S. oil consumption. Although there were voices within the government warning that U.S. dependence on Persian Gulf oil would increase sharply within the coming decade, the official philosophy was determinedly upbeat.

The official position of the U.S. government, as articulated by Assistant Secretary of State for Middle East Affairs Joseph Sisco in congressional testimony in the summer of 1973, consisted of two basic principles. First, the United States had the resources to meet its own energy needs and should not or would not allow itself to become dependent on outside sources for its vital national energy needs. Second, it was asserted that the mutuality of commercial interests between producers and consumers (that is, the consumers' need to buy and the producers' need to sell oil) was sufficient to insulate this essentially commercial relationship from the political effects of the Arab-Israeli dispute. This, in fact, represented the position of many high-level officials within the government in mid-1973. It was to be put to a harsh test before the end of the year.

On the whole, looking back from the vantage point of mid-1973, the United States had every reason to be satisfied with its basic strategy. The political transition to independence by the mini-states in the Gulf following the British withdrawal had been more orderly than almost anyone would have dared hope. The Iranian seizure of some small islands at the mouth of the Gulf in late 1971 had been balanced by the retraction of Iranian claims to Bahrain, and the initial Arab outrage seemed to have subsided into reluctant acceptance of a fait accompli. The Iraqi threat to Kuwait in March 1973, and a nearly simultaneous upsurge of tension between Saudi Arabia and South Yemen, had been managed without the need for any direct U.S. intervention.

Both of the two pillars of U.S. policy, Iran and Saudi Arabia, appeared stable and increasingly self-confident. Iran was providing troops to assist the new sultan of Oman to put down the externally assisted rebellion in Dhofar Province. United States ambassadors had taken up their posts in all the new Gulf states, and the prospects for continued good relations were strong.

Despite the growing importation of oil, the balance of trade between the United States and the Gulf was heavily in the favor of the United States and was expected to stay that way as the oil producers sought Western technology and products with their increasing oil revenues. The 8,000-foot runway and communications station at Diego Garcia became operational in March 1973, providing military support capacity, and the Middle East Command seemed securely established after successful negotiation of a lease with the government of Bahrain, replacing the original British host arrangement.

When James Schlesinger replaced Elliott Richardson as secretary of defense in the summer of 1973, I was asked to write a paper looking at U.S. policy objectives in the Persian Gulf through 1980. I remember writing that if the situation looked as good in 1980 as it did in 1973, we would be able to congratulate ourselves on an unequivocal policy triumph.

THE AFTERMATH OF THE OCTOBER 1973 WAR

That was not to be. The strategic environment was dramatically and fundamentally transformed by the sudden outbreak of a new Middle East war. The Arab oil embargo against the United States and certain other states supporting Israel demonstrated that business and politics in the Middle East could not safely be separated from each other. The resulting panic in the world markets, including massive disruptions in U.S. domestic distribution systems, demonstrated that the United States was much more vulnerable than had previously been supposed. The threat of possible naval actions against shipping destined for Israel drew attention to the vulnerability of oil shipping lanes through the Gulf and the Indian Ocean. The cutoff of fuel to U.S. naval forces required an improvised oil supply system relying on Iran and tankers from the Philippines, some 4,000 miles away. The Bahraini government demanded that the Middle East Command terminate its use of facilities there. The Soviet Union doubled its warship presence in the Indian Ocean in response to U.S. naval deployments.

The initial U.S. response to the war also transformed the earlier minimalist approach of the United States. The U.S.S. *Hancock* carrier task force was ordered into the Arabian Sea in late October, and a greatly increased naval presence was maintained until April 1974.

This was probably related to the global alert of U.S. forces in response to the Arab-Israeli war and a reaction to the shipping threat, as well as a more generalized response to the sudden cessation of oil supplies.

In early November, Secretary of Defense James Schlesinger announced the U.S. intention to return to the (Johnson) policy of more frequent and more regular naval deployments to the region. In January 1974, an emergency request was sent to Congress to upgrade the facilities at Diego Garcia. (Congress refused to take immediate action and postponed the request to the following year.) Also in January, Schlesinger warned the Arabs that they risked violence if they sought to use the oil weapon to cripple the industrialized world, thus implicitly linking U.S. military actions to possible U.S. pressure against the oil producers.

To add to the apprehension of the Arab states of the Persian Gulf, in November 1974, the carrier U.S.S. *Constellation*, which was participating in a routine naval exercise in the Arabian Sea, suddenly broke off from the exercises and conducted air operations during a 36-hour circumnavigation of the Gulf. Although the reasons for this very unusual maneuver were never explained, it certainly captured the attention of the Gulf rulers.

Finally, in December 1974, Secretary of State Henry Kissinger, under intense questioning by a journalist, declared that, in the event of actual "strangulation" of Western economies, the United States could not exclude the use of force. This statement, published in *Business Week* in January 1975, further fueled a public debate that raged primarily in the U.S. media for nearly two years.

Once the initial dust had settled, with the boycott over and the Arab states beginning to reestablish closer ties with the United States in the wake of Kissinger's brilliant negotiation of a disengagement agreement, the U.S. government undertook a comprehensive reevaluation of its Indian Ocean strategy. In the wake of the war, there were a number of changes in perception and strategy.

The most dramatic change was the recognition of Persian Gulf oil as a much more direct and vital interest of the United States in the area. There was a clear understanding that the oil had been turned off at the wellhead for political reasons, rather than any military threat. However, the very act of recognition by senior policymakers that events in the Persian Gulf area could directly affect American security in a profound manner was, in itself, a major watershed in U.S. strategic thinking.

Concomitant with this new awareness of U.S. interests was a heightened suspicion of the growing Soviet military presence in the region. Soviet deployments during the crises of 1971 and 1973 had attracted the attention of military planners, and new information now began to emerge about Soviet military construction in Somalia, including indications of a major airfield and other facilities at Berbera. These concerns were fueled by the signing of a Friendship Treaty between the USSR and Somalia in July 1974.

A third change in U.S. attitudes was the unwillingness of America's allies to lend assistance in the course of the recent crisis. The French had established an Indian Ocean Command in 1973, including a major naval presence, and the British continued to maintain a periodic presence. However, the basic judgment after the October War was that the United States would have to go it alone rather than placing heavy reliance on allied support, as had previously been assumed. This fact, together with the sobering experience of attempting to maintain a carrier task force 4,000 miles from its base of support in the Philippines, led to an urgent reconsideration of the nature and level of U.S. support infrastructure. Diego Garcia assumed a much greater importance.

In light of these new perceptions, the questions to be answered were: What level of U.S. military presence would best serve U.S. interests in the region, and how could that presence most effectively be combined with diplomatic and other policy instrumentalities, including possible arms-control initiatives, to pursue American objectives? Not surprisingly, the policy decision in the first instance, that is, in the early fall of 1974, was to institutionalize the actions that had been taken almost a year before, in the heat of the crisis. These actions had proved operationally feasible, and much of the political cost had already been paid. Thus, it was decided to maintain a contingency naval presence in the form of periodic deployments from the Pacific Fleet. In practice, this took the form of three deployments per year, with every other task force to include an aircraft carrier.

The expansion of Diego Garcia was proposed to Congress, to include a longer runway (12,000 feet) and greatly increased fuel-storage capacity capable of supporting a carrier task force for up to 60 days, in addition to enlarging the anchorage and improving piers and handling facilities. In short, Diego Garcia was to be expanded from its genuinely austere status as a communications station to an intermediate facility capable of supporting major naval and air deployments for limited periods of time. Negotiations also continued with the government of Bahrain to seek continued access there for the three ships of the Middle East Command.

Finally, it was determined that no new initiatives on Indian Ocean arms limitations would be undertaken with the Soviets for the time being. Rather, the United States would pursue a policy of "tacit restraint," with the United States asserting its rights to operate military forces in the Indian Ocean at the new, but still relatively modest levels that had emerged from the 1973 crisis.

There was general recognition that this increased level of military activity was not in itself a solution to the stubborn political issues facing the United States in the area, nor was it a substitute for other diplomatic or economic policies that might be pursued on a bilateral basis with various states of the region. Rather, this enhancement of U.S. military capabilities and presence was regarded as a symbol of U.S. political interest, reinforcing other policy instruments, as well as an assertion of American intent to maintain access to the region.

Again, this policy and its underlying philosophy were not unanimously shared within the national security community in Washington. In particular, there was a small but tenacious group, represented in the Departments of State and Defense, in the Arms Control and Disarmament Agency, and in the White House, which supported a more active pursuit of arms limitations talks with the Soviet Union. Moreover, there was pressure in the same direction not only from the regional states and the UN, but also from some key allies (including the Whitlam government in Australia and some elements of the British Labour government) as well as Congress.

From late 1974 until mid-1975, the debate over U.S. strategy centered almost exclusively around the controversy concerning the expansion of Diego Garcia. A powerful faction emerged in the Senate, led by Senator John Culver, which questioned the operational need for such expansion in the absence of any serious arms-control efforts. A series of hearings was conducted, examining every detail of U.S. Indian Ocean policy, starting with the formation of BIOT in 1966 and the displacement of the approximately 500 original inhabitants of Diego Garcia, by then living in squalid conditions in Mauritius. Nixon had resigned in August 1974 as a result of the Watergate scandal, and President Gerald Ford was left to defend against charges of another government cover-up in the Indian Ocean.

In March 1975, a landmark was passed when Ford, at congressional insistence, signed a formal determination that "the construction of such facilities (Diego Garcia) is essential to the national interest of the United States." This was the first high-level policy statement indicating that essential U.S. interests were at stake in the Indian Ocean region.

The whole matter was resolved in July 1975, after a full day of debate in the Senate, by a narrow vote approving the expansion program. However, the Senate deferred funding until the following spring, pending an administration study and report to Congress on possible arms limitations measures. Consequently, in late 1975, a special panel was convened under the National Security Council to conduct an in-depth study of the technical problems associated with possible Indian Ocean arms limitations.

By April 1976, the arms-control panel had completed its report, concluding that naval arms limitations would pose severe technical problems but would not necessarily be impossible to negotiate. This conclusion was reported to Congress in mid-April 1976 with the further comment that it was the consensus within the administration that no new arms-control initiative should be undertaken at that time, citing, among other things, the apparent lack of interest by the Soviets and their military activities in Angola and Somalia. With this, work began immediately on the expansion of Diego Garcia.

In addition, a number of other events in the region and elsewhere had a direct impact on the overall perception of the security environment in the region as seen from Washington. The sultan of Oman paid his first visit to Washington in January 1975. The visit was very successful in opening up direct lines of relationship with the United States, which provided the sultan with an important alternative to the British. TOW antitank missiles were sold to Oman, and the sultan indicated a willingness to permit U.S. aircraft to use Masirah Island. It was clear by this time that the war in Dhofar was being won by the sultan with Iranian assistance, and this visit represented a key first step in the U.S.-Omani security relationship that was to develop later.

In March 1975, King Faisal of Saudi Arabia was assassinated, with Khalid becoming king in a smooth transition after the initial shock. In the same month, Iran and Iraq resolved their long-standing border dispute through the good offices of the Algerians. This took the U.S. government totally by surprise, and it infuriated Kissinger by introducing an Iraqi element into the Arab-Israeli equation at a moment of great sensitivity in his negotiations. However, it removed one of the most dangerous flash points in the Gulf, and the United States had no choice but to put the best face on it.

In June 1975, the Suez Canal reopened. There was great uneasiness about this in U.S. military circles, as it was felt that an open canal would work to the net advantage of the Soviets, who would now be able to surge forces into the Indian Ocean from the eastern Mediterranean. By contrast, U.S. carriers could not transit the canal due to physical constraints. Senator Henry Jackson even proposed banning *all* military transits, but the idea was rejected as impractical and probably undesirable. That judgment proved correct. The Soviets made no change in their pattern of operations. They have continued to avoid use of the Suez Canal almost entirely for their Indian Ocean squadron—even when it would have seemed tactically convenient—whereas U.S. forces used it with growing frequency. By early 1981, the canal had been widened and deepened sufficiently for U.S. carriers to use it as well, and it assumed growing importance in U.S. naval strategy.

In June 1975 negotiations were successfully completed with Bahrain, permitting continued use of facilities there for the Middle East Command, albeit at a significantly increased rental price.

In late 1975, a Soviet Bear reconnaissance plane overflew a U.S. carrier in the Indian Ocean for the first time, and the Soviets began regular IL-38 patrol flights out of Aden and Somalia. This was the first introduction of Soviet ground-based air in the region, and it was more than a symbolic development. The Soviets had previously lacked any air support for their Indian Ocean squadron, and this development suggested that the Soviets intended to develop an operational naval capability, as opposed to the largely symbolic deployments to date. The sequence of events closely resembled the pattern of Soviet naval buildup in the Mediterranean in the 1960s.

CARTER I: 1977 TO THE SOVIET INVASION OF AFGHANISTAN

During the first years of the Carter administration, the basic policies of the Nixon and Ford administrations in the Persian Gulf and Indian Ocean, which had by that time become fully institutionalized and operationally routine, were retained virtually unchanged. The construction on Diego Garcia, the structure and modus operandi of the Middle East Command, and the triannual task force deployments from the Pacific Fleet were continued without change. The two-pillar policy in the Persian Gulf was reviewed and was retained in the form that had evolved in practice since 1970.

More restrictive guidelines were adopted for the sale of arms, which aroused some concern in Iran. However, many of the worst excesses of the Nixon-Kissinger "blank check" policy had already been remedied—largely through the efforts of former Secretary of Defense Schlesinger—and President Jimmy Carter made it clear in a variety of ways (including the early sale of seven AWACs to Iran) that he intended to maintain an active security relationship with Iran.

Similarly, the new American stress on human rights and a more active concern with North-South issues had little tangible effect on existing strategy. In fact, the efforts that Carter took during 1977 to reassure Iran and Saudi Arabia and to open a dialogue with India could be understood as a continuation and elaboration of the basic principles of the Nixon Doctrine.

The most fundamental change in U.S. policy during this period was Carter's deep personal interest in exploring arms limitations with the Soviet Union. Initially, Carter talked about "demilitarization" of the Indian Ocean. As he became more acquainted with the issues, he revised his terminology to refer to "arms limitations," but his commitment to the concept was clear and was pursued with vigor for a year.

The technical framework for a negotiating position had been worked out in some detail in the report of the special National Security Council panel in early 1976 during the Ford administration, and it was adopted as the starting point by the Carter administration. Formal talks were initiated with the Soviets in Moscow in June 1977, followed by sessions in Washington and Bern, Switzerland. Considerable progress was made in these talks in resolving some of the technical issues and acquainting the two sides with the central concerns of the other.

However, the key dilemma that emerged was the inability of an essentially naval agreement to deal with the more basic issues of regional intervention by other military or nonmilitary means. This problem, which started as a cloud on the horizon and quickly grew in size, was dramatized by the massive Soviet and Cuban intervention in Ethiopia in support of the revolutionary Marxist regime in its battle with Somalia. The talks broke down in early 1978 and remained moribund until the coup de grace was delivered—as it was to other arms-control initiatives—by the Soviet invasion of Afghanistan in December 1979.

Throughout 1978, U.S. policy in the region was dominated by two events: the Arab-Israeli developments, leading to the Camp David accords of September and negotiation of the Egypt-Israel Peace Treaty of March 1979, and the explosion of the Iranian revolution, resulting in the collapse of the monarchy in February 1979 and its replacement by a fundamentalist Islamic regime dominated by the fiercely anti-Western Ayatollah Khomeini.

An analysis of these two events is not possible here, but their outcomes fundamentally altered U.S. strategic perspectives of the Persian Gulf and Indian Ocean region. In the course of the delicate and prolonged negotiations associated with the Egypt-Israel Peace Treaty, the United States developed a relationship with the Egypt of Anwar al-Sadat that was deeper and closer than had ever existed between America and an Arab state. This complex new relationship provided, among other things, possibilities for security cooperation, thus introducing a new dimension into the strategic equation.

At the same time the United States was gaining a new ally in Egypt, it was losing one in Iran. The sudden and total collapse of the shah's regime in Iran at the end of 1978 effectively demolished a decade of U.S. strategy in the Indian Ocean and Persian Gulf. Iran was the indispensable eastern pillar of the two-pillar policy. Without Iran, the entire concept of seeking stability in the Gulf by promoting cooperation between key friendly states became meaningless. Likewise, the Nixon Doctrine, which relied heavily on Iran as the protector of American security interests, was invalidated.

It would be no exaggeration to say that by the beginning of 1979, the United States had a collection of military assets and bilateral relationships, but these were largely artifacts of a previous era and were bound together by no strategic concept for the protection of U.S. regional interests. There was a growing awareness that the policy of the preceding decade had steadily placed more and more reliance on Iran, to the extent that when the shah's regime collapsed, the United States was left strategically naked, with no safety net.

The sense of urgent concern was magnified in February 1979, by reports of an incipient invasion of North Yemen by its avowedly Marxist neighbor to the south. Subsequent information cast considerable doubt on the extent of actual fighting along the border, and many in Washington had serious reservations about the initial panicked reports coming out of Yemen and Saudi Arabia. However, the precise accuracy of the battlefield reports was less important than the indisputable fact that Saudi Arabia felt immediately threatened. Moreover, this event, coming in the wake of the Marxist coup in Afghanistan in April 1978, the conclusion of an Ethiopian-Soviet treaty in November 1978, the assassination of U.S. Ambassador Adolph Dubs in Kabul in February 1979, together with the fall of the shah, risked creating the impression in the region and elsewhere that America had lost all capacity to influence regional events. It was feared that the key states of the Persian Gulf would conclude that they should accommodate to the rising wave of Soviet influence and power before they themselves were swept away. Zbigniew Brzezinski was particularly sensitive to this perception of American power in disarray and retreat, and he began speaking out in December 1978 about the instability in Southwest Asia, which he dubbed the "arc of crisis."

The U.S. government responded to the Yemen crisis with a series of measures intended to reassure American friends in the region and to demonstrate U.S. resolve. A carrier task force was dispatched from the Pacific to the Arabian Sea, establishing a new baseline of constant American military presence for the remainder of the year. Secretary of State Cyrus R. Vance issued a formal warning to the Soviets about any Soviet or Cuban involvement in the Yemen affair. A long-standing $390 million package of military assistance to Yemen, including 12 F-5E fighter aircraft, was expanded and rushed to Yemen on an emergency basis. AWAC early warning aircraft were deployed to Saudi Arabia for joint training and to bolster Saudi air defenses.

Almost simultaneously with these events in March 1979, two other developments occurred that symbolized the transformation of the strategic environment in the region. The end of one era was marked by the quiet demise of the Central Treaty Organization, as Turkey and Pakistan followed Iran by withdrawing. What may have been the beginning of a new era was celebrated with considerable fanfare in Washington as Egyptian President Sadat, Israeli Prime Minister Menachem Begin, and President Carter met to sign the first peace treaty between Israel and an Arab state.

The effort to develop a new U.S. strategy for the Indian Ocean and Persian Gulf began even before the Yemen crisis and the climactic events of March 1979. As it became evident that the shah's regime was disintegrating, Brzezinski initiated a series of studies within the National Security Council to begin to identify the elements of a strategic approach. Throughout 1979, it was Brzezinski who pressed the bureaucracy and who personally shepherded through the system what came to be known as the "security framework" for Southwest Asia.

The first serious effort to articulate some of these ideas came as a result of the trip by Secretary of Defense Harold Brown to Saudi Arabia and several other Middle Eastern states in mid-February 1979. Although there were widespread reports at the time that he had gone to Saudi Arabia seeking bases for U.S. forces, his objective was in fact much more limited. He sought to reassure the Saudis and others that the United States was conscious of the need for greater U.S. efforts to counterbalance Soviet activities in the region and to enlist regional cooperation in joint efforts to bolster security. The objective was not to press the Saudis for base rights—which was certain to be rejected for reasons of Saudi political sensitivity—but to initiate a more explicit dialogue on matters of mutual security interest.

A similar message was carried to the area by Brzezinski and Deputy Secretary of State Warren Christopher in March. In both cases, the Saudis and other regional states listened politely, but declined to undertake any substantial new security relationship with the United States, pending some tangible progress on the overriding political issue of Palestinian rights.

In April 1979, the issue of U.S. Persian Gulf policy was examined at the cabinet level in a Special Coordinating Committee meeting in the White House. That meeting approved maintaining an increased U.S. naval presence in the Indian Ocean in the form of a carrier task force, and it set in motion the interagency process to assemble the political, diplomatic, economic, and military elements of a new "security framework." This process proceeded at a deliberate pace throughout 1979, with Brzezinski goading an often reluctant bureaucracy.

By the end of 1979, well before the Soviet intervention in Afghanistan, the outlines of a strategy had been sketched in, including initial identification of U.S. forces for a rapid deployment force, operational planning for an increased U.S. military presence, and preliminary discussions with Oman, Kenya, and Somalia about possible use of some facilities in those nations. These efforts provided much of the underlying structure and planning for the events of the following year.

The other signal event of 1979, of course, was the taking of American hostages in Tehran on November 4. Although this development had little immediate impact on U.S. military activities in the region, it was important for several reasons. First, it prompted a thorough review, at the highest levels, of U.S. military capabilities in the region. The sobering conclusion of that review was that U.S. ability to project military power in the region—beyond a show of naval force—was extremely limited. Second, it dramatized the perpetual dilemma of the inadequacy of military power alone to influence internal political events in regional states. In fact, it was quickly concluded that indiscriminate show or use of force might well be counterproductive to fundamental U.S. interests. Finally, it led to a detailed examination of a possible rescue mission. Although it was initially determined that such a capability was lacking, secret efforts were launched to develop such a capability for possible use later, if required.

In late November, when there were serious fears that the hostages were in danger of being killed, and when the attack on the Grand Mosque in Mecca threatened to trigger a wave of attacks on American citizens and property throughout the region, a partial evacuation of U.S. diplomatic personnel and dependents was ordered. The U.S. naval presence was augmented by a second aircraft carrier and the assignment of two additional destroyers to the Middle East Command. The principal rationale for the military buildup was not to threaten, but rather to be prepared in the event an evacuation had to be carried out on short notice.

CARTER II: THE CARTER DOCTRINE (1980–81)

The Soviet invasion of Afghanistan in late December 1979 set off a series of U.S. actions that had, in many cases, been under consideration for a year or more but, until that time, had remained little more than a collection of option papers.

President Carter's widely quoted statement to the effect that he had learned more about Soviet intentions from this event than from all his previous experience in the presidency was subject to a great deal of derision for its apparent naivete about the Soviet Union. The choice of words may have been infelicitous, but the underlying message was of critical importance.

Jimmy Carter, perhaps more than any recent American president, believed deeply in the importance of dialogue and mutual accommodation between the United States and the Soviet Union on fundamental issues of peace and international security. He was truly prepared to walk the second mile in pursuit of nonviolent solutions to issues of East-West competition, and he stubbornly resisted the advice of his more hawkish advisers for a more confrontational policy throughout three years of his presidency, in the hope that the USSR would respond to a historic opportunity to develop peaceful means of resolving disputes. In practical terms, this was reflected in his primary reliance on the policies and advice of Secretary of State Vance as opposed to those promoted by Brzezinski. His candid remark early in 1980 was, in effect, a public admission of the failure of those policies and an implicit decision to rely henceforth on a more confrontational approach.

In terms of Indian Ocean policy, the new approach was articulated in his State of the Union address of January 23, 1980, where he stated that "Any attempt by any outside force to gain control of the Persian Gulf region will be regarded as an assault on the vital interests of the United States of America, and such an assault will be repelled by any means necessary, including military force."

The primary drafter of this formulation was Brzezinski, who, in a little-noticed speech in Montreal on December 5, 1979, described the framework of the so-called Carter Doctrine and summarized the steps that had been taken to implement it during its first year. Brzezinski began with an analysis of the American commitment to the independence and security of two central "strategic zones"—Western Europe and the Far East—as it had evolved in the years after World War II. He suggested that "a third strategic zone assumed in recent years vital importance to the United States and its allies: the region we call Southwest Asia today, including the Persian Gulf and the Middle East." The Carter Doctrine, he noted, was in response to the increased Soviet threat in the region; and it resulted in "a new and historically important commitment of the United States, one which has long-term implications for the decade of the 1980s. *It reflects the recognition that the central challenge of this decade is likely to be as massive and enduring as that confronted by American leadership in the first post-World War II decades*" [emphasis in original].

Brzezinski noted that during 1980 President Carter had convened the National Security Council on several occasions, and more than 20 meetings of the Special Coordinating Committee of the National Security Council had been held to develop the concept of the "regional security framework." By the date of his speech in December, the following had been accomplished:

- A rapid deployment joint task force had been established.
- Seven prepositioning ships with mechanized equipment, ammunition, fuel, and other supplies had been deployed in the Indian Ocean (at Diego Garcia).
- Three hundred jet transports and 500 turboprop transports were available for airlift.
- Congress was reviewing an administration request to purchase eight fast roll-on, roll-off, freight and troop carriers that could reach the Suez Canal from the east coast of the United States in 11 to 12 days.
- Exercise deployments of small parts of the force to the region had taken place that fall, most recently to Egypt.
- Deployment times had been reduced significantly. Tactical air forces could be in the region within hours, a battalion within 48 hours, and a division within two weeks.

The military program was accompanied by a series of political and diplomatic initiatives. Access agreements for the use of regional facilities were signed with Oman (April 9), Kenya (June 27), and

Somalia (August 22). A high-level emissary was dispatched to India in January 1980, in an unsuccessful attempt to build some degree of consensus about the nature of the Soviet actions in Afghanistan.

United States concern about Pakistani efforts to acquire a nuclear capability had resulted, less than a year earlier (April 1979), in the termination of all U.S. military and economic aid to Pakistan. Those concerns were now relegated to secondary importance and a two-year $400 million package of aid was proposed during the visit of a high-level delegation to Islamabad. Although Pakistan rejected the package as insufficient, important talks continued between U.S. and Pakistani defense officials.

Also on the military side, but not mentioned in the Brzezinski speech, the United States initiated reconnaissance flights into the Indian Ocean by B-52 aircraft for the first time. An amphibious ready group, with an 1,800-Marine detachment aboard, was deployed into the area, also for the first time.

The Iraqi invasion of southwest Iran in September 1980 led to a further upward ratcheting of direct U.S. military presence. At the end of September, there appeared to be a real danger of an escalation of the war to the southern Persian Gulf, which could have involved Iranian air strikes against oil targets on the Arab side of the Gulf. At the urgent request of Saudi Arabia, four AWAC early warning aircraft, together with their necessary support elements, were deployed to Saudi Arabia to enhance air defense capabilities. At about the same time, a guided missile cruiser was positioned in the Gulf with additional air defense capability, and U.S. warships maintained a more active patrol posture in the vicinity of the Strait of Hormuz.

One final incident of increased U.S. military activity during 1980 was the failed attempt to rescue the American hostages in Tehran in late April. The rationale for the raid, and the reasons for its failure, cannot be assessed here, although both deserve more careful analysis than they have been accorded in the literature to date. Suffice it to say that the attempted raid reflected a greater willingness on the part of the U.S. government to employ military instruments in the pursuit of its policy objectives than had previously been the case, and that the attempt itself could never have been made without the additional military presence and supporting infrastructure that had been developed over the preceding months.

By the time the Reagan administration arrived in Washington in January 1981, it would have been accurate to say that the U.S. security structure in the Indian Ocean and Persian Gulf region was more symbol than reality—at least as measured in purely military capacity to project meaningful power. Nevertheless, it was equally apparent that the developments of 1980 marked a major threshold in the evolution of U.S. strategy in that region. Not only was U.S. military presence at its highest level in history but there was also an underlying conviction that this region represented a major strategic zone of U.S. vital interests, demanding both sustained attention at the highest levels of U.S. policymaking and direct U.S. engagement in support of specifically U.S. interests. That was without precedent.

THE REAGAN ADMINISTRATION

During the first years of the Reagan administration, policy with regard to Southwest Asia consisted almost entirely of a continuation and consolidation of the policies initiated by the Carter administration. There was a slight shift in terminology. Whereas Brzezinski referred to a "security framework," the Reagan administration spoke of a "strategic consensus" for the region. At the start, the distinction may have been greater than it later appeared, for the new administration genuinely seemed to believe that it could weld a regional consensus around mutual opposition to a Soviet military threat, subordinating political concerns to the search for security. However, as the political realities of the region began to make themselves felt, the more ambitious objectives of a strategic consensus seemed quietly to yield to a set of goals and means entirely compatible with—if not indistinguishable from—those of the Carter administration, at least as articulated by Brzezinski.

On the strategic side, the most important development was the continued buildup of the rapid deployment force and its establishment in early 1983 as a unified command. Although the commander of the RDF, Lieutenant-General Robert C. Kingston, reportedly conducted talks with regional states in the search for a forward headquarters for the new command, this initial effort was quietly shelved, and the RDF staff of more than 900 personnel remained at MacDill Air Force Base in Florida.

The new unified command had earmarked a total of some 230,000 military personnel from the four services and was given responsibility on the political-military side for recommending to Washington which weapons systems would be sold to which regional states as part of the security assistance program. The basic mission of the RDF, however, was defined in classical military terms. The Department of Defense was quoted in the *New York Times* as follows: "Our principal objectives are to assure continued access to Persian Gulf oil and to prevent the Soviets from acquiring political-military control directly or through proxies."

In order to accomplish this mission, the RDF was projected to eventually include five Army divisions, two Marine divisions with supporting air wings, ten tactical Air Force fighter wings, three Navy carriers with appropriate escort vessels, and five squadrons of Navy anti-submarine warfare aircraft. In addition, thirteen shiploads of equipment and weapons were prepositioned at Diego Garcia, and the Defense Department purchased six additional container ships to improve mobility. Construction of support facilities began at the Egyptian Red Sea port of Ras Banas, although funding was delayed due to congressional insistence that Egypt sign a formal access agreement with the United States, a step the Mubarak government refused to take for political reasons. Military cooperation talks proceeded with a number of states in the region, and transit rights were secured from Morocco for U.S. military forces in circumstances which were not spelled out publicly. The second "Bright Star" joint exercises were conducted in the Egyptian Western Desert in late 1981, and a third exercise was scheduled for the summer of 1983.

In June 1981, the Reagan administration announced a package of $3.2 billion in economic and military aid to Pakistan, plus the sale of 40 F-16 aircraft. This agreement represented a significant new departure in recent U.S.-Pakistani relations. The subordination of concerns about Pakistani nuclear development was made formal by the congressional waiver of provisions of the Symington Amendment to the Foreign Assistance Act, which would have prohibited such aid in the absence of progress on nonproliferation.

Although the Reagan administration was understandably reluctant to endorse a policy that the press insisted on calling the Carter Doctrine, neither did the new administration renounce its substance. In fact, President Ronald Reagan, in a press conference in October 1981, paraphrased it by stating: "There's no way that we could stand by and see [Saudi oil resources] taken over by anyone that would shut off that oil." In the same news conference, he also offered what might be called the Reagan Corollary to the Carter Doctrine: "We will not permit [Saudi Arabia] to be an Iran." Although not spelled out in any detail, these two statements seemed to imply, first, a fundamental emphasis on Saudi Arabia as the only remaining "pillar" of U.S. Persian Gulf policy, and second, a willingness to consider U.S. intervention in response to domestic instability in at least certain key states in the region. However, neither of these propositions has yet been tested in practice, and it is not clear how the Reagan administration might react to an actual crisis in the region.

GENERAL OBSERVATIONS AND CONCLUSIONS

After this necessarily abbreviated summary of nearly a third of a century of U.S. policy and practice, it may be helpful to identify some of the basic trends and the evolution of U.S. assumptions, perceptions, and attitudes toward the Indian Ocean and Persian Gulf region.

Perhaps the greatest change has occurred with respect to the perception of U.S. interests in the region. As late as 1970, the region was seen as a distant backwater of international politics where U.S. interests were relatively low. In 1980, only a decade later, the U.S. government had formally decided that U.S. interests in the area were vital to the preservation of its own security.

This change was paralleled by, and was to some extent a function of, a radical shift in U.S. attitudes toward the Soviet presence and Soviet objectives in the region. Initially, the region was perceived as an area of U.S.-Soviet competition for political and economic influence. But after a series of crises, culminating in the Soviet invasion of Afghanistan, the region came to be regarded more and more as an area of military competition and direct military threat.

Both of these changes were directly affected by the politics of oil. What was initially regarded as a European and Japanese requirement for access to the oil of the Persian Gulf was replaced with a profound awareness of U.S. vulnerability as a result of greatly increased U.S. dependence on foreign oil, the demonstrated chaos in the U.S. economy created by the oil boycott of 1973–74, and the global economic effects of skyrocketing oil prices. It is particularly significant that the devastating surges in oil prices had to be understood as a function of Middle Eastern political turmoil rather than the mechanical operation of a purely economic model. In fact, purely economic calculations and projections have repeatedly been thrown into a cocked hat by the pressures of political events.

All of these changes, in turn, are reflected in the transformation of U.S. attitudes about the need for a major U.S. military presence in the region. In 1970, the U.S. government felt it could confidently rely on a tiny, symbolic military presence while looking to friends and allies for protection of U.S. regional interests. By 1980, that view had been replaced by the conviction that the United States could rely only on its own resources, and a major effort was launched to develop the requisite infrastructure to support a very considerable U.S. military presence.

If the Indian Ocean and Persian Gulf may now be regarded as the "third strategic zone" of U.S. global policy, it is instructive to consider some of the problems that presents for the policymaker. Unlike Europe or Asia, where the United States has fought major wars, there is necessarily a problem of U.S. credibility. Rhetoric aside, just what price is the United States willing to pay to defend what it believes to be its interests in the region? Which interests are truly considered vital and which are only secondary? What would be interpreted as a genuine threat, requiring some degree of U.S. active intervention? It is not clear that the answers to those questions are always available in Washington, let alone in Moscow or in the region.

Furthermore, unlike Europe and Asia, where the United States has acquired an extensive array of military infrastructure, together with the routine budgetary line items to support a major military endeavor, in the Persian Gulf and Indian Ocean, the United States is starting from scratch. Even today there is only the most rudimentary military support structure, and each effort to expand that very thin base requires new political and budgetary commitments and entails severe political costs both in the region and at home.

Finally, in Europe and Asia, nearly half a century of intense and often painful experience has established some generally reliable "rules of the game" in terms of deterrent doctrine and lines of permissible and impermissible behavior by the Soviet Union and its allies on one side and the United States and its allies on the other. Berlin, for example, is no longer a burning East-West issue only because some basic understandings have been developed by trial and error over the years. In the Indian Ocean and Persian Gulf, there is no effective doctrine, and even the most rudimentary rules of the game have yet to emerge in any recognizable form. Uncertainty prevails—about interests, intentions, capabilities—with all the perils of misapprehension, suspicion, and improvisational politics which that entails.

Looking at the record of U.S. strategic thinking in this region, one can only conclude that it has been neither farsighted nor particularly wise. On the contrary, with few exceptions, it has consisted of after-the-fact adjustments to unanticipated and largely unwelcome developments. In one sense, the history of the past decade in this part of the world can be described as an inexorable shift in the policy center of gravity from the eastern Mediterranean and the Arab-Israeli dispute toward the Persian Gulf. Bureaucratic and U.S. domestic political realities have consistently inhibited even the mere acknowledgment of this fact, let alone a systematic evaluation of its implications.

The record of U.S. behavior in this instance represents a classic case of the response of a status quo power under assault. United States objectives have tended to be vague and ill-defined. Essentially, the United States in each instance has desired nothing more than to have the situation remain as it was. When this proved impossible or impracticable time and again, U.S. objectives were progressively narrowed to defend more vigorously what remained. The nature of the process has not been so much a growing awareness of U.S. interests as a realization that nothing can any longer be taken for granted. Unfortunately, there is scant evidence that this process is yet understood or that it has played itself out.

In responding to the recurring crises of the past quarter century, successive administrations in Washington have tended to rely on a limited set of policy instruments, consisting primarily of arms sales and military deployments, occasionally reinforced by economic assistance or incentives. Although several generations of U.S. policymakers have known, or at least suspected, that military instrumentalities are inadequate to prevent or resolve essentially political problems, these instruments are the most readily available to the policymaker, particularly in moments of international stress.

This dilemma has been rendered even more poignant by the absence of policy objectives that were both feasible and well defined. It is impossible to plan a sensible, economical, and farsighted policy and to muster the necessary resources to carry it through unless one has a clear sense of direction. Smaller powers understand very well that objectives must not be allowed to outrun capabilities. The United States, accustomed to behaving as a superpower with almost limitless resources, has not stopped to make that sobering calculation, despite the inescapable fact that its resources today are entirely finite.

Until an administration in Washington is prepared to ask itself soberly what is truly vital to U.S. interests in this region and then to balance that against a realistic appreciation of U.S. political, economic, and military capabilities, there is little reason to expect that the future will be more than a perilous reprise of an old refrain.

4

Soviet Policy Toward South and Southwest Asia: Strategic and Political Aspects

Alvin Z. Rubinstein

The 1980s ushered in a new era in Moscow's relations with the nations of South and Southwest Asia. For the first time in its long imperial history, the USSR has become a source of concern to every nation in the region, and not only, as previously, contiguous Iran and Afghanistan. With the fall of the shah of Iran in January 1979 and the Soviet military occupation of Afghanistan in the waning days of December 1979, the Soviet Union's geopolitical situation and future prospects in the Persian Gulf-Indian Ocean area greatly improved in ways that are not yet fully clear, but that will be in the decades ahead.

As with any cataclysm, after the shock is absorbed, time is needed to reveal the full consequences. Still, the immediate changes in the environment can be ascertained and their effects tentatively assessed. This chapter will focus on Soviet policy toward key actors in South and Southwest Asia since the late 1970s with the aims of identifying continuities and changes in Soviet perceptions and behavior and speculating on the probable pattern of the Soviet approach, especially as it relates to the ongoing rivalry with the United States.

STRATEGIC TRENDS

From the mid-1950s, when Stalin's successors launched their multifaceted and extensive forward policy in the Third World, until the late 1970s, when the communist takeover in Afghanistan and the revolution in Iran transformed the political-military situation along the USSR's southern border, Soviet policy toward South and Southwest

Asia was adaptive, low risk, and geared to the long term. At the time of Stalin's death in March 1953, Soviet strategists had been uneasy over the U.S. policy of seeking to establish a network of military alliances with nations located in the general region to the south of the USSR's underbelly in order to exploit its vulnerability to penetration by nuclear-armed long-range bombers. This threat was reason enough in the premissile age to discard Stalin's deleterious legacy of hostility toward newly independent bourgeois-nationalist regimes in the Middle East and South Asia and to explore ways of thwarting U.S. policy.

Afghanistan and India were natural targets of Soviet attention. Perceiving Pakistan, America's military ally, to be their primary security problem, they responded favorably to Moscow's overtures for diplomatic normalization and offers of economic assistance. Their shared interest in thwarting Washington's design for the region paved the way for rapidly improved political and economic relationships, a swift reversal of what had existed during Stalin's later years.

The polarization of regional conflicts, which were aggravated by internal, intrasystemic, and external factors quite separate from U.S. policy, whetted the interest of Afghanistan and India for Soviet arms. Moscow gave generously, first to Afghanistan, then to India, in the process entrenching its presence, undermining U.S. efforts to promote regional stability, and slowly altering the strategic environment in ways conducive to the advancement of long-term Soviet aims.

The adage whom the gods would destroy, they first deprive of reason was tragically demonstrated in Afghanistan. At the behest of Prime Minister Prince Mohammad Daoud Khan (1953–1963, 1973–1978), who was eager to exploit Pakistan's internal unrest and to press territorial claims to its Pathan-speaking tribal areas, the Afghan government broke with tradition and turned to the Russians for military assistance and advisers. Daoud's ambitions increasingly clouded his judgment. In his desire to modernize and strengthen the country militarily, he relied heavily on the Soviet Union, seeming to forget a century of Russian pressure. Even his removal from power by the king in 1963 did nothing to arrest the excessive reliance on the USSR, because inertia brought ample benefits: Kabul found taking Soviet economic and military assistance the path of least trouble.

A decade later, Daoud seized power in a coup that depended on the support of the military, whose officer corps had by this time become honeycombed with communists trained in the USSR. After a few years, in the waning period of his rule, Daoud sensed the danger and tried to return the country to an approximation of the policy of *bi-tarifi* (literally, "without sides") that had traditionally been used to preserve independence, but it was too late. In his attempt to use the Soviet connection for the attainment of his ambitions, Daoud, the autocrat turned republican, had lost his bearings. He had lost sight of the nature of the relentless imperial power on his northern border and misjudged the susceptibility to subversion of a small traditionalist elite in a backward Third World country by the very social stratum of educated, but impatient, ideologues and idealists that modernization had spawned.

The Soviet Union's relationship with India was an outgrowth of their shared opposition to the U.S. policy of arming Pakistan. Its program of economic assistance, begun in 1955, was broadened to include military equipment in 1962, when, worried by Pakistan's acquisition of advanced aircraft from the United States, China's pressure in the north, and America's unwillingness to sell arms on favorable terms, India turned to Moscow. The Soviet leadership, hoping for a reconciliation with China, delayed implementing the Indo-Soviet agreement reached in August 1962 for delivery of 12 MiG-21s.[1] By 1964, however, it moved to become India's principal arms supplier, entering into a number of coproduction agreements and providing tanks, naval vessels, and combat aircraft on favorable terms. Moscow also became an important source of economic assistance for capital investment in the public sector, notably in the steel, oil, and heavy machinery industries.

By the 1970s, Moscow, no longer fearful that India might ally with the United States, sought, through the Indo-Soviet Treaty of Friendship and Cooperation of August 9, 1971, to cement the overall structure of political, economic, and military relationships. At a time of U.S.-Soviet détente, the treaty helped allay suspicions in India concerning the reliability of the Soviet Union as a patron-protector. It also legitimized the USSR's involvement in the affairs of the subcontinent, inter alia through Article 9, which provides that when either country is subject to an attack or threat of attack by a third country, the "contracting powers shall immediately enter into mutual consultations in order to remove such threat and to take appropriate effective measures to ensure peace and the security of their countries." The treaty assured Moscow of India's nonparticipation in any military alliance directed against the USSR and of its recognition of the geopolitical necessity of close relations with the Soviet Union.

Although Moscow has not obtained any tangible military privileges in India or any special position in India's domestic system, it expects that the extensive network of relationships assiduously nurtured over the past generation, of which the treaty is the capstone, will dispose New Delhi toward continued accommodation, notwithstanding the startling turnabout in the geostrategic situations of Afghanistan, Iran, and the Soviet Union. The Reagan administration's decision to upgrade Pakistan's military capability and expressed willingness to sell military equipment to China serve to remind India of the USSR's importance to it. As long as Pakistan remains India's central security concern, Moscow is not fearful that New Delhi's uneasiness over the presence of Russian troops at the Khyber Pass will overshadow the convergences that make for continued cooperation.

Integral to the USSR's objective of thwarting the U.S. policy of containment was its policy toward Iran. It required a different approach from that used in South Asia, entailing accommodation with a country possessed of a long memory of Russian imperialism and allied with the United States.

In the 1950s and 1960s, Iran (like Turkey) was a key Soviet concern. It is not exaggeration to suggest that the USSR's courtship of the non-Arab Muslim states situated along its southern border was strategically the most important component of Moscow's overall Middle Eastern policy; and it is in the changed policies of Turkey, Iran, and Afghanistan that Moscow may be considered to have achieved its most significant gains in the Third World.[2] The post-Stalin Soviet desire to normalize relations with Iran did not get very far, notwithstanding the 1955 settlement of boundary and financial claims, an agreement on the sharing of the waters of the Aras and Atrek rivers, and the shah's visit to Moscow in July 1956. Moscow's strong criticisms of Iran's participation in the Baghdad Pact and deepening military involvement with the United States, coupled with the shah's suspicions of Soviet designs on Iran, limited diplomatic normalization. The breakthrough came in September 1962, when the shah informed Moscow that Iran would never permit its territory "to become an instrument of aggression against the territory of the Soviet Union," and it, specifically, "will not grant any foreign nation the right of possessing any kind of rocket bases on Iranian soil."[3]

Having obtained assurance against the establishment of bases in Iran, Moscow quickly improved relations with the shah. Economic ties expanded enormously, epitomized by the construction of the Isfahan steel mill and the natural gas pipeline (IGAT); and the shah purchased more than $1 billion in arms during the 1967–78 period. Indeed, during the halcyon decade prior to the shah's fall, relations between the two countries had never been better: The border was quiet, with no large-scale deployments on either side; defectors were returned with quiet regularity; Soviet propaganda was restrained and said little to embarrass the shah's persecution of local communists. This pragmatic accommodation extended to their pursuit of divergent policies in the Gulf without any adverse consequences for their fundamental relationship. True, Moscow developed an increasingly close relationship with Iraq, Iran's main regional rival. This courtship started soon after the military coup in July 1958 had overthrown the pro-Western monarchy and brought to power a radical nationalist, anti-Western regime whose withdrawal from the Baghdad Pact immediately assured the Iraqis a warm reception. But relations with Iran were sufficiently important for the Kremlin to urge restrain on Iraq when, on November 30, 1971, in the wake of the British military withdrawal from the Gulf, Iran occupied the islands of Abu Musa and the two Tunbs at the entrance to the Gulf. Moscow was eager not only to avoid any unnecessary tension with the shah but also to discourage any Iraqi behavior that might provide the British with an excuse to maintain a military presence in the region.

Iraq was the other prime target of Soviet policy in Southwest Asia, that is, the Gulf. The Soviet-Iraqi Treaty of Freindship and Cooperation of April 1972 was intended to expand Soviet-Iraqi cooperation, persuade Baghdad to regularize Soviet naval access to Umm Qasr, and convince the ruling Baath party of Moscow's determination to shield it from possible Iranian attack and back its campaign to solve the knotty Kurdish problem and nationalize Western oil holdings. However, the treaty had the unanticipated effect of alarming Saudi Arabia, which feared the Baath's hegemonial ambitions in the Gulf. Thus, for the remainder of the decade, it frustrated Moscow's efforts to normalize relations with the Arab states of the lower Gulf and made the Soviet Union a marginal actor in the region. Not until after the fall of the shah and the crystallization of the subversive threat to the Sunni Arab monarchs of the Gulf from Khomeini's Shiite-based revolution would the USSR, newly in control of Afghanistan, find the environment conducive to new diplomatic overtures.

SOVIET AIMS

A brief review of key Soviet pronouncements purporting to represent the USSR's principal objectives is in order. The statements are a convenient starting point and the useful gauge for evaluating Soviet aims and behavior.

In May 1969, Premier Aleksei Kosygin proposed a pact of regional economic cooperation among the USSR, Afghanistan, Pakistan, India, and Iran. A few weeks later, on June 7, 1969, at the International Conference of Communist and Workers' Parties in Moscow, CPSU leader Leonid Brezhnev went a step farther, declaring: "We are of the opinion that the course of events raises the question of creating a system of collective security in Asia."[4] Judging by the context of the speech, however, his aim was to isolate China rather than to organize the noncommunist countries of the region into a special grouping. The proposal languished, attracting little interest in Moscow for several years. Its presumptively anti-China intent was further evidenced by Brezhnev's raising the idea on March 20, 1972, one month after President Richard Nixon's visit to China and the startling Sino-American reconciliation.

In the early 1970s, the USSR's policy in Southwest Asia focused on improving relations with the regional rivals, Iraq and Iran. Moscow assured the shah of its peaceful purposes in the Gulf and deplored Iran's projected high level of arms procurement. Soviet broadcasts combined professions of friendship with warnings of the dangers of arms races and "warmongering" policies. After the October War and OPEC's demonstration of the West's vulnerability to a cutoff of oil, the Soviet media intensified their attention to the Gulf-Arabian Peninsula region, emphasizing the threat that inhered in U.S. efforts to establish a military presence that could be used against the Arab oil-producing countries.

Diego Garcia, an islet in the British colony of the British Indian Ocean Territory, created in 1965, became a convenient whipping post for lashing U.S. policy. An 11-mile island in the Chagos Archipelago, centrally situated in the Indian Ocean, it was leased to the United States by Britain in 1966 as a communications facility and subsequently upgraded to a major naval base.[5] Soviet writers repeatedly warned that this militarization of the Indian Ocean was a threat to all the littoral states, and especially to the Gulf Arabs, whose oil fields the United States sought to control; that the United States was promoting an arms race by building up Iran and Saudi Arabia; and that the entire American approach bore the imprint of Washington's pro-Zionist orientation—a theme calculated to heighten receptivity to the overall condemnation of U.S. policy.

At the Twenty-fifth Congress of the CPSU in February 1976, Brezhnev called for support of proposals that opposed "any of the powers setting up military bases in the region of the Indian Ocean," implying Diego Garcia. By 1978, Moscow was warning also of U.S.

plans to expand its presence in the Gulf by creating "quick reaction forces" (the rapid deployment force established in 1980!) for use by the Pentagon "to coordinate its actions with local reactionary forces to suppress national liberation movements."[6]

Soviet analysts conveniently ignored—and still do—the role that the USSR's rapid and major military buildup in Somalia in 1974, 1975, and 1976 played in spurring the United States to upgrade the Diego Garcia facility. Moreover, while the littoral states gave lip service to concern over the growing U.S. military presence in the Indian Ocean, in private, representatives of these governments acknowledged that the U.S. base did not threaten their independence; and some welcomed the development. I recall delivering a lecture to an Indian military group in New Delhi in January 1976 and not being questioned about Diego Garcia. When I raised the matter in discussion with several of the senior officers, they said they did not regard it as a threat to India—in contradistinction to official statements issued by the foreign ministry. The contrast between public and private comments is important to consider in any assessment of how the superpowers are perceived in the region.

As a newcomer and marginal actor in the Gulf, having diplomatic relations only with Iraq, Iran, Kuwait, and the geographically distant two Yemens, the USSR aimed at "the weakening of the Gulf States' ties with Western countries and the encouragement of alternative governments or policies more congenial to Soviet interests."[7] It denounced the shah's role in the suppression of the Dhofari rebels in Oman on behalf of Sultan ibn Said Qabus and played on Arab fears that Iran, under the guise of stabilizing the Gulf region, would seek "to reanimate the CENTO bloc and pave the way to the creation of a new military-political line-up."[8] By exploiting the historic animosity and deep-rooted suspicions between Iran and the Arab regimes of the Gulf, Moscow hoped to promote ties with the latter.

The fall of the shah in January 1979 was a boon for Moscow and a grave defeat for Washington. In one fell swoop, the United States lost its enforcer and ally in the Gulf, a network of electronic and military services, and credibility as a reliable patron-protector—a consideration that the Kremlin knows must figure prominently in the decision making and diplomacy of the regional actors, as it no doubt did in Moscow's. On the other hand, the Soviet Union acquired a new salience, particularly after its military occupation of Afghanistan. It was now the only superpower with a palpable presence and convincing force capability in the region; and it was to be approached carefully. Pakistan's president, Mohammad Zia ul-Haq, put the sentiment pithily, several weeks after the Soviets moved to his border: "You can't live in the sea and create enmity with whales. You have to be friendly with them. The Soviet Union is on our doorstep. The USA is 10,000 miles away."[9]

Moscow sought to allay regional apprehensions over its intentions, first, by offering a variety of proposals for arms limitation, demilitarization, and nuclear-free zones, and second, by contrasting its desire for peaceful coexistence with the bellicosity of the United States. During a visit to India soon after Khomeini's triumphant return to Iran, Kosygin strongly criticized Washington's reported plan to maintain a carrier task force in the region: "We by no means approve of it. We advocate the Indian Ocean to be an ocean of peace. We have no base whatever in the Indian Ocean, and any reports to the contrary are baseless and slanderous."[10]

The comment was well received by the Janata government, which was on far better terms with the United States than Indira Gandhi's had been; and the joint communique expressed regret that the Naval Arms Limitation Talks (NALT) between the Soviet Union and the United States had been suspended and called for their immediate resumption. (NALT, started in June 1977, at President Jimmy Carter's initiative, was suspended by Washington in February 1978, because of displeasure with the Soviet intervention in Ethiopia.)

After occupying Afghanistan, Moscow tried to justify its action (and deflect criticism) by emphasizing the danger to the area of U.S. bases, military moves, and threats. In a major statement that appeared in the form of an interview in *Pravda*, Brezhnev denied that the national interests or security of the United States or other countries were in any way affected by events in Afghanistan, which he held to be solely a domestic Afghan matter:

> Also absolutely false are the allegations that the Soviet Union has some expansionist plans in respect of Pakistan, Iran or other countries of that area. The policy and psychology of colonialists is alien to us. We are not coveting the lands or wealth of others. It is the colonialists who are attracted by the smell of oil.[11]

In the months that followed, Soviet media and officials hammered at the following themes: It is the United States, which as early as August 1977 had approved the creation of a rapid deployment force, that was fueling tensions; Moscow does not harbor any aggressive intentions against either Iran or Pakistan; it is the "Carter Doctrine," not Soviet policy, that threatens the use of force in the Gulf; it is unthinkable that the United States should arrogate unto itself preemptive rights in a region that is in the USSR's backyard; it is the imperialists (that is, the United States) which seek to prevent independent advances and the social and economic progress of developing countries under the guise of defending them against an alleged Soviet threat; and it is the United States, not the Soviet Union, that seeks to eliminate détente from the mainstream of world politics.[12]

In December 1980, amid severely deteriorating U.S.-Soviet relations over Afghanistan, Poland, and SALT, Brezhnev visited India to urge its acceptance of the new situation in the region. Playing on India's disquiet over the U.S. rearming of Pakistan and a possible disruption of Gulf oil as a consequence of a spread of the Iraq-Iran war that had broken out the previous September, he strongly defended Soviet policy in Afghanistan in a major speech before the Indian parliament. Soon, he averred, normal conditions will return, "the fog of misinformation will gradually disperse," and "Afghanistan's southern neighbors will realize that a good neighborly accord with the Afghan Government is the only real path. As a result, conditions will emerge for a complete political normalization of the situation, including the withdrawal of Soviet troops from Afghanistan."[13] Brezhnev's message was unmistakable: The USSR will not be dislodged from Afghanistan, so let us work to make the best of the new situation.

Utilizing the uneasiness over the increased tension in the Gulf-Indian Ocean region, and desirous of emphasizing the objectives shared by the Soviet Union and India, Brezhnev put forth a five-part proposal for all interested parties to consider:

> 1. Not to establish foreign military bases in the area of the Persian Gulf and adjacent islands; not to deploy nuclear or any other weapons of mass destruction there;
> 2. Not to use and not to threaten with the use of force against the countries of the Persian Gulf area, not to interfere into their internal affairs;
> 3. To respect the status of nonalignment, chosen by Persian Gulf states; not to draw them into military groupings with the participation of nuclear powers;
> 4. To respect the sovereign right of the states of the region to their natural resources;
> 5. Not to raise any obstacles or threats to normal trade exchange and the use of sea lanes that link the states of that region with other countries of the world.[14]

The self-serving and vague character of Brezhnev's formulations was not lost on the Indian parliament, which applauded only "when he referred to Soviet-Indian relations or Indian achievements. His references to the Iran-Iraq war, Afghanistan, peace in the Persian Gulf area and other issues did not evoke any response."[15] To mollify the Indians and remind them of the value of friendship with the Soviet Union, he left agreements on continued Soviet economic assistance, including oil deliveries on concessionary terms, arms sales, and expanded trade. Already important, they became even more so after the Reagan administration agreed to sell advanced F-16 fighters to Pakistan; witness the military delegation, the largest Moscow ever has sent outside the Soviet bloc, that went to India in March 1982.

In September 1982, during Prime Minister Gandhi's visit, Soviet leaders reaffirmed their readiness to provide expanded economic and military assistance, further cementing close ties by offering to build a nuclear power plant in India.[16] Friendship with India remains the hub of Soviet policy in South Asia. With it, and its control of Afghanistan, the Soviet Union has a strong axis for exerting political leverage in the region.

Looking to Southwest Asia, which is accorded special attention because of the Iranian upheaval and the importance of Gulf oil to Western economies,[17] Moscow sees Iran, not Saudi Arabia, as the strategic prize.

Khomeini's Iran

The USSR had enjoyed excellent relations with the shah, but Moscow welcomed the Iranian revolution, which ended the shah's political-strategic alignment with the United States, shut down the two U.S.-manned electronic intelligence-gathering stations, and sharply reduced arms purchases. Khomeini quickly adopted an intense anti-Americanism and withdrew Iran from the Central Treaty Organization (CENTO) and the role of gendarme for the Gulf, thus depriving the United States of its surrogate in the region. He even permitted the communist Tudeh party to end its underground existence and function openly. The Kremlin anticipated long-term benefits from being the only superpower able to project power effectively in the area and watched with understandable satisfaction the blow to U.S. credibility, the second dramatic demonstration (Vietnam was the first) in less than five years of Washington's inability, or unwillingness, to protect close clients at any cost.

Political and especially economic missions were regularly exchanged. Trade expanded, and more than 100 Soviet-assisted industrial projects started to rise on the Iranian landscape. Political ties were pragmatic and compartmentalized into their cooperative and competitive components. Neither party had any illusions about the other: The Kremlin viewed the shah's alliance with the United States as inherently anti-Soviet, but not threatening in light of the shah's pronouncement in September 1962 that no foreign military bases or missile sites would be permitted on Iranian territory; and the shah suspected the USSR's expansionist ambitions and subversive activities. But both accorded primacy to their mutual interest in a peaceful, stable border and regarded their rivalry in the Gulf as imperial not national, hence limited and low key. Though criticizing Iran's military buildup, Moscow knew that it was directed toward promotion of the shah's aims in the Gulf and not against the USSR, hence Soviet commentaries invariably combined warnings of the dangers of arms races with assurances of friendship.

Their relationship rested on mutual sensitivity to the core security concerns of each and on a readiness to deal with the other on the basis of mutual advantage. Despite different systems, antithetical ideologies, and membership in rival military blocs, they developed valued economic relations, kept their borders quiet, and handled their regional rivalry pragmatically and prudently. Moscow expected no less from the new regime.

Relations with Khomeini's Iran, however, have proved pricklier than Moscow had reason to expect. The issues that loom large in Soviet-Iranian relations wax and wane in importance, largely as a consequence of the vagaries of the domestic turmoil in Iran, but also because of Iran's absorption with the United States during the period from February 1979 to January 1981 (when the 444-day hostage crisis ended) and with Iraq since its invasion in September 1980. The main issues are as follows: Soviet attempts to normalize relations, the USSR's takeover of Afghanistan, the Iraqi-Iranian war, the inability to agree on a price for Iranian natural gas, and Soviet interference in Iran's internal affairs.[18] A few remarks about each should indicate the strained and self-limiting character of Soviet-Iranian ties and the difficulties the Soviets face in their courtship of Iran.

The Soviet Union's quest for normalization and continuation of the good state-to-state relationship that it had had with the shah has been hampered by the suspicion of communism shared by Khomeini's supporters; by the traditional Iranian fear of the covetous colossus to the north; by the communist coup in Afghanistan in April 1978; and by Moscow's insistence on reaffirming, despite Tehran's repeated repudiations, the application of Articles 5 and 6 of the 1921 Soviet-Iranian treaty. These articles stipulate that Soviet forces may intervene in Iranian affairs if a third country threatened to attack the USSR from Iranian territory or if Moscow considered its border threatened. The latter has been a particularly sore point, a reminder that for more than 150 years successive generations of Russian leaders have looked on Iran as their natural sphere of influence and that Moscow's support for the principles of equality between nations and noninterference in the internal affairs of other countries bears little resemblance to the way it, in practice, deals with weaker powers.

Soon after coming to power, the Khomeini regime criticized the USSR's intervention in the internal affairs of Afghanistan, and Ayatollah Khomeini exhorted the Afghans to resist their communist puppet rulers. Moscow's attempts to ingratiate itself with Tehran by adopting a pro-Iranian position in the hostage crisis that erupted on November 4, 1979, when militants seized the U.S. Embassy, failed to silence Iranian criticisms. Since the Soviet military intervention of December 1979, the issue has been a running sore in their relations. Not even the Iraqi attack on September 22, 1980, and Iran's obvious desire that the Soviet Union be a disinterested observer instead of a partisan patron of Iraq, as could be expected from the Soviet-Iraqi friendship treaty, mitigated Tehran's hostility on the Afghan issue.

The Iraqi-Iranian war has posed dilemmas for Moscow, which seeks to avoid alienating either side. The essential Soviet position, set forth in *Izvestiia* the day after the war began, is that the conflict was a vestige of the two countries' colonial past; that the United States seeks to exploit the situation in order to establish control over the region's oil; that Washington hopes the conflict will lessen Iran's ability "to resist the imperialist pressures that are being brought on it"; and that the United States sees the conflict as an opportunity to reorient Iraq's foreign policy toward the West.[19]

Thus far, what is clear is Moscow's inability to use the war to promote its courtship of Iran, without placing in jeopardy its long-term relationship with Iraq. For the moment, in an extremely complex situation, the Soviet government is trying to maintain existing ties with both countries and to forestall a shift by either toward the United States. The balancing act is a play for time, an effort to avoid irrevocable decisions in the hope that a settlement will permit Moscow to pursue its diplomatic friendship with Tehran and Baghdad as well.

A major Soviet disappointment was Iran's cutoff, in 1979, of natural gas shipments, because of Moscow's refusal to meet Iranian demands for a fivefold price increase to world market levels. The Russians, ever the tough negotiators, are reluctant to pay more than absolutely necessary and undoubtedly expected that Iran's long preoccupation with the hostage crisis and fear of a U.S. attack, plus the protracted internal unrest, and the costly Iraqi war would force Iran to agree to a lower price. Iran's stubbornness has been a surprise; its dire economic condition would seem to give Moscow the upper hand, but a settlement of the pricing issue still is not in sight. Moreover, statistics can be misleading. For example, trade figures for 1981, issued by Moscow, show a twofold increase over 1980 in Soviet-Iranian trade, prominent among which is the USSR's first purchase of Iranian oil.[20] Iran needs the money for arms, spare parts, and food, and the Soviet Union is under growing pressure to alleviate the energy shortages of its communist allies. In a word, business is business. Too much should not be read into the visit to Moscow in February 1982 by Iran's minister of energy, which resulted in the signing of a protocol on Soviet-Iranian technical cooperation concerning two power plants that are being built in Ahvaz and Isfahan. The protocol is only a follow-up agreement to a contract that had been previously signed.[21] There is no known agreement as yet on natural gas pricing, which holds the key to future prospects for Soviet-Iranian economic relations.

Whatever the pattern of economic ties, it would be a mistake to use measures of economic interactions to judge the Soviet-Iranian political relationship and anticipate its future. Khomeini's toleration of the pro-Moscow Tudeh party for so long was due to several facts: its support for him when he was in exile, at which time the communists "regularly broadcast his declarations recorded in Iraq" over Radio Iran Courier, operating out of East Germany; its strident anti-Americanism; its acceptance of the Islamic Republic; its link to the Soviet Union, for which Khomeini feels ideological antipathy but whose open antagonism he prefers not to trigger; and its relative weakness among the leftist opponents of the ruling Islamic Republican party (IRP).[22] In May 1983, however, he outlawed the party.

Khomeini's former sufferance reflected political shrewdness, not diminished ideological hostility. Indeed, the Soviet media often complain that the Iranian government unfairly tarnishes the USSR with the same brush of intrigue and greed that it uses for the Western powers, for example, recently objecting to Tehran Radio denouncing

Soviet, as well as Western, exploitation of the "natural wealth of the Islamic nations," at the very time that Moscow was signing an advantageous protocol with the visiting Iranian minister of energy.[23]

Tehran has good reason not to antagonize Moscow. The ethnic unrest and ongoing war with Iraq mandate care and a working relationship with the Soviet Union, which could, if it desired, seriously worsen the domestic situation by shipping large quantities of weapons to Kurdish, Azerbaijanian, or Baluch separatists or to Iraq. Yet one should be skeptical of breathless and unsubstantiated accounts that say the IRP has turned to the Soviet KGB for assistance to stay in power.[24] The Soviet Union is still very much an outsider in Tehran.

Moscow does not feel impelled to act. It encourages the regime's anti-Americanism, watches with satisfaction the growing polarization of political alignments and factions, offers closer government-to-government ties, and waits upon developments. Taking a long-term view comes easily to the Kremlin rulers.

When on turns to the Arab part of Southwest Asia, Soviet diplomacy has less to show in tangible terms. Its aims are, first and foremost, to stymie American initiatives and policy and, second, to improve and normalize relations with leading Arab actors.

Iraq

A quasi-casualty has been the once close ties between the USSR and Iraq. The 1972 Soviet-Iraqi treaty brought Moscow ephemeral benefits–primacy as Iraq's supplier of arms and industrial equipment; participation in oil exploration and development; a role for the Iraqi Communist Party (ICP) in the Baathist government; and involvement in the sequence of events that ended the Kurdish threat to the Baath and led to a political settlement in March 1975 of the dispute between Iraq and Iran, as a result of which Moscow strengthened the Baath, seemingly consolidated its special ties to the regime, and was enabled to proceed with its preferred policy of improving relations with the Baath and the shah. Militarily, at the height of the Ethiopian-Somalian war in late 1977, Soviet aircraft en route to Aden (where arms were transshipped to Ethiopia) were allowed to refuel in Iraq, though this convenience was ended in the spring of 1978 because of policy differences over Eritrea (the Iraqis supporting the Eritrean Muslim separatists against the Christian Ethiopian rulers); Soviet naval vessels may still call at Umm Qasr, though they must obtain permission for each port visit.[25]

By the end of the 1970s, however, even these advantages were in jeopardy. Moscow watched uneasily as Iraq's strongman Saddam Hussein signed major arms agreements with France and Brazil in a move to diversify his suppliers; increased purchases of Western rather than Soviet technology; cracked down on Iraqi communists, executing 21 of them in May 1978, allegedly for setting up party cells in the army; edged toward normalizing relations with Western countries and the monarchical Arab regimes of the Gulf, especially Saudi Arabia, with which Iraq had long been at odds; and condemned the interference by the Soviet Union in the domestic affairs of Afghanistan, Ethiopia, and the People's Democratic Republic of Yemen (PDRY). In addition, there was the degrading order to relocate the Soviet Embassy because of Iraqi suspicion that the Soviets were engaged in electronic spying on Iraqi officials in nearby government buildings. Stung by the Baath's denunciations of local communists, Moscow "imposed a total news blackout on domestic events in Iraq, with no major article on that country appearing in a Soviet newspaper or journal in the eight months prior to the outbreak of the [Iraq-Iran] war," on September 22, 1980.[26] In the spring and summer of 1980, with the buildup of tensions between Iraq and Iran, the Soviet report of the Iraqi government's expulsion of thousands of Iranian Shiites and raids by "armed bands" crossing into Iran from Iraq showed signs of a tilt toward Iran, then in the middle of the hostage crisis with the United States.

The war has not brought Moscow any discernible benefits; on the contrary, it has occasioned sharp setbacks. For the moment, however, the situation is complex and ambiguous. The failure of Iraq to achieve an expected easy victory over the demoralized post-shah Iranian army ushered in a period when the Gulf Arabs were distracted from the Soviet military intervention in Afghanistan and Khomeini's IRP reconsidered the consequences of unnecessarily aggravating relations with the Soviet Union—both developments reminding Iraq of the necessity for maintaining ties with Moscow, if only to prevent Moscow from becoming a partisan of Iran. Despite some occasional reporting in the Soviet press that implicitly portrayed Iraq as the responsible party, the general tenor has been nonpartisan, with reiterations of regret at the fratricidal situation and castigation of U.S. imperialism for aggravating the crisis to obtain military facilities in the Gulf and provoking both sides. Interestingly, of the major Soviet newspapers, the one that has been most partisan toward Iran is *Krasnaia zvezda* (Red Star), the organ of the Soviet army.[27] On a number of occasions, Brezhnev called for an end to the hostilities and a start to negotiations, but neither side has been receptive.

The continued chill in Soviet-Iraqi relations was evident at the Twenty-sixth Congress of the CPSU in early March 1981, when Aziz Muhammed, the first secretary of the Iraqi Communist Party, sharply criticized the Baathist regime, which had not, in contrast to the previous congress, sent a delegation. The Israeli destruction of the Iraqi nuclear reactor at Tammuz, near Baghdad, on June 9, 1981, elicited nothing more substantial from the Soviets than expressions of solidarity. The Soviet media exploited the event to denounce "the Tel Aviv terrorists" and the United States, not to repair ties with Iraq. In December 1981, on the occasion of Brezhnev's seventy-fifth birthday, there were not the customary friendly greetings sent by one treaty partner to another, but *Pravda* published lengthy congratulations from Azia Muhammed, who did eschew any criticisms, this time, of the government of Saddam Hussein.[28]

Moscow would like to play the role of "honest broker" and maintain good relations with both protagonists. It does not want to jeopardize either relationship, and its big fear is that the United States will somehow intrude itself in a way that might lead to restoration of its diplomatic relations not only with Iraq but eventually with Iran as well. It also fears that the war will enhance the appeal of the U.S. offer of "strategic cooperation" with the other Arab states in the region.

This view was expressed by Leonid Zamyatin, a member of the CPSU Central Committee and chief of its international relations department, in an interview with an Arab journalist in the summer of 1981:

> The Americans are of course interested in the expansion of the war and seek to escalate it because this would help in realizing the possibility of the intervention of the United States and those who cooperate with it in Iraq and Iran. The United States wants to weaken both countries. The measures adopted by the United States against Iran are clear proof of bad intentions, the exacerbation of economic losses, the destruction of oil resources and the instigation of conflicts within both Iran and Iraq. The imperialist countries are still exerting overt and covert pressure on Iraq. . . . We are convinced that the governments of the two countries will eventually understand the real situation and will not allow the intervention of Western military forces.[29]

The Iraqi-Iranian war seems to have made more difficult, if not ended for the foreseeable future, Moscow's ability to develop simultaneous close ties with both countries and foster (as it did during the hostage crisis) the anti-American animus in the policy of each. The war may well have sounded the death knell of Soviet hopes to manage regional relationships as the British once did, albeit under vastly simpler circumstances, and to discourage Iraq and Iran from exploring improved relations with the United States.

Kuwait

The other Arab country in the Gulf with which the Soviet Union has formal diplomatic relations is the city-state of Kuwait. For almost two years after Kuwait was granted independence by Great Britain on June 19, 1961, the Soviet Union vetoed its admission to the United Nations out of deference to Iraq's claim that Kuwait was an integral part of its territory. However, soon after the overthrow in February 1963 of Abd al-Karim Qasim, who had toppled the pro-Western Hashemite monarchy in July 1958, relations between Moscow and Baghdad deteriorated because of the anticommunist and anti-Soviet tenor of the new regime. One result was that Moscow readily agreed to a proposal by the Kuwait government in March to establish diplomatic relations:

> For Kuwait this was a very important event, for as long as her independence was denied by the Russians, there was the chance, however remote, that Iraq could find support for a renewed claim to Kuwait. For the Soviet Union, it was not simply an expression of displeasure at Iraqi actions. Most important, the establishment of active and friendly relations with Kuwait might represent an opportunity to extend her presence and perhaps influence in a region, the Persian Gulf, which had traditionally been of interest. Thus Ambassadors were exchanged, and when the Kuwait application for membership in the United Nations was put forward again in May 1963 the Soviet representative enthusiastically endorsed it.[30]

After a slow start, Soviet-Kuwaiti relations quickly improved. There were exchanges of missions, and trade expanded. Most of Kuwait's fishing fleet has been outfitted by the Soviet Union, and Soviet technicians have assisted on road building and construction projects. Though Soviet commentaries were frequently critical of Kuwait's bourgeois socioeconomic system, its close ties to the West, and its reliance on Western arms, Moscow welcomed the permission to maintain a large embassy, which serves a valuable intelligence-gathering purpose, and has cultivated the Kuwaiti leadership.

Kuwait had been alarmed by the 1972 Soviet-Iraqi treaty, though Moscow had not conceived of it as a blank check for Baghdad to do as it pleased in foreign policy, and considered friendly relations with the USSR a form of insurance against an expansionist-minded Iraq. And indeed Moscow did not support Iraq's brief invasion of Kuwaiti territory in March 1973 and its attempt to force Kuwait to relinquish "part of its coast and the islands of Warbah and Bubiyan (off the port of Umm Qasr) to Iraq."[31] Nonetheless, the treaty did seriously hamper Soviet efforts to normalize relations with the Arab regimes of the lower Gulf, all of which mistrusted Iraq's radical, antimonarchical, military leadership. The resolution of the crisis taught Kuwait that the USSR's support was useful, but that its independence rested ultimately on tacit Western pressure and the restraints imposed by fellow Arab countries, none of which wants Iraq to add Kuwait's vast oil reserves to its own for fear that it would become too powerful.

After the October War and the OPEC price hikes, Kuwait's incredible wealth made it increasingly nervous about its security. Among its varied and fidgety diplomatic probes was an approach to Moscow for the purchase of Soviet weapons. The agreement signed in Moscow in December 1975 during the first official visit to the Soviet Union by a Kuwaiti foreign minister may have been prompted by a number of considerations: to buy Soviet goodwill as an added measure of protection against Iraq; to demonstrate to Iraq that it was not a client of Saudi Arabia (the two were then at odds); to signal the United States that the USSR was available as an alternate arms supplier, should Washington ease its pressure on Israel to return Arab land and settle with the Palestinians; to buy weapons for Egypt, which was suffering from a slowdown in arms shipments as a consequence of deteriorating Soviet-Egyptian relations; and to placate the Arab left and especially the Palestine Liberation Organization (PLO), whose adherents constitute the rogue force in Kuwait's hybrid and potentially volatile labor force.[32]

The joint communique issued at the end of the visit stated, among other things, that both sides opposed foreign interference in the Gulf (an allusion to reports that the United States was prepared to occupy the Gulf in order to safeguard the flow of oil). In addition, "the Soviet side" confirmed its support for the right of the Gulf states "to establish national control over the use of their natural wealth, including oil," a pointed reference to Kuwait's nationalization of the remaining 40 percent share of Kuwait's oil held by British and American oil companies.

There were, however, repeated delays, and not until the spring of 1977 were arrangements completed and did weapons begin to arrive. Apparently fearful of subversion in the army, Kuwait had insisted that the training be supervised by Egyptians and Syrians, not Russians. Accordingly, when the problem was finally resolved, no Soviet instructors were allowed to come to Kuwait and no Kuwaiti soldiers were sent to the Soviet Union.[33] The arrangement was evidently more trouble than it was worth, because in August the Kuwaiti minister of interior and defense announced that his country had decided to stop purchasing arms from the Soviet Union.[34] On February 9, 1980, however, the Kuwaiti ministry of defense announced that the Soviet Union had delivered surface-to-surface missiles—the first time that the receipt of Soviet arms had been acknowledged.[35] Whether these were the weapons ordered in 1977, or subsequently, was not revealed.

After the fall of the shah, Moscow used Kuwait as a conduit for reassuring the other Arab states of the lower Gulf of its peaceful intentions. Thus, at the end of January 1979, it sent Oleg A. Grinevskii, chief of the Near East Department of the Ministry of Foreign Affairs, to convey this message from the Kremlin. But by the end of the year, the Soviet occupation of Afghanistan (which Kuwait condemned) exacerbated anxieties in the region and gave new impetus to Kuwait's efforts to minimize superpower involvement in the region and encourage the regional actors to act more assertively and cooperatively to safeguard their security.

Kuwait believes that adaptation to the new strategic situation in South and Southwest Asia requires better relations with the Soviet Union. Kuwaiti newspapers regularly sound the theme, for example, on July 27, 1980, an editorial in *Ar-ra'y Al-'Amm*, deploring U.S. hostility to the Arabs on such issues as Israel's occupation of Arab lands and the establishment of a Palestinian state, observed:

> The Soviet Union is a power to be reckoned with and it is not easy to be hostile to it. . . . Moreover, it has been proved through many experiences that relations with the Soviet Union on the basis of mutual interests do not mean the advent of communism . . . the United States must stop taking it for granted that we are its allies because of our intractable aversion to free dealing with the Soviet Union.[36]

The editorial reflected the official view expressed three weeks earlier by Sheikh Sabah al-Ahmad al Jabir al-Sabah, the Kuwaiti foreign minister, who declared that "the Soviet Union is not thinking of invading the Persian Gulf region to establish its control over the oil deposits there":

> The propaganda racket raised by the United States in this connection is totally groundless. The concentration of American naval fleets in the zone of the Persian Gulf, the Arabian Sea and the Indian Ocean is also quite unjustified.[37]

Indeed, it is precisely this military buildup, he noted, that increases tension and threatens still graver consequences.

During a visit to Moscow in April 1981, his first since December 1975, Sheikh al-Sabah received a warm welcome. His views were music to the Kremlin. In the joint communique of April 25, he joined with Moscow to condemn "Israel's aggressive actions," oppose the Camp David agreements, and support "the convening of an international conference on the Near East, with the obligatory participation of the PLO on an equal basis with other participants."[38] While criticizing Soviet policy in Afghanistan and upholding the right of the Afghan people to determine their own fate, he opposed any foreign interference or presence in the Gulf, noting, "We do not want anybody to volunteer to defend our region nor do we want foreign forces to compete for spheres of influence in the form of military facilities or bases or even in the form of the so-called Rapid Deployment Force which the United States has formed."[39] Moreover, he called on the Gulf Arab states to give careful consideration to Brezhnev's five-point proposal for the neutralization of the region, presented the previous December in New Delhi and at the CPSU congress in February 1981. Sheikh al-Sabah's emphasis on the essential congruence of views between the two countries may have been intended to dispel Soviet suspicion of the newly created Gulf Cooperation Council for which Kuwait has great hopes (see below).

In July, a Kuwaiti military delegation went to Moscow to discuss a new arms agreement. In September, Kuwait's emir, Sheikh Jaber al-Ahmad al-Sabah, made a ten-day visit to Hungary, Romania, Yugoslavia, and Bulgaria, as part of the campaign to persuade other Gulf states to develop closer ties with the Soviet bloc. In February 1982, the Kuwaiti News Agency opened an office in Moscow, symbolizing the official policy of expanding links between the two countries. Kuwait's policy has been described as no more "than balancing the relationship with the superpowers. It is a case of chopping some pieces off the U.S. relationship and adding bits to that with the USSR."[40]

For its part, the Soviet Union hopes the relationship with Kuwait will advance a number of objectives. First, there is the desire for normal diplomatic relations with the Arab states of the lower Gulf, that is, Bahrain, Qatar, the United Arab Emirates, Oman, and of course Saudi Arabia. Moscow wants good relations with Kuwait to show that normalization is not a prelude to Sovietization or subversion and that Kuwait "does not accept the slogan of the mythical 'Soviet threat' which Washington is foisting" on the region.[41] The Soviet relationship with Kuwait is the model that Moscow hopes will reassure the Gulf states and demonstrate that its support for the Marxist-oriented PDRY and the conservative Yemen Arab Republic (YAR) is evidence of opposition to imperialism (the United States) and not of any drive to destabilize the Arabian Peninsula; and that its evenhandedness in the Iraq-Iran war, notwithstanding its treaty relationship with Iraq, is really a desire to see the conflict end and regional stability preserved. Second, through a benign courtship of Kuwait, Moscow seeks to encourage Kuwait's independent initiatives, especially its open questioning of the utility for the Gulf states of too close a strategic relationship with the United States. But whether its diplomacy is flexible enough to strengthen the potential of Kuwait's Gulf-first approach without stumbling over the ruling Sabah family's preponderant economic ties to the West is not at all certain. Third, Moscow undoubtedly would welcome an increase in Kuwaiti investment and trade. At present, the amount of each is very small. Finally, and most important, Moscow hopes good relations with Kuwait will open the way for normalization of relations with Saudi Arabia.

Saudi Arabia

Ironically, although the Soviet Union was the first country to recognize King Abdul Aziz Abdur Rahman ibn Saud's newly created kingdom in 1926, it has no diplomatic relations with Saudi Arabia. In 1932, the Saudi foreign minister visited Moscow, but trade connections never took hold. Since 1938, when Moscow, then in the final throes of the Great Purge, recalled all of its personnel, there has been no official contact between the two countries. The Saudi example has been emulated by Bahrain, Qatar, the United Arab Emirates, and Oman, all of which have kept the Soviets at a distance.

However, Moscow has worked very hard since the mid-1950s to establish footholds on "al-Gezira Arabiya." Armed with checkbook and olive branch, and quick to use regional conflicts as an entree into extensive economic and military relationships, it acquired footholds on the perimeter, in Iraq, Kuwait, the Yemen Arab Republic, and the People's Democratic Republic of Yemen. It is persistent, accepting of the dilemmas that are inherent in trying to court opposing sides in regional rivalries and careful not to foreclose any possible lines of contact with Riyadh.

Soviet commentaries have long maintained a balance of sorts in their coverage of Saudi Arabia. Thus, prior to the fall of the shah, while criticizing Saudi Arabia's military relationship with the United States, its consorting with imperialist monopolies, and its opposition to progressive forces in the Middle East, they often recalled the establishment of diplomatic relations between the Soviet Union and Saudi Arabia in February 1926 and, stressing their common opposition to Israel's aggression, suggested that diplomatic normalization could strengthen the Arab position in the world. While condemning Saudi efforts to bring about a settlement of the Arab-Israeli conflict in league with the United States, Moscow's radio service in Arabic gives great play to occasional Saudi remarks about the importance of the USSR. For example, in September 1976, the Saudi foreign minister, Prince Saud ibn Faisal, acknowledged to an Egyptian journalist the importance of Soviet arms in helping to achieve "a national victory in the October War," and added: "The nonexistence of Saudi Arabia's diplomatic relations with the Soviet Union does not mean that we do not recognize it; in its magnitude and international influence, the Soviet Union is one of the two superpowers; moreover, logic dictates that we have mutually advantageous relations with all countries."[42] This sentiment had also been expressed more than a year earlier by King Khalid ibn Abd al-Aziz.

Saudi disenchantment with Anwar al-Sadat, whose dramatic decision to go to Jerusalem in November 1977 opened the way for an Egyptian-Israeli settlement, could not be turned to advantage by Moscow, because of the USSR's military intervention in Ethiopia, its buildup of the PDRY, whose ambitions make Riyadh uneasy, and the communist coup in Afghanistan in April 1978. Moreover, Soviet accusations of Saudi complicity in the complex drama of assassinations and coups in the Yemens in June 1978 mirrored Saudi views of Soviet involvement. Notwithstanding all of this, Saudi officials continued to drop hints that Moscow took as signifying a desire to normalize relations—witness the interview of December 8, 1978, by Crown Prince Fahd and his brother Salman, the governor of Riyadh, with the Lebanese weekly *al-Hawadith*, in which they said that Saudi Arabia "cannot base its international policy on enmity towards a third country although we oppose communism and atheism. . . . There is no benefit in the struggle against the USSR."[43]

A persistent if forbidding suitor, the Soviet government thought the agitation in the Arab world over Egypt's reconciliation with Israel and the cataclysmic chain of events that brought down the shah created a propitious time to renew its courtship of Saudi Arabia. In late January 1979, O. A. Grinevskii, head of the Near Eastern Department of the Ministry of Foreign Affairs, made a special trip to Kuwait to ask that reassurances be conveyed to the Arab leaders in the Gulf about the USSR's peaceful intentions and lack of responsibility for what happened in Iran. At the same time, Igor Beliaev, a leading Soviet journalist, published an article suggesting the time might be ripe for a Soviet-Saudi rapprochement.[44]

Beliaev noted that "the Soviet Union and Saudi Arabia have never been at war with each other and they have never had any implacable conflicts." Though they have different social systems, there is no basis for enmity. He argued that their shared desire to see a Near East settlement and aversion to the Camp David accords were common ground for "a new interpretation of many vitally important problems," and he implied that better relations between their two countries would be in the best interests of a just solution to the Middle East problems. The overture was familiar, the timing precise, the theme clear: the desire to normalize relations with Saudi Arabia. For Moscow, this was a necessary step in order to establish a Soviet presence everywhere in the Gulf, entice the oil-rich monarchical Arab regimes to disengage from the United States and opt for a policy of nonalignment, and further undermine the U.S. position in the region. A Saudi connection might well accelerate the radical realignment of allegiances in the Gulf in the post-shah era.

In early March the Saudi foreign minister told *al-Hawadith*: "We want to stress that the lack of diplomatic relations with the Soviet Union does not mean that we do not recognize the Soviet Union or the important role it plays at the level of international politics. On the contrary, we have more than once expressed thanks to the Soviet Union for its positive attitude toward Arab problems."[45] The compliment, an echo of earlier ones, was noted by Soviet media, but without fanfare.[46] Several weeks later a secondary Soviet newspaper, commenting on Soviet-Saudi relations, said there was no objective reason for the lack of diplomatic relations between the two countries.[47]

There was an Arab report of a meeting between Crown Prince Fahd ibn Abd al-Aziz and Soviet diplomats,[48] but no signs of diplomatic movement. In the months that followed, very few pieces that could be considered as written specifically to convey a favorable image of the Saudis appeared in the Soviet press, suggesting that Moscow was not optimistic about the resumption of diplomatic ties. Two may be mentioned. In July, Beliaev and a colleague published an interview with the Kuwaiti foreign minister, whom they commended for Kuwait's opposition to the Egyptian-Israeli treaty and whose praise of Kuwaiti-Soviet relations ("the Kuwaiti people know, in these times of difficulty for the Arabs, who their real friends are and who their real enemies are") they hoped would be heard in Saudi circles, at a time when the United States was trying to pressure the Arab states into accepting a greater U.S. military presence in the Gulf.[49] In the middle of August an article entitled "On New Trends in Saudi Arabia's Policy" lauded the Saudis for showing "greater flexibility and independence in foreign policy" and hoped that they and the Jordanians would draw closer to the National Front of Steadfastness and Confrontation in order to oppose the Egyptian-Israeli accords.[50]

Three aspects of Moscow's policy undermined its diplomatic initiative: the USSR-PDRY treaty of friendship of October 25, 1979, increased arms sales to the Yemen Arab Republic, and the military occupation of Afghanistan. As long as Moscow arms the Yemens, it intensifies Saudi anxieties and gives Riyadh second thoughts about the value of diplomatic normalization. This major stumbling block is seen by the Saudis as Moscow's unwillingness to make concessions.

Not unexpectedly, Saudi criticisms of the Soviet invasion of Afghanistan did not discourage occasional friendly Soviet references to the Saudis. A Soviet broadcast to the Arab world on the occasion of the fifty-fourth anniversary of the establishment of diplomatic relations between the Soviet Union and Saudi Arabia stressed, among other things, that the USSR "has good relations with a whole range of monarchies where Islam is a state religion and where Islamic ideas are cherished by the leaders just as much as they are cherished by the Saudis" and that, notwithstanding the "slanderous" allegations of the "Western propaganda machine" about the Afghan events, the Soviets do not harbor any hostile intentions toward the countries of the Gulf.[51] In a major article, a leading journalist, V. Kudriavtsev, cautioned the Saudis against being distracted by U.S. allegations of a Soviet threat.[52] In July, Beliaev, again writing on the need for a restoration of Saudi-Soviet relations, contended that "the limited contingent of Soviet troops temporarily" sent to Afghanistan is no threat to Saudi Arabia; rather, it is the United States and excessive reliance on U.S. protection and expertise that endanger the regime. He believed that "Saudi Arabia's domestic political and international position is changing," and sensed concern in the ruling family about "the immediate future. No trace remains of the former certainty that the special relationship with the United States is a panacea for all ills, external and internal."[53] The time is ripe, he suggested, for a resumption of diplomatic relations with the Soviet Union and the other socialist countries.

Shortly thereafter, in reply, Saudi Foreign Minister Prince Saud al-Faisal stated that an end to the Soviet occupation of Afghanistan would end Saudi inhibitions to the development of good relations with the Soviet Union. He appreciated the USSR's pro-Arab position, but emphasized that Soviet policy in Afghanistan "does not give any healthy signals to encourage countries to have relations with the Soviet Union, because it shows complete disregard for the interests of sovereign, independent states":

> Superpowers should be consistent in their postures. . . . Backing one issue here does not give them the right to interfere in the internal affairs of other countries. . . . Once the Soviet Union achieves this consistency in its policy in the region, I think any inhibition that exists in the Third World . . . and in the Islamic world about evolving and developing good relations with the Soviet Union will be removed. . . . If the Soviet Union has any legitimate concerns in the region, the way to resolve them is through an aboveboard policy toward the countries in which it has objective and legitimate interests. The best way to achieve those interests is through the legitimate channels, and not through occupation and intimidation.[54]

Essentially, the official Saudi position comes back to the occupation of Afghanistan. It is this situation that prompted the Saudis to boycott the Moscow Olympics, remove their embassy staff from Kabul, and react tepidly to Brezhnev's New Delhi proposals for regional security. King Khalid's opposition also derived from a deep-rooted aversion to permitting representatives of godless communism to operate on Saudi soil and from suspicion that the USSR armed its surrogates—the PDRY and Ethiopia—in order to destabilize the Saudi monarchy. After the June War, in the debate among Saudi leaders, some argued that Soviet-Saudi relations should be normalized to induce Moscow to support the Arab cause even more fully, but King Faisal, sharing his father's profound mistrust of the Soviet Union, rejected these counsels, as did King Khalid. For the moment at least,

King Fahd, who succeeded to the leadership on the death of King Khalid in June 1982, has followed the already well-established course.

Meanwhile, with periodic gestures on both sides, the unrequited flirtation goes on, the Soviets persistent suitors, the Saudis wary targets. Much of the back-and-forth, tentative explorations go on in private; messages are frequently "passed by the Soviets through intermediaries such as the PLO," and "Foreign Minister Saud has confirmed that Saudi and Soviet diplomats meet regularly in various regions of the world as part of an ongoing dialogue between Riyadh and Moscow."[55] On one occasion a high-ranking Soviet official, asked if Syria was trying to mediate between the Soviet Union and Saudi Arabia, replied "I know nothing about it."[56] This, not a categorical denial, suggests that secret exchanges may be more than rare.

If Moscow is frustrated by the Saudis' massive economic bonds to the United States and by its inability to extract more political capital out of their coolness to the Egyptian-Israeli peace process, it can take solace from the Saudis' refusal to accede to the Reagan administration's intense effort to forge a "strategic consensus," from their unwillingness to grant military bases on Saudi soil, and from the perennial political strains between Riyadh and Washington occasioned by partisans of Israel lobbying against the sale of advanced weaponry to Saudi Arabia, despite the AWACs decision.

Moscow knows that the Saudis hold the key to the establishment of diplomatic relations with the Arab states of the lower Gulf: the road to Bahrain, Qatar, the United Arab Emirates, and eventually Oman lies through Riyadh. In this, it hopes Kuwait can help; and it gave much publicity to the comment made in June 1981 by Sheikh Zayid ibn Sultan al-Nuhayyan, president of the UAE, who said that the Soviet Union sent its troops into Afghanistan at the request of that country's lawful government, criticized U.S. action to create a rapid deployment force in the region, and rejected allegations that the presence of Soviet troops in Afghanistan posed a threat to the Gulf.[57]

PLO leaders, too, serve a useful role in urging the Arabs to develop closer ties with the Soviet Union—witness the comments by Yasir Arafat's deputy, Salah Khalaf, who is better known by his nom de guerre, Abu Iyad, over the Voice of Palestine on October 21, 1981:

> We must consider the Soviet Union not only as a source for arms but also as a political and military power with which to ally ourselves in order to combat the American-Israeli alliance . . . we must ensure that

all the Arab Gulf states will recognize this superpower to which we are so strongly indebted, or, to be more precise, with which we have a common interest in striking at and checking the advance of the American-Zionist intervention in our region.[58]

For the foreseeable future, the USSR's minimum aim is to forestall the establishment of a permanent U.S. military presence on the Arabian Peninsula. Reiterating its own peaceful intentions, it plays up U.S.-Saudi differences, especially on the Palestinian issue, exploits the rich lode of anti-Americanism in the region, and lashes the United States for fostering an arms buildup for selfish reasons that are detrimental to the countries of the region.[59]

MOSCOW AND REGIONAL COOPERATION

A past master at exploiting endemic regional rivalries and upheavals, the Soviet Union has viewed efforts to promote unity and cooperation warily and more often than not manifested disapproval. Stalin's formula ("socialist in content, and national in form") for dividing and more easily controlling the diverse ethnic groups in the Soviet Union has its counterpart in the USSR's diplomacy in the Third World. So Moscow gives lip service to periodic chimerical Arab efforts at unity, but it prefers to deal with a large number of weak nation-states and fears mergers might be at the expense of pro-Soviet and communist minorities. Thus, it disapproved of the merger of Egypt and Syria in 1958, the fleeting suggestion of unity between Nasser's Egypt and Qasim's Iraq, and the Iraqi rationale for trying to absorb Kuwait. Though upholding the PDRY's calls for Yemeni unification, the Soviet record suggests that Moscow is quite satisfied with the existing situation.

Prior to the shah's fall and the demise of CENTO a few months later, Moscow had bitterly criticized all efforts by the Gulf states to fashion a regional security arrangement "or even a federation of some or all the Sheikhdoms. It was convinced that the independence granted to them was nothing but a farce to justify the continued presence of Western or American hegemony."[60] It opposed the idea of "any Gulf security pacts," an idea first aired by Iran and Saudi Arabia in 1968, after the British announced their intention to withdraw from the Gulf, though because of the Iranian-Iraqi-Saudi triangular rivalry, nothing was done. Moscow also took a dim view of the Saudi initiative in convening a conference in Muscat in November 1976 to discuss the issue of the preservation of security in the Gulf-

Indian Ocean area. When the conference ended without any action, Moscow Radio (in Arabic on November 29) declared that "the idea of setting up a military bloc was tactically not a viable idea at all, and inevitably it had to be abandoned."[61]

The Soviets saw the efforts as one more move directed by the United States to mobilize the region against the PDRY and Iraq, both closely associated with the USSR. For example, in the spring and summer of 1978, Moscow warned of Washington's ambitions to dispatch forces to the Middle East to set up an alliance among the "local reactionary regimes" in the Persian Gulf and Red Sea regions, which the United States regards "as an important strategic zone and as a bridgehead for the struggle against progressive regimes."[62] Apparently distressed that the United States might permanently station troops in Sinai as part of an Egyptian-Israeli settlement, these statements represented a veiled warning against attempts to depose the "progressive" regimes in the PDRY and Ethiopia or to stampede the Gulf states into an alliance out of fear of a possible spread of the Afghani revolution or revival of the Dhofari rebellion.

By the end of the 1970s, the strategic setting had dramatically changed. The upheaval in Iran and fear that Khomeini's Islamic revolution might spill across the Gulf and provoke trouble from the Shiite underclass, the growing Soviet military involvement in the PDRY, YAR, Ethiopia, and Afghanistan (especially after December 1979), the expansion of the superpowers' naval presence in the Indian Ocean, and the reports that the Soviets might need Gulf oil after the mid-1980s prompted the Arab states of the lower Gulf to explore ways of enhancing their security and stability. In October 1979, representatives of Saudi Arabia, Kuwait, Bahrain, Qatar, the UAE, and Oman met in Taif, Saudi Arabia. Notably not invited was Iraq, whose ambitions and military buildup were viewed with considerable suspicion by the other Arab states in the region, at least until late September 1980, when it became bogged down in its abortive invasion of Iran. While publicly supporting Iraq, privately the Arabs of the lower Gulf are relieved at the humbling of Iraq's radical military leadership.

The group criticized by Moscow as "the reactionary regimes in the Persian Gulf area, obviously promoted by Washington," seeking to form a military alliance,[63] convened again in Taif in late January 1981 and established a new regional organization, the Gulf Cooperation Council (GCC), which formally began operating on May 26, 1981. Though Iraq's President Saddam Hussein attended the January meeting, Iraq was not made a member, suggesting that the other Gulf

Arabs preferred to insulate themselves from the Iraqi-Iranian war and that Saudi Arabia preferred not to have a powerful rival in the organization. The impetus for the GCC's establishment probably came from the technocrats who sought a way of institutionalizing the elaborate network of more than 100 bitlateral and multilateral trade, economic, and technical agreements that these governments, including Iraq's, had concluded during the 1968–80 period. However, whereas in January the talks were conducted mainly by technocrats, in May they were dominated by the political leaders, whose growing fear of Iran was the catalyst and who agreed to restrict membership to "like-minded states."[64]

Moscow's initial reaction was predictably critical.[65] Kuwait's foreign minister tried, during a visit to Moscow in late April, to dispel the Soviet reservations about the council, stressing that it "is not inspired by any side," but is the result of a desire to eliminate foreign influence in the region; it "is not directed against anybody, and is not an opponent of any bloc nor is it a supporter of any side. We hope that our friends in the Soviet Union will view our attempts in a positive spirit."[66] Gromyko was noncommittal. The Kuwaitis also tried to convince Moscow to support their own efforts to reconcile Oman and the PDRY, arguing that "if you are really disturbed by the U.S. military presence in the area," remember that "Sultan Qabus has pledged to abrogate the facilities agreement with the Americans if his country's borders with South Yemen are secured by a guarantee."[67]

A basic difference between the GCC and the USSR may inhere in the former's view, expressed at its meeting in November 1981, that "the security and stability of the Gulf are the responsibility of the Gulf states themselves," whereas the latter, judging by a revealing comment made to the Kuwaiti newspaper *as-Siyasah* by L. M. Zamyatin of the CPSU Central Committee International Information Department, believes that the Soviet Union and the United States must take part in discussions on ensuring the security of the region: "I believe that you agree with me that non-participation by either of these two countries in discussing the question of Arab Gulf security would make the decisions taken in those discussions absolutely nonbinding on them, in which case the process of turning the area into an area of peace would be back where it started."[68] Though alluding to Brezhnev's proposals for promoting security in the region, he seemed to imply that no fundamental decisions purporting to safeguard the region could command universal acceptance unless there was a superpower input.

In late January 1982, worried by Iran's seditious activities in Bahrain, the GCC's defense ministers announced that measures for collective defense were being drafted; a month later, on February 24, meeting in Riyadh, the GCC representatives signed "a comprehensive joint security agreement."[69]

There is no reason to suppose that Moscow regards the GCC as anything more than a shell–fragile and unable for long to contain the strains and pressures that beset it from within and without. The restrained Soviet criticisms doubtless reflect Moscow's awareness of the diverse motives that impel the members: Saudi Arabia's desire to find some way of offsetting U.S. pressure for closer strategic cooperation, Kuwait's aim of persuading Oman to retract the military privileges granted to the United States on Masirah Island and the Ras Musandam Peninsula, and Bahrain and the UAE acceding to Saudi pressure. Also, Soviet leaders may not want to do anything that would complicate Kuwait's active effort to reconcile Riyadh to Moscow and to persuade members of the GCC to open commercial contacts with the Soviet bloc, a possible prelude to diplomatic normalization.[70] Yet Moscow is also uneasy at what is sees as the growing importance of the United States in the GCC's planning and defense preparations. Moscow Radio suggested on a number of occasions that Washington intends through arms sales to create a subservient GCC and to transform it "into a tool for the imperialist alliance's policy," and that the "so-called defensive umbrella" provided by the AWACs typifies the subservience Washington seeks to nurture.[71]

CONCLUDING OBSERVATIONS

A long discussion begs for brief observations. South and Southwest Asia are of considerable strategic importance to the Soviet Union. The area has oil; it has the regional animosities that have been the boon to Soviet advances in the Third World; and it is uneasy over the lengthening shadow of Soviet power, America's tarnished credibility, and the intensifying superpower rivalry. The extent to which developments there since 1979 have benefited the Soviet Union is open to speculation, but this much seems clear. Moscow's military power has swept to the Khyber Pass for the first time in its long imperial history. The USSR's domains now border directly on the subcontinent, and as a result its diplomatic options and political leverage have been enormously increased, unquestionably making its policies crucial to the region's future stability. More than ever before, the threat of intrusive and potentially disruptive Soviet power and subversion must condition the policies of the regional actors. There is no doubt that "the Soviet Union has become," as a distinguished Indian journalist observed, "a contender for dominant influence in the region."[72] But only time will tell how the Soviets can translate the "demonstration effect" into increments of influence.

The threat of a Soviet military intervention in Iran is serious, but should not be exaggerated. Afghanistan is not a model for future Soviet risk taking. Though Iran is the most logical next target, paradoxically, for the foreseeable future, it may well be a most unpromising one. The Khomeini regime is strongly anti-Soviet, critical of Soviet policy in Afghanistan, and cool to Moscow's repeated overtures for better economic and diplomatic relations despite its relatively benign position in the Iraqi-Iranian war. At the turn of the century, Captain A. T. Mahan observed that "from the standpoint of military advantage" a Russian naval presence in the Persian Gulf "would be most eccentrically placed as regards all Russia's greatest interests" unless Moscow could acquire a communications network that was permanent, "coherent and consolidated."[73] Lacking this, Moscow is not perceived as a "clear and present danger" by Iran or Pakistan, much less the noncontiguous countries in the region.

Soviet policy is to court key countries, encourage their nonalignment or unalignment with the United States, stress its desire for diplomatic normalization, convey peaceful intent while securing its position in Afghanistan, dispense arms and cater to the myopic national aims and parochial rivalries of regional actors, avoid actions such as blocking the Strait of Hormuz or the flow of Gulf oil, strengthen ties with India, and wait for developments. In the "Great Game," which will be a long one, what Washington does in the region may count for more than what Moscow wants.

NOTES

1. P. R. Chari, "Indo-Soviet Military Cooperation: A Review," *Asian Survey* 19, no. 3 (March 1979): 232.

2. Alvin Z. Rubinstein, *Soviet Policy Toward Turkey, Iran, and Afghanistan: The Dynamics of Influence* (New York: Praeger, 1982).

3. Quoted in Rouhollah K. Ramazani, *Iran's Foreign Policy 1941-1973* (Charlottesville: University Press of Virginia, 1975), p. 316.

4. *Pravda*, June 8, 1969.

5. Joel Larus, "India's Nonalignment and Superpower Naval Rivalry in the

Indian Ocean," in *The Indian Ocean in Global Politics*, ed. Larry W. Bowman and Ian Clark (Boulder, Colo.: Westview Press, 1981), p. 43.

6. Yuri Glukhov, *Pravda*, May 19, 1978.

7. Shahram Chubin, *Soviet Policy Towards Iran and the Gulf*, Adelphi Paper no. 157 (London: International Institute for Strategic Studies, 1980), p. 14.

8. Dimitry Volsky, "Security or Confrontation?" *New Times*, no. 2 (January 1976): 8.

9. Quoted in *Los Angeles Times*, January 16, 1980.

10. *New York Times*, March 14, 1979.

11. *Pravda*, January 13, 1980.

12. For two comprehensive statements of this position, see the address delivered by USSR ambassador to France, S. V. Chervonenko, to the International Diplomatic Academy (Paris) on April 15, 1980, and the press conference held by Soviet Foreign Minister Andrei Gromyko in Paris on April 25, 1980. Foreign Broadcast Information Service [hereafter referred to as FBIS/USSR], April 28, 1980, pp. G1–G7. The United States was repeatedly blamed for the disruption of the Naval Arms Limitation Talks. For example, A. Alexeysev and A. Fialkovsky, "For a Peaceful Indian Ocean," *International Affairs*, no. 2 (February 1981): 90.

13. FBIS/USSR, December 11, 1980, p. D7.

14. Ibid. A number of Brezhnev's proposals were familiar, having apparently been discussed before the SALT talks were suspended, for example, "stabilization" or "freezing" by the United States and the Soviet Union of military activities in the Indian Ocean, and assured maritime access. See *Pravda*, January 18, 1978.

15. Pran Sabharwal, reporting from New Delhi, *Baltimore Sun*, December 11, 1980.

16. *Washington Times*, September 23, 1982.

17. Useful analyses of Soviet policy as of the end of 1978 are Aryeh Yodfat, "The U.S.S.R. and the Persian Gulf Area," *Australian Outlook* 33, no. 1 (April 1979): 60–72; David Lynn Price, "Moscow and the Persian Gulf," *Problems of Communism* 28, no. 2 (March–April 1979): 1-13.

18. The issues are developed in Alvin Z. Rubinstein, "The Soviet Union and Iran Under Khomeini," *International Affairs* 57, no. 4 (Autumn 1981): 599–617; Mikhail Volodarsky and Yaacov Ro'i, "Soviet-Iranian Relations During Two 'Revolutions,'" *Slavic and Soviet Series* 4, nos. 1–2 (1979): 33–58.

19. *Izvestiia*, September 23, 1980.

20. *8 Days*, February 20, 1982, p. 40.

21. FBIS/USSR, February 17, 1982, p. H2.

22. Eric Rouleau, "Khomeini's Iran," *Foreign Affairs* 59, no. 1 (Fall 1980): 18.

23. FBIS/USSR, February 18, 1982, p. H1.

24. Patricia Blake, "Iran: Big Brother Moves In: Soviets Are Influencing Security, Military and Economic Affairs," *Time*, November 23, 1981, p. 44; William Safire, *New York Times*, March 15, 1982.

25. Stephen S. Kaplan, ed., *Diplomacy of Power: Soviet Armed Forces as a Political Instrument* (Washington, D.C.: Brookings Institution, 1981), p. 509.

26. Karen Dawisha, "Moscow's Moves in the Direction of the Gulf—So Near and Yet So Far," *Journal of International Affairs* 34, no. 2 (Fall/Winter 1980/81): 220. For details of the Soviet-Iraqi relationship, see also Shahram Chubin, *Security in the Persian Gulf: The Role of Outside Powers* (Totowa, N.J.: Allanheld Osmun, 1982), pp. 86–109.

27. *The Soviet Union and the Middle East: A Monthly Summary and Analysis of the Soviet Press* [hereafter referred to as *SUME*] 6, no. 1 (1981): 4.

28. *SUME* 6, no. 12 (1981): 10.

29. FBIS/USSR, August 28, 1981, pp. H2–H3. See also *Izvestiia*, January 20, 1982.

30. Stephen Page, *The USSR and Arabia* (London: Central Asian Research Centre, 1971), p. 81.

31. A. Yodfat and M. Abir, *In the Direction of the Persian Gulf* (London: Frank Cass, 1977), p. 86.

32. Of Kuwait's approximately 1.3 million inhabitants, about 550,000 are native Kuwaitis. The Palestinians are the largest component of the foreign population—about 450,000 of the 750,000.

33. FBIS/Arabian Peninsula, June 21, 1977, pp. C1.

34. FBIS/Arabian Peninsula, August 10, 1977, p. C3.

35. *Middle East Economic Digest*, February 15, 1980, p. 35. According to the article, "Kuwait is also believed to have ordered SA-6 'gainful' and SA-7 'Grail' surface-to-air missiles from the Soviet Union, but delivery of these has not been confirmed. The value of each order is reported to be $100 million."

36. FBIS/Arabian Peninsula, July 31, 1980, p. C2.

37. FBIS/USSR, July 14, 1980, p. H10.

38. FBIS/USSR, April 29, 1981, p. H4.

39. Ibid., p. H2.

40. Quoted in *Weekly Media Abstract*, Report no. 112, November 22, 1981. A far more unflattering assessment has been advanced by J. B. Kelly, a renowned scholar of the region and a critic of Western illusions about the Gulf. The ruling al-Sabah family's response, he writes, "to every actual or apprehended danger to their rule has been, as general policy, to buy it off, either with money or by the adoption of fashionable political attitudes. Kuwait is the weathercock of the Gulf. It was the first of the minor states to terminate its treaty relationships with Britain, the first to erect a facade of constitutionalism, the first to enter into diplomatic relations with the Soviet Union and China. Most recently it has also become the first to acquire Russian arms and Russian military instructors. It was the earliest and most vocal supporter, as well as the principal financial backer, of the Palestine Liberation Organization, and of late years it has provided a haven for terrorists. It has been the foremost practitioner of the art of appeasement, paying Iraq to drop its claim to sovereignty over the sheikhdom and purchasing immunity from the unwelcome attention to the more extreme Palestinian groups by means of bribes.

"Kuwait's voice has been the most shrill in denunciation of a Western imperialism, which served it very handsomely in the past, the most strident in demanding that the price of oil to Western consumers be raised ever higher. Yet for all this there is a remarkable persistence on the part of many Western commentators in viewing Kuwait as the most advanced of the Gulf states and in lauding its government as the most enlightened and able. It is a view as ill-considered as any conclusion about the shaikhdom's future, based upon its present appearance of stability, is unwise." J. B. Kelly, "Saudi Arabia and the Gulf States," in *The Middle East: Oil, Conflict and Hope*, ed. A. L. Udovitch, Critical Choices for Americans, Vol. 10 (Lexington, Mass.: Lexington Books, 1976), p. 438.

41. G. Kuznetsov, "The Persian Gulf: Real Paths to Peace," *International Affairs*, no. 7 (July 1981): 104.

42. FBIS/USSR, September 24, 1976, p. F4.

43. Quoted in *Middle-East Intelligence Survey*, December 1–15, 1978, pp. 132–33.

44. Igor Beliaev, "Saudi Arabia: What Next?" *Literaturnaia gazeta*, January 31, 1979, p. 14.

45. FBIS/USSR, March 6, 1979.

46. *Izvestiia*, March 6, 1979.

47. *Sovetskaia Rossiia*, March 27, 1979.

48. Radio Free Europe—Radio Liberty, "On the Eve of a New Saudi-Soviet Relationship?" RL 163/79, May 29, 1979, p. 3.

49. FBIS/USSR, July 6, 1979, p. H11.

50. FBIS/USSR, August 15, 1979, p. H3.

51. FBIS/USSR, February 20, 1980, p. H6.

52. *Izvestiia*, April 6, 1980.

53. FBIS/USSR, July 14, 1980, p. H9.

54. Interview with Mona as-Said in *Monday Morning* (Beirut), July 21-27, 1980, as cited in FBIS/Arabian Peninsula, July 28, 1980, p. C4.

55. William B. Quandt, *Saudi Arabia in the 1980s: Foreign Policy, Security, and Oil* (Washington, D.C.: Brookings Institution, 1981), p. 71.

56. Interview by the Lebanese newspaper, *as-Safir*, with Karen Brutents, deputy chief of the CPSU Central Committee's International Department, in Beirut, as cited in FBIS/USSR, January 29, 1982, p. H1.

57. Tass report of an interview in the Paris-published weekly *al-Mustaqbal*, cited in *Krasnaia zvezda*, June 7, 1981. See FBIS/USSR, June 15, 1981, p. H4.

58. Quoted in Jon Kimche, "The PLO's Second Front," *Midstream* 28, no. 2 (February 1982): 4.

59. A. Vasilyev, *Pravda*, March 11, 1982.

60. Yodfat and Abir, *In the Direction of the Persian Gulf*, p. 70.

61. *USSR and Third World*, 12 September–31 December, 1976, p. 216.

62. *Pravda*, May 19, 1978.

63. FBIS/USSR, January 2, 1981, p. CC7.

64. For this insight, I am indebted to Dr. John Duke Anthony. See his "The Gulf Cooperation Council," *Journal of South Asian and Middle Eastern Studies* 5, no. 4 (Summer 1982), pp. 3–18.

65. *Pravda*, February 10, 1981.

66. FBIS/USSR, April 29, 1981, p. H2.

67. FBIS/Arabian Peninsula, May 13, 1981, p. C6.

68. FBIS/USSR, May 13, 1981, p. H7.

69. FBIS/Arabian Peninsula, February 25, 1982, p. C3.

70. *8 Days*, January 9, 1982, p. 17.

71. FBIS/USSR, February 23, 1982, p. H4.

72. Giralal Jain, *The Times of India*, January 30, 1980.

73. A. T. Mahan, "The Persian Gulf," *National Review* 40, no. 140 (1902): 37.

Part III

THE MIDDLE POWERS

5

Western European Perceptions of Europe's Stake in Persian Gulf-Indian Ocean Security

Shahram Chubin

The policies of Western European countries toward the Persian Gulf-Indian Ocean area are today discussed primarily with reference to the Western alliance, to their needs in light of the upheavals in the region and the extension of Soviet power. They are seen in terms of the necessity for alliance unity and a division of labor in an era when Western Europe's security is threatened by events outside the formal treaty area, when relations with the United States are in transition, and when the old nostrums are no longer valid.

Historically speaking, it is only recently that the major European states have wound down their commitments in this region, encouraged in part by the United States. Only recently France had the largest naval presence. Barely a decade ago Britain was the security manager of the Gulf region. Although the policies of the European states (and the perspectives that inform them) in the coming decade are our immediate concern, it is well to consider the issue more generally. What will be the role of medium-sized industrialized states in the coming years? What will be their responsibility for contributing to international security and order? Historically, this responsibility has not been merely a function of great (or superpower) status.

At a time when international order is threatened by a variety of dangers, the capacity of the superpowers to manage affairs is increasingly in doubt. Even were it possible for them to maintain order, it is doubtful that it would be desirable. Yet what kind of international system can we anticipate, and what role, if any, can the European states play beyond their immediate setting? What are the trends in the international system, especially in the area with which we are concerned?

The role of the Western European states must be set in context, with reference made to their past, to their relations with the United States and one another, and to the prevailing perspectives and policies that seek to safeguard their interests, be they values or tangible assets. If, in an era of multipolarity, diffusion of power, and difficulties of management, the international order is no longer the exclusive domain of the superpowers, it is not yet clear that other states can contribute to its management, or in what ways.

In the immediate postwar period, in which decolonization coincided with an era of bipolarity, fear of superpower confrontation was ever present. Bipolarity circumscribed the margin of maneuver for many states, including those of Europe. For some less developed countries, nonalignment seemed an avenue of escape. For the Europeans, the security produced by alliance overshadowed doubts about its other shortcomings, for example, entanglement elsewhere and loss of independence.

Differences occurred between Western European states and the United States with regard to third areas, but these were secondary issues that accelerated, together with other pressures (indigenous nationalism and competing claims on resources), decolonization and the process of disimperialism. The buffer provided by U.S. nuclear and economic supremacy contributed to a narrowing of perspective from the global to the regional and created a psychological dependency on U.S. leadership in all areas, including the Third World.

In recent years, U.S. supremacy has been challenged in both the military and economic spheres. Economic competition within the alliance and nuclear parity between the blocs, together with the uneven record of U.S. leadership, especially in relation to issues in the Third World, have caused rifts in the alliance's structure.

The relationship between NATO's strategy and the redistribution of roles within the alliance and events in third areas is complex and circular. The perennial Western European fear of superpower "collision or collusion" persists. Differing estimates of the value of détente and arms control and of their linkage to Soviet behavior in the Third World aggravate misgivings on both sides of the Atlantic. Whereas the Europeans are no longer as deferential as in the past, the United States is no longer prepared to pay the bills in the alliance without commensurate deference.

The differences between the global perspectives of the United States and its more regional-minded partners in Europe have been accentuated as the former sees its allies benefiting from its exertions, even while they snipe at it or doubt its sagacity. The free ride enjoyed by the Europeans for so long must, the United States believes, end with a greater European defense contribution in Europe and greater solidarity with U.S. efforts in the Third World. It is in these areas, especially in the Persian Gulf, that Europe, Washington argues, faces its gravest threats and this requires recognition that threats there are not in practice distinguishable from direct threats to Europe. Threats in the Gulf are unlikely to come separate from threats in Europe, and threats to Europe are likely to include simultaneously moves in the Gulf.

The Europeans do not deny the essence of the thesis but differ somewhat on the nature of the threat, the appropriate response, and particularly their most useful contribution in meeting it. The differences do not stem merely from American military and global responsibilities versus European provincialism, nurtured for more than a generation by dependence on the United States and now blended with dependence on the Arab oil producers, which encourages a European deference rather than decisiveness. The differences—and they are not as major as one might infer from the heat of mutual recrimination in 1973 and the 1979–81 period—stem from two principal sources: a psychological incapacity or unwillingness after a generation of dependence on the "nuclear umbrella" to accept the need for rethinking alliance strategy and the inevitably greater financial and military contributions that will be demanded of Europe. (This manifests itself in criticism of the United States on issues such as "lack of consultation" but rarely sees any sustained attempt by European states to make constructive suggestions.)

The international system that one contemplates is not a simple one of hierarchies, clear alignments, and dominant issues; rather, it is characterized by a diffusion of power, multiple crosscutting cleavages, and a simultaneity of issues that obscures rather than clarifies any definition of power or responsibility. The European states, as they emerge from a period of semienforced seclusion, will necessarily consider the range of possible policies in the Gulf-Indian Ocean area against their assessment of the following:

1. The future role of the alliance, relationships with the superpowers, and the scope for unilateralism, or a united Europe.
2. The sources and nature of conflict and instability in the Third World, their roots and consequences. Related to this is the issue of the Soviet role in exploiting these, whether a prime cause or complicating factor, and the best response by the West.
3. Attitudes toward the utility of force and intervention in a period where each is constrained.

4. The more general issue of the North-South relationship, the interconnection between development, change, and order and between enlightened preventive diplomacy and the incidence of disorder.
5. Whether in the evolving international system the role of medium powers will be to assist, prevent, or accept transformations in the status quo and power hierarchy and to do so unilaterally or multilaterally through the Western alliance—and possibly to engage local states in the management of order through the encouragement of regional structures of security.

Too much should not be made of the classification "European." These states differ in histories and historical memories, in their perspectives, in their interests vis-a-vis either superpower, and in their orientation toward the Third World. Living in a security community has only sublimated their competitiveness vis-a-vis each other. Britain and France, colonial rivals in the Middle East, still compete there aggressively for markets, and the memories of the Atlanticist-Gaullist strains of 1973 are still fresh. France periodically contrives ostensibly persuasive and ingenious reasons for pursuing its own interests in the guise of the wider interests of an alliance. The relationship between France and West Germany historically is equally mixed, alternating between embrace and balance, inclusion and reinsurance. Until recently, France has pursued a delicate policy to offset any possible revanchist tendencies in Germany by balancing with the USSR. Today its worry has shifted to fear of German neutralism, and it has correspondingly altered its course to anchor Bonn more firmly in the alliance, by taking up a firmer anti-Soviet stance in Europe. (For France, Britain's role in the alliance assumes importance in this respect.)

Varying degrees of capability, differing assets, and comparative advantages, in addition to these other differences, account for variations in the European states' policies toward the area. There are also divergencies stemming from different views of the current and evolving international system and the requirements for an attainable measure of order.

The European states, despite these differences, have substantially similar interests in the Persian Gulf region. Though their level of dependence on the region for oil varies—three-fifths for West Germany, two-thirds for France, three-quarters for Italy—generally it remains high. Imported oil accounts for 45 percent of Europe's total energy, and 70 percent of its oil, in the 1970s, came from the Middle East. Furthermore, the region as a whole is extremely important in terms of trade. Arab purchases from the European Community accounted for 13.3 percent of the extra-Community trade, more important than trade with the United States and Japan together. Also, the region, for reasons of proximity and geopolitics, is the most natural area for European states' interest. And despite the differences in emphasis between the European approach and the approach to problems of security in the region, there is a very substantial agreement on the issues and aims, whether in deference to the Arab-Israeli issue or to Persian Gulf security.[1] Nevertheless, there is also a vested European interest in differentiating itself tactically from the United States and its overidentification with Israel and its overestimation of the Soviet threat. Domestic and continental European pressures to build European autonomy in separation from, if not in opposition to, U.S. policy is not a recent phenomenon[2] and may be expected to continue.

Let me summarize some related arguments as far as the international environment is concerned. First, security in the Third World will be the principal issue of East-West competition for the foreseeable future. Europe and the West in general will be more vulnerable in the Gulf region than in Europe itself. Second, the Persian Gulf region will remain of paramount importance with or without the oil factor, as the Soviet Union will continue to be interested in the region. Similarly, regional instability and conflict will continue, with or without the Soviet Union (or indeed the Arab-Israeli dispute). Third, the "psychological gap"[3] between Europe and the United States is a reality that may continue, if not increase. Europe appears to be "out of phase"[4] with both superpowers, and this may take a while to resolve itself. This gap may be attributable in part to the atrophy of the habit of thinking globally, or strategically, which was perhaps a natural accompaniment of a shrinkage of power. It may also be due both to the nature of threats today, which are obscure and fuzzy, and to the difficulties of mobilizing democracies to sacrifice lives for such murky causes. Fourth, wars—civil wars, wars of national liberation, and wars of natural resistance—are endemic to the Indian Ocean region.

This raises more general questions for the Western European states: What is the nature of conflict in the Third World, and what management role is there, if any, for the medium powers? In the past, the fear stemming from such conflicts was one of great power entanglement leading to nuclear confrontation. Today the converse is the case, with fragmentation and decentralization the norm as conflicts persist unmanaged, weakening the basis of international order without threatening it with a cataclysm. As middle powers, the

European states will have to consider their potential role in a system of renewed East-West competition and Third World conflict. Learning to live with this instability while confining it and preventing the USSR from harnessing it for Soviet purposes will be the continual challenge for European diplomacy.

There is no doubt that in the Gulf-Indian Ocean region the Europeans enjoy certain advantages, especially a receptivity to them as more acceptable, less intrusive, less polarizing partners in the development process. This regional acceptability—an irony given their historical antecedents—is of course flattering to the European states, which pride themselves on a sophisticated understanding of complex societies derived from historical contact.[5] But regional acceptability is not without its costs; the Arab states count on using the Europeans as a pressure group to weaken U.S. ties with Israel.

The region itself is a complex political environment resisting simplification as grand strategy. There is no single dominant issue in the region. There is no consensus on the role of the great powers, but there exists strong support (albeit often rhetorical) for nonalignment. Given its salience to the East-West competition, even limited conflicts in this region contain the seeds of major power confrontation. At the same time, local conflicts quickly seem to become regional and internationalized—witness Lebanon or Iran-Iraq. Here, in contrast to other areas of the Third World, the threat of confrontation arising from local conflicts is high. This emphasizes the potentially important role to be played by both regional and other states in containing conflict.

THE HISTORICAL BACKGROUND

There is a temptation during periods of crises to contrast current problems with previous eras of seemingly glowing unity and stability. This tends to impart to the past a unidimensionality that it rarely possessed. Certainly in the case of the European states' encounter with the Indian Ocean-Persian Gulf, there was always diversity. In the postwar period, Anglo-French rivalry in the Middle East was as constant as it had been before and during the war. France, suspicious of British motives, held on to its foothold in Lebanon, which its interventions had helped stabilize since the mid-nineteenth century. Britain and America continued their rivalry over oil in the Gulf. The United States continued to distrust the ambitions of the colonial powers. European and American unity was somehow achieved in response to Iran's oil nationalization in the 1952–54 era, but it gave way eventually to a greater American stake in Iran's oil industry.

By the mid-1950s, the United States sought to fashion regional alliances against the USSR, but did so without wishing to block indigenous nationalism, which it considered a positive force. It found itself in the anomalous position of undermining its European allies regionally by encouraging their rapid disimperialism, while stepping into their shoes with local pacts. In practice it found this difficult. Unable to join the Baghdad Pact (or CENTO), it had to rely on Britain's full membership as a substitute—that is, to accept the value of its European allies' role. In 1956, in Suez, the United States took a position directly opposed to its major European allies, apparently in the belief that the dispute was essentially a colonial one, not a priority East-West or global issue for the alliance. The results of that episode were to mark a turning point both in the relations of the major European powers with the Middle East and in France's relations with the alliance. Yet a year after Suez, the United States proclaimed the Eisenhower Doctrine, asserting the right to unilateral action in the region—precisely what it had denied its allies.[6]

The United States was thus at best ambivalent about its European allies' continued commitments in third areas, seeing in them relics of a discredited colonialism that might harm the United States in its relations with the Third World. At the same time, the West clearly benefited from these relations. Who could doubt, for example, Britain's stabilizing role vis-a-vis Jordan, and even more so in the Persian Gulf where Britain acted as security manager until 1971? Here, at a minimal cost in personnel and resources, Britain's presence ensured local security.[7] It insulated the area from Soviet involvement, froze regional conflicts or the implementation of irredenta (for example, Iraq or Kuwait, in 1961), and managed change in the region (sometimes by preemptive coups, as in Abu Dhabi, in 1966, and in Oman, in 1970) in the interests of stability.

Britain's role here and in southern Arabia was generally unacknowledged as an alliance contribution until after it was terminated. Britain's decision to withdraw by 1971, though often discussed in financial terms, did not stem principally from this consideration. Rather, it represented the culmination of a long process of post-imperial retrenchment that had started nearly 20 years earlier in the Indian subcontinent and zigzagged its way across the Mediterranean and Middle East back to the Gulf. A related consideration was that the British military presence was now deemed counterproductive—attracting Arab nationalist antagonism rather than insulating the region from upheaval. In any event, Britain's involvement in CENTO continued as long as that treaty lasted (1979), bringing with it annual naval exercises (Midlink) with Iran, Pakistan, Turkey, and the United States. In addition, Britain's various acquisitions and leases in the Indian Ocean area–Diego Garcia, Gan, Masirah (Oman)–proved exceptionally useful for the United States, which gradually sought to improve its strategic position in the region as the full import of Britain's withdrawal–no longer obscured by Vietnam–began to register.

France was treated more suspiciously than Britain and reciprocated the feeling. What two French authors in a changed political context referred to as "a lonely battle against destabilization" was seen as France's rather selfish fixation on its empire and colonies.[8] Despite France's dismal record in Indochina and Suez, there appears to have been substantial domestic support for the continuation of a role outside Europe. France managed to maintain the largest permanent Western naval presence in the Indian Ocean until 1979. Allowing for its various possessions from Djibouti to Reunion, it was still a considerable feat of determination in an era when defense costs were under attack and the military instruments' limitations constantly trumpeted.

The United States, barely acknowledging its allies' contribution, persisted in a policy of unilateralism. After 1967, it aligned itself increasingly with Israel. In 1973, it saw the issues primarily in East-West terms, while the European allies were concerned with the availability of oil and its price. They saw the U.S.-Israeli connection as the problem and something they did not wish to identify with in the provision of facilities and overflight rights. The United States in turn saw little value in the European states dealing with the major issues that concerned it: balancing the USSR and settling the Arab-Israeli dispute. It therefore pursued its unilateralism (1973–79) with little change, except in the energy dimension of the problem, where it sought a multilateral approach. Unsurprisingly, France refused to fall into line with an American initiative, especially since, unlike the Suez period, the United States was not in a position to make it worthwhile by providing assurances regarding U.S. oil supplies to Europe.[9]

The Europeans had dismantled their empires in the Indian Ocean area with difficulty and with little sympathy from the United States. Their residual commitments were rarely accepted as contributions to an allied or Western position in world politics or to the need for a presence. In the 1960s, the European states in turn came to see American involvement in third areas first as an embarrassment and later as a potential threat: It might entangle the European allies in American adventures elsewhere, or it might serve as a diversion of

American energies and resources from Europe, thus blurring the focus of NATO and diluting the U.S. commitment to the alliance.

American policies in the Middle East-Indian Ocean were no more reassuring. Since 1956, a reversal of alliances had taken place: the United States shifting from support for the Arabs to backing for Israel, while France and the United Kingdom shifted in the other direction. By 1973 and after, each saw the other's support for its preferred local state as the encouragement of its intransigence. More generally, the Europeans watched incredulously as American policy, which had supported local nationalism in the 1950s and 1960s (recall John Kennedy's initial support for Nasser in the Yemen) and maintained its unilateralism, allowed the erosion of its strategic infrastructure in the region and rationalized its retrenchment by the Nixon Doctrine, thus reversing itself. Overnight in January 1980, after the Soviet invasion of Afghanistan, the Carter Doctrine was proclaimed; the search for "facilities" was initiated, and allied solidarity demanded.

Suddenly, it seemed, the Russians were everywhere, the alliance was being tested, and the fate of the West hung in the balance. If the Europeans reacted lethargically and cynically saw in all this a ploy for a revival of American leadership in the alliance, or judged their reactions in the light of their possible repercussions in Europe, this was regrettable—and understandable. The European presence in the region had been considerably unsung in the councils of the alliance. American policy had been to ignore it and pursue its own policies unilaterally.

The European states—principally France and Britain—though unhappy with the United States, were not united vis-a-vis one another. Rivals, first as colonial powers and later as traders, each felt a sense of *amour propre*, especially in relation to the Middle East.[10] As great powers, each state had a strategic perspective extending beyond merely territorial possessions. Its recent historical experience, combined with a habit of reliance on the United States for ultimate security—which could be offered in an era of nuclear superiority—had contributed to the narrowing of that perspective. Whether it can be relearned or revived is uncertain. But the historical experience of the European states both vis-a-vis each other and the United States has never been as even as it may sometimes appear.

THE EUROPEAN STATES' PERSPECTIVES

The European states' interests in and historical contact with the region vary, as do their relationships with the United States and the

USSR. Yet the major European states have more in common with each other than they do with either superpower. Their general perspectives on international relations inform their specific view of regional politics and the forces at play therein. Having become dependent on the United States for broader strategic thinking, they have grown used to interpreting events elsewhere with reference to Europe's needs. In so doing there is a reluctance to interpret events elsewhere in ways that might harm Europe, whether by "linking instabilities," by making détente (or arms control) conditional on the Soviets' "responsible" conduct,[11] or by the outlay of arms for other areas, which might weaken Europe.

An unwillingness to interpret developments elsewhere in a manner that would increase Western Europe's responsibilities leads to a certain degree of optimism and wishful thinking, as well as conservatism. This last is obvious in relation to détente and trade, where the use of trade as an incentive is applauded, but as a sanction rejected. Symptomatic of this approach has been the Europeans' tendency to downgrade the importance of the Soviet role in exploiting regional tensions, to see Soviet ambitions for parity as understandable, and to argue that the key to the stabilization of the region is the settlement of the Arab-Israeli issue and the pursuance of a sensible North-South policy. This focuses on the "diplomatic" route or "playing the politics of regions" (in Stanley Hoffmann's phrase[12]); and the emphasis on preventive diplomacy contrasts strongly with that of the United States. The Europeans see U.S. reactions (for example, to Afghanistan) as volatile, with a tendency to simplify a complex problem by overemphasis on the short term and the military dimension. Whether in Afghanistan–which the Europeans consider an exceptional case, only incidentally strategic and a potential liability for Moscow–or in the Middle East–where American responses since 1967 are viewed as excessively East-West in character–the Europeans are more worried by injudicious U.S. responses and demands than Soviet gains.

To be sure, much of this is traditional European camouflage for indecision or impotence. Romanticism about the South dressed up as neo-Gaullism by Giscard or *Tiers Mondainism* by Mitterrand simply reflects a French propensity for carving itself a distinctive niche, however implausible. Similarly, the emphasis on the long term, on regional politics, on Soviet liabilities, and even on the lack of alliance "consultations" and, alternately, American vacillation or American precipitateness underscore Europe's ambivalence about directly confronting the problems of instability.

The emphasis on preserving détente and Europe's security, though strongest in West Germany, exists everywhere, and it is through this prism that issues like the Gulf and its environs are seen. Unlike the Americans, the Europeans do not have the luxury of pursuing the "ethics of convictions"; for them it is a question of the "politics of survival."[13] Having experienced war on their territory and having now to live with the USSR nearby, they cannot adopt postures that indefinitely foster tensions and instability: "The fear of confrontation and the claims of tranquility loom far larger than the problems of the military balance, Soviet opportunism, or instability in the Third World."[14]

European feelings of insecurity in the light of the new pressures toward bipolarity are understandable, not only because it reduces their flexibility but also because it occurs at a time when the United States no longer has a comfortable surplus of nuclear superiority. The emphasis in Europe on "Europe without the superpowers," and the differences on issues relating to the Third World, are to some extent symptoms of this. But while the Europeans are used to objecting both to American decisiveness and indecision and to underestimating the potential effectiveness of constructive proposals,[15] they are still themselves divided on a policy toward the Third World.

The European perspective on the Gulf-Indian Ocean area is undoubtedly conditioned by both the inherent limitations of their potential role and the priority they assign to their immediate environment in Europe. Differences do exist among the European states in their perspectives and policies toward the region, but these are not major (see discussion below). Necessarily, differing historical experiences, degrees of dependence (and vulnerability), and varying assets in relation to the region give rise to divergent views and emphasis. Yet there is a core of common perspective, some of which have been alluded to:

1. Dependence on the region for oil gives European states not just a stake in stability for the flow of oil but also for markets to recycle the oil revenues. European states are thus sensitive not only to the independence and stability of Gulf governments but to their preferences and displeasure.
2. Perhaps because they are militarily weaker, they assign a higher value to other dimensions of the threat and to remedial measures other than the military.
3. Perhaps because of the need for a link of participation and responsibility, and/or because they simply distrust U.S. judgment and policies, they seek a collective solution in which a European contribution is included. European

involvement is thus necessary, at best as a complement to U.S. policies, at worst as a means of dissociating from the excessively close ties of the United States with Israel.

4. Because of the Europeans' dependence on the United States for ultimate security, differences among allies on non-NATO questions should not be allowed to affect the cohesion of the formal alliance.
5. The contraction of power, the shrinkage of perspective, the erosion of consensus, the fuzziness of the threats, the competing demands on resources, the constraints on the use of force and its inherent limitations, together with the rise of other powers, have made the attainment of a sharp perspective on issues in the Third World difficult. Inherently complex, these issues, which encompass all the problems associated with modernization, intra- and interstate conflict, and regional rivalries, are resistant to simple solutions. While the Europeans have emphasized one part of the set of problems—the relationship between development, security, and stability and the centrality of the Palestinian issue—the Americans have taken the other, the need for a balance of power and regional order. While the Europeans have been tolerant of change—even disruptive changes, which they see as largely inevitable in the process of development—the Americans have been alert to the degree to which Soviet machinations have encouraged, used, and furthered change with a strategic purpose in mind.

But these differences should not obscure the common interests of Europe and the United States: access to the region, the flow of oil, the denial of preponderant influence to the USSR, a just and durable peace that guarantees the sovereignty of existing states, and the security and independence of all states in the region—from Egypt to India, from Iran to Kenya. The Europeans, of course, see their diplomacy constrained by the tight U.S.-Israeli bond. They seek opportunities for a better deal with oil producers by being flexible on the issue of Palestine. It is this that has made the European states more acceptable security partners for the Gulf states than the United States. There is an irony that the European colonial powers should find themselves more welcome in the region than the United States, which encouraged their disimperialism.

Soviet interest in the region will persist with or without the oil question, posing a long-term problem and, given increased Soviet military power and indigenous instability, a long-term strategic threat. The Europeans, too—quite apart from the oil question—will remain sensitive to developments in Southwest Asia. Their objection to the U.S. emphasis on military means has been that it obscures the other dimensions of the issue. They emphasize the reduction of opportunities for exploitation through stabilization by economic instruments. Subconsciously, perhaps, the Europeans have lower expectations; they seek preventive measures and want to limit damage and diversify sources of supply and political relations and to avoid overidentification with any particular regime, country, or cause, lest it mortgage future relations. In short, the aim is to learn to live with the problems of revolutions and coups, fragmentation and secession, irredentas and regional conflicts, and Soviet intervention–not to solve them.

EUROPEAN POLICIES

There has been no such thing as a European policy toward the Indian Ocean area, for the European states differ in approach among themselves, and the Indian Ocean is rarely conceived as a whole but as a set of subregions and issues. Thus, despite the increased interconnectedness of issues in the region–the linking of the traditionally insulated Gulf with the Arab-Israeli issue, the new ties between Pakistan and the Islamic world, the growth of Soviet power-projection capabilities, which have tended to make Southwest Asia (or the northwest quadrant of the Indian Ocean) a single strategic arena–the habit of separating this vast region into its constituent elements continued until 1979.

The interests of the European states in the region are twofold. The first, which gains its salience from oil dependence, relates to the set of issues that may impede the flow of that oil or set conditions on it. This includes the replacement of friendly regimes, the radicalization of the region, or regional conflicts. The second, more general, interest is in the promotion of workable relations and the maintenance of a modicum of order in those countries that cannot be considered strategically important but that nonetheless lie in geographic or political proximity to the region and therefore affect its stability. The latter interest is unexceptional; it could be a description of interests with all countries and regions. It is the first, the issue of oil and the sense of immediacy about the issue, that has been a distinctive feature of European states' policies.

Perhaps understandably the European states had shown no great interest in the Arab-Israeli issue before 1973. To be sure, Britain and France had been involved in the Tripartite Declaration of 1950, limiting arms transfers to the contestants. But this was a bow to the colonial status of these states. Britain, as the former mandatory power in Palestine caught between conflicting nationalisms, had finally managed to extricate itself from the issue; it was in no rush to take it up again. Still, Britain's ambassador, Lord Caradon, had put together UN Security Council Resolution 242 in November 1967 to patch over the differences. France, after a special relationship with Israel, separated itself in 1967 and drifted toward the Arabs. Germany, for historical reasons, remained close to Israel, despite the damage to its relations with the Arab states.

The European states' failure to adopt a common approach is easily understood, for the individual states vary greatly in the priority attached to the issues and to their style of diplomacy. France is self-centered; Italy, poor and divided. Britain, America's most loyal ally, is constrained primarily by financial considerations. Germany is handicapped by its historical experience and legal restrictions and is exposed to nearby Soviet power and pressure. Not only different, European states' policies have often been competitive vis-a-vis each other, as well as with those of the United States.

Despite this, two events in the past decade have shocked the Europeans into action: the 1973 war and the 1979 Soviet invasion of Afghanistan. Both focused attention on the issue of oil; the first led to a political-diplomatic approach, and the second sparked a more explicitly strategic assessment.

The 1973 war opened a breach between the two sides of the Atlantic on the question of how to address the problem of ensuring the supply of oil. The Europeans, with their greater oil dependence, were loathe to alienate the producing states and fearful of the prospects of continual conflict in the region. They focused on the settlement of the Arab-Israeli conflict as the key to a number of problems, first as a means of reducing Soviet opportunities, second for defusing a source of radicalization, and third as a symbol of the new European relationship with the Arab world. Already in November 1973, while Kissinger was negotiating an Israeli disengagement, the European Community had made its position clear by adopting the Arab states' interpretation of UN Security Council Resolution 242. In subsequent years, the Palestinian issue, previously a "refugee" question, and especially the role of the Palestine Liberation Organization (PLO), assumed centrality in the European approach to the problem.

The details of the European approach or initiative are of interest primarily because of the European states' belief (or at least professed belief) that it represented a key to ensuring stability in the Southwest Asia region—and as such reveals both a certain perspective and a yardstick for assessing the Europeans' diplomacy.

The European approach was to emphasize the importance of a comprehensive rather than step-by-step approach to the problem, articulate the centrality of the Palestinian question in any settlement, and use their influence on the United States to pressure Israel toward a settlement. This strategy had undoubted advantages. It could show the Arabs that the West (and especially the Europeans) could be sensitive to the stakes in the issue, and thus maintain an open Western line to the Arab moderates. Within the Atlantic alliance, the Europeans could point to their separate path as a complementary role, a fruitful division of political labor. On the level of principles it could be argued, as did France, that it gave the Arabs a choice—an alternative to the superpowers.

Therefore, the European states, after 1973, embarked on a more active diplomacy in the Middle East, with France and Italy taking the lead in seeking preferential arrangements with the oil suppliers in exchange for arms and technology, including nuclear. If sometimes the timing or emphasis of a particular communique appeared to share by a fraction the common European position on the Middle East question, this was considered par for the course. At the same time, a Euro-Arab dialogue was set up to increase communication, and presumably understanding, between the two sets of states, which had, fortuitously, now discovered how much they had in common.

The United States, meanwhile, continued its unilateral peacemaking efforts: first the disengagement agreements, later a brief and aborted discussion of a Geneva Agreement (1977), followed by the Camp David process initiated by the brave and visionary Anwar al-Sadat. When these appeared to grind to a halt, due primarily to Israel's intransigence in 1979, the European states became concerned. The civil war in Lebanon, the revolution in Iran, the divisions within the Arab world about whether Sadat's approach was a model or a separate peace and a sellout—all of these convinced the European states of the need for some movement on the issue, to show the Arab states that the Europeans at least remained sensitive to their needs.

The result was the Venice Declaration of June 1980, which put the case for a comprehensive approach to peacemaking and the centrality of the Palestinians in this—in a way that appeared to undermine the American-sponsored Camp David approach. This declaration appears to have been the high point of the European initiative. On the level of signaling the European interest in and concern with developments in the region, it made sense. To the extent that it sought to signal Western sympathy and understanding for the more beleaguered Arab states, it was also useful. But it could be useful only as part of a Western, not a European, strategy.

Dependent on the Arabs for oil and on the United States for security, the European states were in no position to offer the Arab states very much. Lacking strong ties with Israel, they could not furnish the Arabs with a settlement; lacking military strength, they could hardly ensure the local states' security against major threats. And good ties with the Arabs could not guarantee Europe oil. Conversely, as part of a Western strategy, they could be very useful in providing a conduit to Washington for Arab views and pursuing policies in the region that Washington might be unable to sanction for a variety of domestic reasons. But this complementary role required harmonization of policy in the West and flexibility rather than a willingness to score points off allies, without commensurate responsibility.[16] No matter how much the European states felt impotent because of Israel's obduracy and U.S. passivity, the European initiative could not exist on its own. To the Americans, the Europeans often appeared to be indulging in futile, and even harmful, grandstanding. For the Arab states, the Europeans were seen as essentially a channel of influence on Washington, an alternative to excessive dependence on the United States, and a source of arms and political diversification.

On the general European level, the European states had the elements of a common approach, but this homogeneity dissolves on closer examination. The European states came to the issue from a variety of backgrounds. France, for example, has been self-consciously activist on Middle East issues, cultivating the Arab states since 1967 and pursuing a policy that intended to reflect neither short-term nor purely commercial considerations but to affirm its broader interests: "Pour la France, le Moyen-Orient s'inscrit dans un dessein politique mondial que caractérise sa volonté de transcender un rôle purement régionale."[17] France's dependence on Middle East oil (74 percent), its interest in a mediating role in East-West and North-South issues, the special importance it attaches to providing a third choice to developing countries, and its belief in its own destiny have inclined it to play an active diplomatic role. To this end, France, in the name of a division of labor, has kept in close touch with all elements in the Arab world (including Iraq, Libya, Algeria, and Syria). It has been receptive, with qualifications, to the PLO; imaginatively elastic in its formulations regarding Palestinian rights; and insistent on a comprehensive approach to a settlement, that is, a formula that includes its own political participation. To this end, it had no hesitations in energetically pursuing the Venice Declaration under Giscard, even if it appeared to compete with and undermine Camp David and antagonize Israel.

In the name of precisely the same principles, Giscard's successor moved French diplomacy toward equidistance between the two contestants, jettisoned the Venice Declaration, and endorsed the piecemeal Camp David approach. The position of Mitterrand's France, sympathetic to the Palestinians and the Israelis, is more harmonious with that of the United States. French support for the multinational Sinai peacekeeping force and receptiveness to the eight-point Fahd plan, genuinely complement the American approach.

Germany's situation has been different. It has been unwilling to pursue any activist policy in the Middle East that might undermine its position vis-a-vis either the United States or the Soviet Union or weaken it in Europe. Its policies have adapted to the European consensus. Bonn moved away from its pro-Israeli policy during the 1970s, but has been reluctant to embrace the PLO. Support for Egypt and the United States made it receptive to the Camp David formula, and since 1978, German diplomacy has been more active in the region in an attempt to reduce the schism between Egypt and its Arab brethren.

Britain's diplomacy has been guided by support for the United States, competition with France, and a belief that it has a special role to play in the area. France's commercial penetration of Jordan and the Gulf has been irksome—particularly because it is clearly abetted by the government's diplomacy, which included presidential visits to the Gulf in 1980 and 1981. For Britain, the question of oil is less important than general commerce. But this has not prevented it from supporting Sadat and the Americans while accepting, for example, the Venice Declaration. Britain upholds the right of the Palestinians to a "homeland," but has not used the expression "self-determination" or formally accepted the PLO as the official Palestinian spokesman. Under the Conservative government of Margaret Thatcher, Britain's position has shifted toward greater support for the Fahd plan and away from Camp David.[18] Apparently it was British reluctance to offend the Arabs that delayed the setting up of the multinational Sinai force.[19]

Since Israel's invasion of Lebanon in June 1982, and especially after President Ronald Reagan's proposal of September 1, 1982, calling for some link between the Palestinians and the Jordanians, European and American diplomatic policies have moved closer. However, none of this guarantees future harmony. The European emphasis on the PLO remains and may increase if Israel is seen to be obdurate. Europe's most effective role is an adjunct to U.S. diplomacy. This is dependent, however, both on European relations with the United States and American Middle East policy. When strains occur either as a result of America's pro-Israeli tilt or from other differences in the alliance, the temptation for a separate European approach increases. The reduction of the sense of urgency on the oil issue, grave inter-Arab disputes, or PLO extremism also condition European diplomacy. The failure of the Euro-Arab dialogue, the futility of seeking preferential oil supply arrangements (not least because of regional instability), and the essential barrenness of a purely commercially oriented foreign policy for great powers have hastened the convergence of European-American diplomacy in the Middle East. Given the variety of threats in the broader region, and the range of instruments required to manage them, there is ample room and indeed a necessity for a flexible Western approach in which the European states, less stigmatized by their ties with Israel, make a contribution.

EUROPE AND REGIONAL SECURITY

Until 1979, Europe was not required to take a strategic view of regional stability; in 1973, it had insisted on the primacy of the regional issue, not the Soviet dimension. Security in the Indian Ocean was considered an abstract concept made up of equal parts of superpower balance and regional forces. Actions in specific areas by individual European states were contributions not to some general good but in the service of national interests. In this period, détente and general deterrence were deemed adequate. American nuclear power and conventional military capability, including maritime forces, could deter Soviet aggression. Defense of the periphery was a case of "lesser included cases" in relation to general deterrence on the central front. This view was shattered by the revolution in Iran and the Soviet invasion of Afghanistan. Coming on top of an energy crisis and a crisis of confidence in the American leadership, defense of the Gulf clearly needed reassessment.

The matter of mutual recriminations apart, the events of 1979 demonstrated the collapse of the regime for Gulf security that had succeeded Britain's paramountcy. If the regional powers were powerless as local substitutes, what alternative security arrangements were feasible? The question was less easy to answer than before. The Gulf states were more politicized than a decade earlier. The limits of

American power and judgment, first in Vietnam, now in the Gulf, had been amply demonstrated. Soviet power had grown and with it the means to exploit instability and intimidate local states. Local instability, in any case, was inescapable and gave the USSR an indirect means of expansion less easy to block.

For the first time in recent years the European states were faced with a direct challenge: how to contribute to security in the Gulf in the face of a transformed strategic situation. Any inclination to wish the issue away or to return to traditional formulas ("settle the Arab-Israeli issue") would not, this time, wash. The U.S. alarm at developments transformed these into alliance issues and a test of allied unity. In addition, 1979 showed that the European policy of seeking preferential arrangements with the local states had been superseded. The threats now were no longer of embargoes but rather of inadvertent interruptions (and price increases) arising from instability and conflict.

The initial caricatured debate on both sides of the Atlantic suggested how novel the situation was, both for the Europeans to face such responsibilities and for the United States to have to ask them to do so. It was scarcely surprising that both parties made up labels for the other: reckless, militaristic, and geopolitical versus pusillanimous, political, and regionalist. But the serious issue remained how European states, individually or collectively, could assist the United States, or work in parallel, to maintain the security of the region. All agreed that there were many sources of instability—not all of which were unhealthy—and all agreed that there were a variety of needs in the region affording the European states ample choice in their particular role.

The gaps between the Europeans and the United States were soon found to be bridgeable. A substantial consensus emerged:

1. Threats to the region's security came from many sources, including domestic, but Soviet power and proximity were paramount considerations requiring a military counterpoise. This was a precondition for any diplomacy and would deter aggression and reassure friends.
2. The continuation of the Arab-Israeli dispute would leave the region open to Soviet influence, and the U.S.-Israeli connection complicated any Gulf defense policy.
3. A U.S. military presence in the region could be politically counterproductive, even if it made the most military sense.
4. The contingencies in which a rapid deployment force could and should be used required rigorous analysis.
5. The political components of a security structure, the Arab-Israeli issue, cooperation with the Gulf Cooperation Council, etc., should be emphasized.

6. The Europeans, less stigmatized regarding Israel, and in some cases with historic ties to the region, could play a useful role, especially in lesser contingencies.
7. In any case, a European contribution to the security of the region was essential in order to give a signal that a "Western" not a U.S./USSR issue was at stake, to share the risks of security with the United States, and to alleviate the burden on the stretched assets of the United States.[20]

How to give concrete expression to these principles has consumed much time since then. However, before discussing these, it is well to note the specific contributions individual countries can make.

The United Kingdom

Britain's political relationship with the Gulf states has remained excellent over the past decade. The fund of knowledge of the area derived from intimate historical contact has stood it well since its withdrawal, giving Britain a reputation and acceptability matched by no other European state. The past significant presence has not been totally lost, even if the quality of political intelligence so ably collected by field officials has diminished with time. Britain has consciously retained a discreet security relationship with the Gulf states. In Oman, there are 340 British officers and noncommissioned officers; approximately half are serving officers, the remainder contract officers or on loaned service. The heads of all three services are commanded by British officers. In Kuwait, there are 170 British serving officers. Britain sells arms to most of the Gulf states, including Iran and Iraq (and has offered to service and repair their Chieftan tanks), and has personnel working for the Saudi air defense. Although lacking a direct military presence in the Gulf, Britain has access to Masirah and Diego Garcia. Its past involvement in the Dhofar rebellion suggests a willingness and competence to get involved discreetly and without excessive introspection on the side of a friendly government.

Britain's importance cannot be overemphasized. Of the European states, it is the ally most willing to cooperate with the United States, the most able to see the military dimension of the issues, the most pragmatic in its approach toward the form of cooperation. The present Conservative party is particularly disposed toward an emphasis on the military requirements of security. Earlier in their tenure there was some discussion of a possible Persian Gulf patrol comprised of four frigates as an adjunct to the U.S. naval force based in Bahrain.

Although this has not materialized, Britain's potential naval contribution is important. In the past, annual exercises in CENTO entailed cruises for prolonged periods in the Indian Ocean. In 1978 a helicopter cruiser, five frigates, and four support ships were deployed there. In 1979, a helicopter cruiser, a nuclear-powered submarine, a type 42 destroyer, four frigates, and three support ships were again dispatched. In 1980, Britain participated in an allied naval patrol in the Gulf of Oman to signal the West's concern about the Iran-Iraq war.

Its naval experience, willingness, and contact with the littoral states make Britain an important potential contributor. But a major constraint in future years will be relentless demands for cuts in the defense budget. With a choice among three areas, the nuclear deterrent, the British army on the Rhine, or the navy, the outcome is hard to predict. The desire to specialize may serve to protect the navy[21] (especially after the Falkland Islands war), but political considerations make it unlikely that cuts in Britain's continental commitment will be easy, and the nuclear deterrent carries with it Britain's prestige.

France

As the European power most conscious of its wider responsibilities, France has had a diplomacy intended to advertise its independence and the value of its commitments. Although its diplomacy has often seemed to serve a remarkable French chauvinism, there are few who question its ultimate value to the West. In relation to the Third World, France has always seen for itself a special responsibility. Its present government sees the problems of development as the root cause of much of the instability in these countries, views revolutionary movements with a degree of romantic acceptance, and seeks to play a role of intermediary or alternative for these states in relations with the superpowers. Although exceedingly skeptical about the Soviet military buildup and Soviet policy in Europe, France has been more reluctant to see the Soviet Union behind problems elsewhere. It has therefore declined to impose an East-West matrix onto regional problems and has argued that the Soviet threat there is primarily indirect, requiring an equivalent response but containable mainly by the reduction of opportunities for Soviet exploitation.

This emphasis on a third choice for the developing countries (besides the two superpowers) and on the regional causes of instability has certain benefits for France's diplomacy. It allows it maximum flexibility and rationalizes departures from a Western position, for example, in selling arms to all comers, cultivating the radical states, or going beyond standard formulations on certain issues. Presumably, French diplomacy is far too sophisticated to believe that these policies are models for the West. Rather, it is predicated upon a different set of Western policies to which it is an adjunct. In brief, France's approach to security in the region is not offered as a substitute but as a complement to the military underpinning provided largely by the United States.

France's diplomacy, however, has not been confined to posturing or drafting communiques. Its interests in the Indian Ocean region are considerable. Seventy percent of France's imported oil came from the Middle East in 1981, and the same region accounted for 75 percent of France's weapons exports.[22] That region accounts for 20 percent of France's exports and 13 percent of its imports. While France has jealously reserved its independence of action vis-a-vis its alliance commitments, it has also zealously guarded its interests and prestige in the Third World, intervening with military force on a number of occasions.

Before 1979 France maintained the largest permanent Western naval presence in the Indian Ocean. The fleet operated from bases in Mayotte and Djibouti, its standard composition being 14 ships. These are periodically augmented by deployments of an aircraft carrier or submarines. In early 1982, for example, two submarines were sent (as they had been in 1976).[23] France has also shown a readiness to intervene on behalf of threatened client-states. Troops specifically earmarked for such missions are labeled assistance forces and include the Eleventh Parachutist Division (12,500), the Ninetieth Naval Infantry Division (8,000), and the Thirty-first Brigade (35,000). In addition, some 14,000 military personnel stationed in Djibouti are capable of rapid deployment.

France's force projection capability and demonstrated willingness to act on behalf of friendly regimes, and not only in Africa (for example, French assistance in the November 1979 Mecca incident was significant), are important Western assets. They are by no means diminished by the physical limitations on the French contribution—namely, the inability to deploy heavy equipment over long distances (for example, Shaba II) or maintain an aircraft carrier on a permanent basis in the Indian Ocean.[24] France's willingness to coordinate its deployments informally with those of the United States and Britain during crises is a considerable contribution.

West Germany

Of all the major European states, West Germany has had the greatest difficulty in admitting to itself that threats to the alliance outside of Europe may be as serious as those within. It has made the greatest investment, material and psychological, in détente and is reluctant to admit its demise. It has encountered great domestic political strains, a crisis of confidence and even of identity, that make its structure fragile and its capacity for undertaking new tasks problematic. Germany appears to fear change and is reluctant to acknowledge, let alone embrace, the shifts in East-West relations. A certain distrust of U.S. leadership, and especially the U.S. tendency to oscillate between extremes, has encouraged it to deny the security dimension of the problems in the Indian Ocean. In the extreme formulation this takes the form of assessing Soviet actions as defensive and regional instabilities as merely symptoms of development. This tends to rationalize German preferences to continue normal relations with the USSR and to provide development assistance to those states requiring it. The idea of German troops to defend oil fields or states in the Middle East or the Indian Ocean is inconceivable. Quite simply, Germany is incapable, psychologically or politically, of thinking or acting in the region in strategic terms.

This does not deny Germany some role similar to that of other European states. Germany relies on the region for oil (particularly Saudi Arabia) and markets (Iraq and Saudi Arabia).[25] As a result of Saudi pressure, Germany has started to reconsider its restrictive arms exports policies, but it has been unable to provide Riyadh with the Leopard tanks that it wants. Other, more discreet, forms of assistance have been provided, including training of the air force and assistance to special forces dealing with insurgencies and other contingencies.[26] Germany has extended financial assistance to key countries in the region, especially Turkey, Egypt, and Pakistan. Aid to Turkey has been especially important, both bilaterally and multilaterally as part of an overall aid package put together by 17 countries led by Germany and the United States in May 1981 but deferred in March 1982.[27] In 1982, Bonn was in the forefront of extending economic assistance ($100 million) to Egypt, and in 1981 its economic aid to Pakistan exceeded that of the United States.[28]

Germany contends that such assistance is a substitute for direct military assistance in that it helps these countries to stabilize their internal situation, which is basic to their security. Also, because West

Germany's assistance helps Turkey to modernize its air bases (this is politically possible for Bonn because of Turkey's NATO membership), it constitutes a direct contribution to Western security in that these bases may have to be used in the future to project power in the Persian Gulf area.

Be that as it may, the United States does not consider this or the extension of the German navy's patrol area in Europe as serious contributions to the Western problem of coping with threats in the Gulf-Indian Ocean region. U.S. ambassador in Bonn Arthur Burns put it bluntly, observing that Germany had not been helping to support U.S. policies outside NATO or U.S. policy in the Middle East or in registering displeasure over Poland.[29] A sympathetic European view also believes that despite the very real constraints on direct German military contributions, there is scope for improvement. Germany must provide more help elsewhere, possibly to earmark troops for operations outside the NATO area, both to impress U.S. public opinion and to buy influence over how force is used.[30]

While this may appear to be desirable, it is, for the time being, psychologically unattainable. For the foreseeable future, West Germany's contribution to security in the Gulf-Indian Ocean area will remain an economic one.

Italy

Italy's contact with the Indian Ocean area has not been as significant as its involvement in North Africa. A strong dependency on Arab oil and a desire to forge preferential ties with the oil producers have made Italy reluctant to offend Arab sensibilities. At the same time, however, it has retained a measure of balance and sympathy for Israel. Its willingness to act on some of the strategic issues posed by regional instability has surprised its NATO partners. Besides the alacrity with which it volunteered to support and participate in the Sinai force, it has shown a readiness to pursue a more activist policy generally.[31] Thus, in June 1982, Italy offered to mediate the Iran-Iraq conflict. Also, like France, it provided a contingent of soldiers for the multinational force deployed in Beirut in August and again in September 1982.

Since 1979, when the United States shifted one of its aircraft carriers from the eastern Mediterranean to the Indian Ocean, Italy has agreed to increase its naval contribution in the Mediterranean, to free U.S. naval forces for a wider role elsewhere. This will assume increasing importance, because much of the oil from the Gulf no longer passes through the Strait of Hormuz but flows through the new Yanbu pipeline, the older Sumed line, and the northern line when it is operating.

Potential European Contribution

The Western European states have a range of capabilities that could be of immense value in the service of a coordinated Western approach to security. There are several different areas in which this contribution could be used. First is an increased European contribution to European defense, which would permit the United States greater flexibility in other areas. In addition, guaranteed rights to the United States to use Western European bases and facilities in the event of extra-NATO contingencies would seem to be a form of minimal contribution.[32] Moreover, the Europeans must accept the right of the United States to deploy its troops in Europe freely to third areas, as necessary.[33]

A second area is indirect military contributions to contingencies in the Persian Gulf-Indian Ocean area. These could be of a permanent or temporary nature and be either unilateral or collective in character. Their most impressive manifestation would be an allied deployment force earmarked for contingencies outside of NATO.[34] A looser variant would be an ad hoc contribution in a crisis or the deployment of national contingents into crisis areas without formal commitment or schedule. A third form of European assistance could be in the economic field, for example, helping to finance the costs of base construction and modernization, weapons purchases, and the like. This would presumably be most attractive to countries like Germany (and Japan), which find themselves inhibited in the military arena.

These suggestions are only illustrative of a variety of contributions that the European states could make. Other analysts have discussed in greater detail the value that even small European contributions may have in stretching Western resources, by improving deployment cycles and by the specialization of individual functions.[35] Short of such military and economic contributions, however, there is still a clear need for joint threat assessment, the exchange of information, contingency planning, and joint exercises. Intellectually, the Europeans recognize the problems posed both by a new international environment and a redistribution of burdens within NATO; whether they are able to meet the challenge, which is demanding and painful, remains to be seen. The deeply imbedded habits of second-guessing and of taking refuge in formal obligations or procedural objections to avoid confronting the inescapable demands made on them will just not do in the 1980s.

PROBLEMS AND PROSPECTS

The issue of a European contribution to a Western security policy in the Gulf-Indian Ocean region is twice complicated, first by differences within Europe and second by strains between the two sides of the Atlantic. The reasons for this inhere in the absence of unity that complicates any coherent European input into an Atlantic dialogue on approaches to Third World areas. Relations between Europe and the United States, exacerbated by changes in the relative balance of power and differing perceptions of threat, are also complicated by the larger problem of how to deal with the Soviet Union. With the advent of parity, the reliability of the U.S. nuclear guarantee is questioned. At the same time, "peripheral" threats appear to be both more likely and as threatening to Europe as those originating on the Central Front. But the response of the European states to this new situation has been equivocal: an uneven recognition of the threats coupled with a slow and reluctant strategic reassessment. The reluctance stems from an unwillingness to jeopardize détente (West Germany), or to act on an analysis that requires greater financial burdens (United Kingdom), or to collaborate with the United States in a much closer fashion (France).

To the United States, the Europeans' reluctance to increase their defense responsibilities in Europe and contribute in some, even token, measure to forces in the Gulf region serves to undermine the Atlantic partnership. Even confirmed Atlanticists doubt whether the disparity between defense expenditures can long be sustained, especially as between one-third and one-half of the U.S. defense budget is devoted to forces in Europe. Unless the European contribution increases, some observers believe, the U.S. commitment will decline, in order to meet other global responsibilities, including those in the Gulf.[36] Strong congressional criticism suggests that with growing economic stringencies the demand on the European allies to do more in Europe and elsewhere will increase.[37] The U.S. argument is firm and unmistakable: The United States does not wish to choose between its interests in Europe and those elsewhere, but it may have to do so for economic reasons.

In Europe there is a growing recognition of the seriousness of the issue. The differing emphases on the two sides of the Atlantic have given way to a realistic recognition that NATO's interests do not stop at the fortieth parallel, and that these interests do require a military underpinning, which cannot be left to the United States alone to secure because it divides the alliance, reduces Europe's influence on when and how force is used, or may cause a miscalculation by the adversary.[38] Though agreement on a coherent approach and detailed specialization of function is far from being at hand, the Europeans recognize that individual contributions will vary with the means and the issue and that different coalitions will aggregate informally in different crises. The principle of sharing the risks by multilateralization is also generally recognized as important. For example, there is little doubt that in the autumn of 1980 the British, French, Dutch, German, and Australian naval contributions in the Gulf of Oman caused less concern in the region than would have a unilateral effort.

Recognition, however, does not guarantee results. Europe will need to improve its own approach to Persian Gulf-Indian Ocean issues much more than in the past. The specific constraints on individual countries are important. For example, in the case of West Germany the trade-offs between stabilizing Third World clients and destabilizing Europe by demanding a greater German military involvement need careful examination.[39] The European contribution should not be underestimated. It is low key, discreet, and effective and potentially extremely important as one part of a Western strategic response to problems in the region. It is, however, not enough if it is confined to noncontentious areas, while the United States is left with the politically unrewarding tasks.

The United States, for its part, will need to be more consistent in its policies and avoid favoring those sanctions vis-a-vis the USSR that mainly require European sacrifices rather than its own. Policies such as lifting the grain embargo and exerting pressure to prevent a Soviet gas pipeline only increase the propensity of Europeans to doubt U.S. seriousness. Ultimately, as regards the USSR and contingencies in the Third World, the alliance will need "a mechanism for sharing more equally the costs of a common policy."[40]

There is little doubt that Soviet strategy is to decouple the Europeans from the United States. It emphasizes American unreliability or militancy while contrasting American and European interests. It seeks to portray the energy problem as largely a European problem and has suggested an "all-European" energy conference as the start of a "collective solution" to the problem. If the USSR can increase

European inhibitions about improving its military posture in the Gulf region and portray the United States as the source of military threat, it may improve its own position as security manager of the Gulf in a position to both guarantee (and deny) European oil supplies.[41]

The Atlantic Alliance remains the cornerstone of Western security. I have concentrated on it because its health will determine whether the individual European states will assume positions that are mutually reinforcing in the Indian Ocean area, or adopt policies that further weaken the collective enterprise. A purposive coherent set of policies, collectively or singly, can only be forged if the European states transcend their largely regional roles to play a wider role in the maintenance of international order. The dismal record of coordinating policies in third areas does not give grounds for optimism. Nor does the weakness of most European governments, the fragility of the domestic consensus, the pressure of other demands on resources, and the analytic and practical difficulties of shaping a constructive course together with the ever present opportunities to play referee or critic rather than committed ally make the task any easier. In the past, European policies tended to be at the mercy of the most activist member, France, which sought to build a European consensus in opposition to the United States. Such a policy of dissociation, I have argued, is doomed to sterility.

With a diminished sense of vulnerability as regards Middle Eastern oil, European governments have begun to look at the Persian Gulf region with greater clarity. Less acutely conscious of their weakness, their differences with the United States also appear less acute. Though gradations in emphasis exist among individual states, there are no significant differences among the European states insofar as their evaluation of the security of Southwest Asia is concerned. The major differences between the European and the American position are still ones of perspective. The Europeans emphasize the political and accept the intractability of problems, of learning to cope with them, of the durability of the competition with the Soviet Union, and of the need for differentiated policies, cultivation of the South, support for independent nationalisms, and assistance to regional arrangements such as the Gulf Cooperation Council. The European states' willingness to cooperate with the United States in the Middle East reflects a change in their relationship. In early 1983, differences between Europe and the United States relating to South and Southwest Asia appeared unlikely to be as significant in the 1980s as they had been in the preceding decade.

NOTES

1. For an article that makes this point clearly, see John C. Campbell, "Les Etats-Unis et l'Europe au Moyen Orient: Interêts Communs et Politiques Divergentes," *Politique Internationale*, no. 7 (Spring 1982): 165-85.

2. Henry Kissinger, *Years of Upheaval* (London: Weidenfeld and Nicholson, 1982).

3. Pierre Hassner, "America's Policy Towards the Soviet Union in the 1980s: Objectives and Uncertainties," in *America's Security in the 1980s*, Adelphi Paper no. 174 (London: IISS, 1982), pp. 35-51.

4. Josef Joffe, "European-American Relations: The Enduring Crisis," *Foreign Affairs* 59, no. 4 (Spring 1981): 842.

5. David Watt referred to this recently in "America's Alliances: Europe," in *America's Security in the 1980s*, Adelphi Paper no. 174 (London: IISS, 1982), pp. 19-26.

6. For a discussion from this perspective, see David Deese, "Oil, War and Grand Strategy," *Orbis* 25 (Fall 1981): 525-55.

7. On the order of 6,000 and 12 million pounds a year by 1971.

8. Dominique Moisi and Pierre Lellouche, "French Policy in Africa: A Lonely Battle Against Destabilization," *International Security* 3, no. 4 (Spring 1979): 108-33.

9. In 1956, American crude oil production increased by about 600,000 barrels a day, of which three-quarters went to Europe, one-quarter to replace lost imports. The United States then could effectively act as the guarantor of Western Europe's energy supply.

10. Recall General de Gaulle's suspicions of Britain's motives in wartime Syria.

11. Already in October 1973, Henry Kissinger had warned the Soviet Union that "détente cannot survive irresponsibility in any area, including the Middle East," speech, *Pacem in Terris*, Washington, D.C. Kissinger, *Years of Upheaval*, pp. 490-91.

12. Stanley Hoffmann, "The Western Alliance: Drift or Harmony?" *International Security* (Fall 1981): 105-25.

13. See Pierre Hassner, "Western European Perceptions of the Soviet Union," *Daedalus* (Winter 1979): 121.

14. Joffe, "European-American Relations," p. 842.

15. Flora Lewis, "Alarm Bells in the West," in "America and the World 1981," *Foreign Affairs* 60, no. 3 (Spring 1982): 571.

16. There are many articles on the subject. See Stephen Artner, "The Middle East: A Chance for Europe?" *International Affairs* (Summer 1980): 420-42; Harvey Sicherman, "Politics of Dependence: Western Europe and the Arab-Israeli Conflict," *Orbis* 23, no. 4 (Winter 1980): 845-57; Adam M. Garfinkle, "America and Europe in the Middle East: A New Coordination?" *Orbis* 24 (Fall 1981): 631-48; Campbell, "Les Etats Unis et l'Europe au Moyen Orient."

17. See Dominique Moisi, "L'Europe et le Conflit Israel-Arabe," *Politique Etrangère* 4 (1980): 836, 838.

18. For example, Lord Carrington, while the EEC's council president, during a visit to Riyadh in November 1981. Also, Selim Turquie, "L'Impuissance de l'Europe en Moyen Orient," *Le Monde Diplomatique* (April 1982).

19. This earned Lord Carrington, the foreign minister, the additional title "duplicitous bastard" from Secretary of State Alexander Haig. For the genesis of the force, see Philip Geyelin, *International Herald Tribune*, March 23, 1982. The link to the Venice Declaration was ultimately dropped.

20. For a moderate expression of the U.S. view on the need for a Western approach to Western interests outside Europe, see Richard Burt, "In Defense of Western Values," *Department of State Bulletin* 82, no. 2061 (April 1982): 65-66.

21. Two weeks before the Falklands crisis, Britain announced a cut in naval manpower of 10,000 over the next four years. *Financial Times*, March 24, 1982.

22. Sales of arms in 1981 alone were considerable: $750 million to Egypt for 20 Mirage aircraft, $1.8 billion to Saudi Arabia for a modernized navy, and $655 million to Iraq. See *Middle East Economic Digest*, May 16, 1982, p. 4; and *Financial Times*, March 3, 1982. Foreign arms sales are important in France for generating employment and keeping unit prices competitive.

23. *Le Monde*, February 1982.

24. With one being overhauled, France is left with only one other on operational deployment.

25. West German exports to the Arab world accounted for 7.4 percent of total exports. Iraq and Saudi Arabia together account for DM 12.8 billion of exports. Saudi Arabia is West Germany's principal supplier of oil. *Financial Times*, February 16, 1982.

26. The latter is through an agreement between the two nations' interior ministers. See *Middle East Economic Digest*, April 23, 1982, p. 53.

27. The fact that this was due to distaste by some European countries for the military regime underscores the utopian views about strategy and security that prevail in Western European states, as well as their dependence on left wing parties for support.

28. *Financial Times*, February 9, 1982; *Die Zeit*, May 29, 1981.

29. See his testimony to the House Foreign Affairs Committee as reported in *Financial Times*, April 14, 1982.

30. *Times* (London), April 1, 1982.

31. *Times* (London), September 27, 1982.

32. The U.S. government insisted on this at the 1981 and 1982 NATO meetings. See *International Herald Tribune*, May 17, 1982.

33. The principle appears somewhat easier to achieve in light of Britain's naval deployment in the South Atlantic, which reminded the Europeans that it might at times be the European states that may need to deploy troops outside Europe. This incident reversed the traditional European role of worrying about U.S. entanglements in third areas.

34. This is the suggestion of Colonel Jonathan Alford, deputy director, the International Institute for Strategic Studies.

35. See especially Dov S. Zakheim, "Towards a Western Approach to the Indian Ocean," *Survival*, January-February 1980, pp. 7-14, and "Of Allies and Access," *Washington Quarterly* (Winter 1981): 87-96; and James Digby, "The Emerging American Strategy: Application to South West Asia," Rand Corporation (N-1700 Fi), May 1981, pp. 36-37.

36. Joseph Kraft, *International Herald Tribune*, January 3, 1982; and James Chace, *International Herald Tribune*, April 23, 1982. See also Jeffrey Record,

"Should America Pay for Europe's Security?" *Washington Quarterly* 5, no. 1 (Winter 1982): 19–23.

37. *Washington Post*, March 27, 1982.

38. For a discussion entitled "Europe in a Wider World," see *Times* (London), April 19, 1982. See also the report of the four Institutes on International Affairs, "Western Security: What Has Changed? What Should be Done?" (1980).

39. "There is already an East German Afrika-Korps in operation; do we really want a West German equivalent?" Joffe, "European-American Relations," p. 849.

40. Armin Guetowski of the Institut für Wirtschaftsforschung (Hamburg), as quoted in *Business Week*, February 22, 1982.

41. For a discussion and citations, see Shahram Chubin, *The Role of Outside Powers in the Persian Gulf* (Gower, U.K.: IISS, 1982), pp. 136–38.

6

India's Relations with Gulf Countries

Bhabani Sen Gupta

Concrete, if disturbing, evidence that under the impact of modern geopolitics the world is getting rapidly smaller is the welding together in less than a decade of the two adjacent regions of South and Southwest Asia into a single geostrategic arena. Strategic linkages between the two regions began to form in the mid-1970s; with the turn of the decade, the security boundaries of Southwest and South Asia virtually disappeared, while instabilities in one region clearly affected the stability of the other. Earlier, in the 1960s, Britain and the United States brought Turkey, Iran, and Pakistan together in the Central Treaty Organization (CENTO), but this cold war alliance could not thrive as it was rejected by a majority of the countries in the two regions. In the 1970s, the Soviets came up with their own concept of Asian Collective Security and mounted a vigorous diplomatic drive to sell it to as disparate a collectivity of countries as Iran, Afghanistan, Pakistan, and India. In 1974–76, India and Iran, the two most powerful states in South and Southwest Asia, respectively, cautiously initiated a policy of security cooperation; the initiative froze in 1978 as the shah of Iran faced waves of domestic unrest. The end of Iran's role as the most trusted ally of the United States in Southwest Asia enhanced the importance of Pakistan for American strategic planners. In response to what Moscow perceived (mistakenly, it seems by hindsight) as an imminent U.S. military movement in the Persian Gulf region, the Soviets intervened in Afghanistan in December 1979 with a "limited military contingent" of 85,000 troops and promptly outflanked Iran. The United States equally promptly conferred on Pakistan the role of a front-line state in the confrontation that now rapidly built up between the two superpowers in Southwest and South Asia. The strategic merging of the two regions was thus accomplished by the two superpowers acting against one another.

The merging has enhanced rather than reduced the insecurities and instabilities of the two regions, whether they are taken separately or in their newly imposed linkage. Taken together, Southwest and South Asia have become the heartland of the Third World and therefore have earned the dubious distinction of being described as the "arc of crises." The oil wealth of Southwest Asia and the vital sea lanes that carry the oil to Western Europe, Japan, and the United States inevitably make the region an arena of close encounters between the superpowers.[1] Because neither superpower can control the region and pilot its internal development and change, these encounters have made Southwest Asia more insecure and unstable than before. The strategic importance and inherent insecurities of Southwest Asia have enhanced the strategic importance of South Asia, which, by itself, is not endowed with a vitally important resource like petroleum, and, and at the same time, have shaken its stability.

The complex intermeshing process of multiple instabilities and insecurities in Southwest and South Asia is both a cause and a consequence of the fragile subsystems of states in the two regions. Nowhere else in the conflict-ridden Third World are sovereign states more divided by historical enmities and hostilities. Of the 15 sovereign states in Southwest and South Asia, only one, India, has the potentialities of a major power. Two others, Pakistan and Iran, have the personnel and resource potential to play significant regional security roles. However, intense enmities among the states of Southwest and South Asia have prevented regional security cooperation; on the contrary, the states of South and Southwest Asia have fought more wars among themselves than have countries in any other Third World region. Furthermore, the vast majority of the 15 states have been found to be politically unstable. Domestic instabilities and interstate conflicts have made all of the 15 states, including India, dependent on one or the other superpower for the defense of national frontiers. Recent events have shown how the superpowers have been sucked into the internal and regional instabilities of Southwest and South Asia. Ironically, the deep involvement has made both superpowers less capable of bringing the volatile currents of change in the region under their firm influence and control.

INDIA IN SOUTH AND SOUTHWEST ASIA

India's position in the Southwest and South Asian region is unique for several reasons. In territory, population, and national resources, India is a potential major power. Slow but steady pace of development over a span of 35 years has promoted India to the status of a middle power. Commanding an economy that is equal to that of France, India ranks among the 12 industrial nations of the world, maintains the world's fourth largest army at the cost of 4.5 percent of its gross national product, and boasts of the world's third largest reservoir of scientific and technological personnel. India has become virtually self-supporting in food grains and will probably be largely self-supporting in petroleum by the end of the decade.

India's political stability and uninterrupted evolutionary political development along parliamentary democratic lines lend it a distinction hardly matched by any other Third World nation. India still carries in its ancient bowels the planet's single largest mass of poor and deprived humanity: 300 million Indians are still abysmally poor and perhaps 500 million suffer from various degrees of malnutrition. However, the fact that the Indian political system is not threatened by this huge mass of deprived and poor people is a tribute to the dynamism of its political system and to the stability of its deeply entrenched social institutions and cultural values.[2]

At the same time, India's slow but steady growth as a major regional power has created aspirations at home and expectations abroad, which the regime is unable to meet. The Indian elite wishes to see India cast in the role of South Asia's leading power, whose voice must be heard and respected beyond the frontiers of the region. There are many in Western Europe who wonder why India, with its military, economic, and political strength, does not chart a course in regional and world affairs that would be as independent of the United States as of the Soviet Union. In contrast with these Indian elite aspirations and Western European elite expectations, India is perceived by its smaller neighbors more or less as an imperial "big brother," determined to bring the entire South Asian region under its hegemony.

The brute reality, however, is that India has not so far acquired the status of security provider in South Asia, not to speak of Southwest Asia. In 1971, India crushed the Pakistani army in the Bangladesh liberation war and emerged as the undisputed leading power in South Asia. However, the strategic divide between India and Pakistan and the three major wars the two had fought between 1948 and 1971 had already opened up South Asia to superpower intervention; the United States (and later China) stood behind Pakistan and the Soviet Union behind India. When, in 1971-73, India put together a security framework for South Asia, it lacked regional endorsement. The three legs of the India-made South Asian security "regime" were the Indo-Soviet treaty of 1971, the India-Bangladesh treaty of peace and friendship of 1972, and the Simla agreement between India and Pakistan concluded in 1972. The regime was formally recognized neither by Pakistan nor by Bangladesh, but they did not possess the power or the will to disturb it. What was more pleasing to the Indians was that the regime was tacitly allowed, though not approved, by the United States and China for most of the 1970s.[3]

In mid-decade, the Indian security regime for South Asia received a shot in the arm when the first skeletal spanners of a bridge of strategic understanding and cooperation silhouetted between India and Iran. The improbable appeared to be happening. Mohammed Reza Shah Pahlavi, America's "unconditional ally," and Indira Priyadarshini Gandhi, a Soviet "ally" if not a Soviet "client," were striving together to unite Iran and India in strategic cooperation for shared objectives in Southwest and South Asia. Indira Gandhi's visit to Tehran in May 1974 and the shah's return visit to India in October expanded bilateral economic cooperation.[4]

In 1979-80, not only the bridge of understanding between India and Iran collapsed with the fall of the shah and the triumph of Iran's Islamic revolution; the Indian security regime for South Asia broke down under the impact of the Soviet intervention in Afghanistan and the cold-warish U.S. response to that traumatic event. All communication came to a halt between India and the Iran of the Ayatollah Rohulla Khomeini. Prospects of Pakistan receiving substantial quantities of military weapons from the United States, including the glamorous F-16 fighter, revived the traditional strategic cleavage in South Asia. Refusal to condemn the Soviet movement into Afghanistan isolated India from the conservative Islamic countries of Southwest Asia. Only with Iraq did India's channel of economic cooperation and political communication remain open. India, which had stood the first big hike in oil prices in 1974-75 rather remarkably well, nearly wilted before the more grievous second hike in 1979-80. In 1980-81, oil imports consumed 80 percent of India's export earnings, and forced India to negotiate massive $5.2 billion FRDs from the International Monetary Fund.

Adversity made it necessary for India to make a fresh bid to build bridges to the oil-rich countries of Southwest Asia. In 1981,

Prime Minister Gandhi made a successful trip to Kuwait and the United Arab Emirates (UAE) and in 1982 an even more successful one to Saudi Arabia. Her talks with the leaders of these Southwest Asian countries covered political and security issues, as well as questions relating to economic cooperation. The most significant result of the conversations was the recognition that the security of Southwest and South Asia had become indivisible and interdependent. Although this did not confer on India a security role in Southwest Asia, it did lend a new dimension to India's regional foreign policy and diplomacy and a certain weight to India's voice on matters of security and stability in Southwest Asia.

HISTORICAL PERSPECTIVE

Britain's imperial power had bestowed a strategic harmony on South and Southwest Asia, reducing the latter to a periphery of the Indian empire, linked therewith for defense and security. The British had pursued two contradictory policies to consolidate and rule their sprawling Asian empire. On the one hand, they knit India and South Asia together for the purpose of defense and administration and promoted the unifying and integrating concepts of nationalism and national identities. On the other hand, they made ample use of the time-tested strategy of divide and rule to keep peoples and cultures apart and at loggerheads with one another. When Britain transferred power to a subcontinent surgically severed into two mutually hostile sovereign states of India and Pakistan, it still hoped, ironically, that both new nations would continue to belong to the British strategic system for Asia and the Indian Ocean.[5] India and Pakistan, however, opted out of that system immediately after independence.

India had a whole new set of frontiers to defend and develop. The dispute with Pakistan over Kashmir led to the war of 1947–48; in India's view, Pakistan became both an independent threat and a symbol of India's own internal religious-cultural cleavage. Less than three years later, China extended its control to the whole of Tibet, ending India's inherited privileges in Outer Tibet. This action also breathed new strategic life to the long-somnolent Himalayan territories of Nepal, Bhutan, and Sikkim. These territories, together with Kashmir, started to dominate India's security scenario. About the same time, Pakistan opted out of "greater India" by concluding a military pact with the United States. This brought the cold war to the subcontinent, as India accepted political support and development assistance from the Soviet Union.

In the 1950s, both India and Pakistan reached out to the Arab and Islamic countries for friends and allies. Pakistan masqueraded its Islamic identity. India rode the tide of nationalism, antiimperialism, anticolonialism, and anti-Zionism. Thus, Indians applauded Mossadegh's bid in 1951 to free Iran from the clutches of the international oil cartels. Later, strong linkages were formed between Nehru's nonalignment and Nasser's positive neutralism. Forces of decolonization mingled with cold war rivalries of two power blocs to divide the countries of the Middle East and the Persian Gulf (Southwest Asia) into two categories: nonaligned and pro-Western. The first group came to be identified as progressive, the second reactionary, Islamic, or pro-Western. India was with the progressive group. Its West Asian policy was Cairo-centric, "so much so that Indo-Egyptian relations came to be represented as Indo-Arab relations."[6] One inevitable result was that India's relations with the pro-Western countries remained cool. Among these countries were Iran, Saudi Arabia, and the tiny sheikhdoms of the Persian Gulf, which in those days carried little political or economic premium, though not Iraq after the revolution of 1958 and the collapse of the Baghdad Pact.

For a while, linkages with Nasserism and anti-Western Arab nationalism proved to be emotionally and ideologically satisfying to the Indians. But the political-diplomatic lag became rudely apparent for the first time in 1962–63, when a majority of the West Asian and Persian Gulf countries refused to back India in the border war with China. Pakistan's pan-Islamic cry met with strong resistance in Egypt and Turkey in the 1950s,[7] but received ample hospitality in the majority of the Middle Eastern and Persian Gulf nations, and India realized during and after the Sino-Indian war of 1962 and the India-Pakistan war of 1965 that many of the Arab states as well as Iran were pro-Pakistan, if not anti-Indian. Indian parliamentary debates on the 1967 Arab-Israeli war manifested unprecedented hostility toward the Arabs and put the government's policy of total support for the Arabs against Israel entirely on the defensive.[8]

India's West Asia and Persian Gulf diplomacy underwent radical change in the mid- and late 1960s after the death of Nehru and the decline of Nasser's influence and finally his demise. The Persian Gulf came, for the first time, in the focus of Indian foreign policy. A number of new power centers emerged and several of them—Iran, Iraq, and Kuwait, notably—were located in the Gulf region, geographically closer to India than Egypt and Syria. Foundations of a new economic diplomacy in Iran were laid in 1965 with an agreement on the establishment of an oil refinery in Madras, South India, with an annual capacity of 2.5 million tons. The agreement's economic, political, and strategic significance became clearer eight or nine years later. It was concluded in spite of the fact that the shah had given strong support to Pakistan in its 1965 war with India, indicating that Pakistan need not be an insuperable barrier to closer relations between Iran and India. Moreover, the National Iranian Oil Company and the American International Oil Company joined together to meet the foreign exchange component of a public sector refinery in India,[9] thus lowering the threshold of political-ideological differences between Tehran and Delhi.

The first visit to Tehran by a ranking Indian political leader took place in 1968, when Deputy Prime Minister Morarji Desai led an economic delegation to seek expansion of Indo-Iranian trade and Iran's involvement in a chemical and industrial complex in Gujarat, on the west coast of India. India's economic diplomacy, however, took time to acquire new pastures in the Gulf region. The first comprehensive economic agreement with Iraq was concluded in April 1973, under which Iraq promised to supply 30 million tons of crude in ten years and $50 million credit in the form of crude supplies to cover the hard currency requirement of a public sector refinery at Mathura, in northern India. On its part, India promised goods and services for a railroad between Baghdad and Ramadi Ali Oain, a steel rolling mill, electric power transmission, manufacture of light engineering goods, and other projects. This was the beginning of Indian participation in development activity in the Persian Gulf.

The new Indian diplomacy in the Gulf-Middle East region was cushioned more on economic interests than on the ideology of anti-imperialism, on noninvolvement in inter-Arab differences rather than on the dichotomy between progressive and reactionary groups of states. Even then Pakistan remained a barrier between India and the Gulf. In 1971, India once again failed to persuade the majority of the Arab and Gulf nations that it had valid reasons to intervene on behalf of the Bangladesh liberation war. Several high-level Indian missions toured these countries, but only from Egypt was a measure of understanding and cooperation forthcoming. India designed the Simla agreement with Pakistan to legitimize the new political map of the subcontinent. But Zulfikar Ali Bhutto, then Pakistan's president, normalized his country's relations with Bangladesh not within the Simla framework, but with the good offices of leaders of the Islamic Conference he was able to convene with great fanfare in Lahore in 1973. The shah of Iran, fearing that India might further dismember Pakistan, committed Tehran in 1972 to the defense of Pakistan's territorial integrity by announcing that any attack on Pakistan would be considered an attack on Iran.[10] The Islamic countries of the Persian Gulf and the Middle East in effect worked together with Pakistan to deny India the political and strategic fruits of its victory in December 1971 over Pakistan and its role as the liberator of Bangladesh.

INDIA AND THE INDIAN OCEAN

An American naval initiative in the Indian Ocean in December 1971 pushed these blue waters into the matrix of Indian strategic thinking 25 years after India's emergence as a sovereign nation. India had begun to develop a strategic view of the Indian Ocean in the mid-1960s when Britain permitted the United States to build naval "facilities" on the island of Diego Garcia. India did not lodge a formal protest, but announced its "strong opposition" to American base building in the Indian Ocean, which was seen by the Indian press as an attempt to preempt Soviet penetration of the ocean.[11] Between 1967 and 1970, contours of U.S.-Soviet naval rivalry in the Indian Ocean emerged in clearer relief. The Arab-Israeli war of 1967 brought the Soviet Union to the Middle East both as a land and naval power. For the first time, the USSR's naval presence in the Indian Ocean came to international notice. The United States and Britain concluded an agreement under which the United States was to build a naval base on Diego Garcia.

India's first perception of the Soviet naval presence was not exactly benign, nor of the American naval presence exactly hostile. What began to be articulated with nationalist fervor was the need for a strong Indian naval role to defend India's interests and ensure the security of its 3,000-mile-long coastline.[12] However, it was not before 1970 that the Indian government was able to formulate a coherent perspective of developments in the Indian Ocean. This perspective rested on two main premises. The first was the limitation of India's power and resources. India, as Defense Minister Swaran Singh confessed in parliament, could hardly do anything to prevent the "tendency" among the more powerful nations to deploy their navies over far-flung areas of the world. All that India could do was to try to ensure the security of its 12-mile-wide territorial waters. This it preferred to do by augmenting its own naval capability "within our resources" rather than by actively trying to set up an Indian Ocean community or by entering into naval defense arrangements with littoral nations.

The second premise was that it was vital for Indian strategic interests that the ocean be not dominated by either of the two superpowers, nor by any one of them in combination with China. If there were an American penetration of the Indian Ocean, it should be neutralized or balanced by a Soviet penetration. Only a competitive and balanced presence would prevent either superpower from building up its naval forces to a level unacceptable to India and other littoral states. It was the best assurance that conflicts between the superpowers in the ocean would remain under control and that intervention in the affairs of littoral states would be minimized.[13]

In India's perception in 1970, neither superpower was about to build a massive naval presence in the Indian Ocean; the two were engaged in a relatively low-profile competition. This reassuring image allowed a relaxed official stance. Protests against American base building on Diego Garcia lacked vigor and were no more than routine reflexes of a government opposed to foreign bases and external intervention anywhere in the Third World. The Soviets were seen only as putting up a naval "presence" in the Indian Ocean and not as building bases, and suggestions that they had acquired base facilities at Vishakapatnam, on the east coast of India, were vehemently denied.[14]

The government's perception of the Indian Ocean situation was reflected in November 1970 in a report printed in the staid and prestigious South Indian daily *The Hindu*. The extension of American or Soviet power to the Indian Ocean, the report maintained, "does not by itself pose any new threat to the countries of the region." There was as yet "no great competition between the U.S. and the Soviet Union." The Russians were simply trying to establish a presence and the Americans a capability; in balance, the American position continued to be "overwhelmingly superior." India had to live with the fact that "the two superpowers are extending their naval power to the Indian Ocean to fill the remaining gaps in their global confrontation." India could only keep a close watch on developments and take measures to prevent either superpower from "getting too many shore facilities in Pakistan."[15]

This relaxed Indian attitude collapsed in 1971. For the first time a war between India and Pakistan was fought both on land and in the Arabian Sea. Fearing that after vanquishing the Pakistani army in Bangladesh, India would turn against what remained of Pakistan, the Nixon administration dispatched a naval task force to the Bay of Bengal led by the nuclear-armed carrier *Enterprise*. The war, however, established a harmony of Indian and Soviet strategic interests in South Asia and the Indian Ocean. India fought the war in close political coordination with Moscow, and with the strategic assurance that the Soviets would take care of any Chinese intervention across the Himalayan border. When the *Enterprise* steamed up to the Bangladesh shore, the Soviet ambassador reportedly assured Mrs. Gandhi that the Soviet navy in the Indian Ocean would see to it that there would be no American naval intervention on behalf of Pakistan.[16]

In Indian strategic thinking in the 1970s, a permanent Soviet naval presence in the Indian Ocean became essential to balance and contain the American buildup.[17] However, India, at the same time, welcomed whatever small steps were taken in the 1970s by the two superpowers to negotiate an agreement for naval arms control in the Indian Ocean.

THE OIL CRISIS OF 1973-74

Meanwhile, India had to absorb the traumas of the Arab-Israeli October 1973 War and the international oil crisis that followed. The war obliged India to take an explicit stand on behalf of the Arabs against Israel; this was no wrench, but only a revival of traditional pro-Arabism. By forceful support of the Arab demand that Israel withdraw from all territory occupied during the war of 1967, India got the oil-exporting Arab regimes promptly to delete its name from the list of countries selected for the oil embargo as well as the oil squeeze.[18] It also gained a measure of belated Arab sympathy for its own claim that the Chinese vacate territory they had occupied along the Indian border as a result of the 1962 war. The political blasts of the oil crisis were easier to weather, though Indians can hardly erase from their memory that the Arabs did initially place an embargo on oil supplies to their country.

The economic blasts proved to be harder to face. India's oil imports have remained more or less static since 1970-71, within the range of 15 to 17 million tons. But the import bill has increased 42 times, from $146 million in 1970-71 to $6.3 billion in 1980-81.[19] Like most other nations, India had to improvise an oil diplomacy. Involved in this enforced enterprise were the need to boost exports, risking domestic shortages of many essential commodities, diversifying sources of oil supplies (the Soviets once again proving to be helpful with a long-term agreement to supply 2.5 million tons of crude annually), obtaining deferred payment facilities in Iran and Iraq, and getting as large a share as possible of the fat pie of Arab petrodollars.[20]

Since 1974, India has been projecting to the Persian Gulf countries an image of a nation that is eminently in a position to meet a sizable portion of the goods and services they need for their dazzlingly ambitious modernization and development projects at rates considerably cheaper than those available in the developed capitalist countries. Furthermore, India's development experience would be more relevant to these oil-rich developing countries than the growth and development concepts of the Western nations. India offered joint ventures, joint commissions on industrial and technological cooperation, turn-key projects, consultancies, and new patterns of trade relations. By the late 1970s, India's vigorous economic diplomacy was rewarded with promising returns. Iran came up with offers of investments totaling $1 billion. Indian public and private sector companies built railroads, airports, townships, housing projects, an electric power supply plant, a water filtration plant, a sponge-iron plant, and a fertilizer factory in countries in the Persian Gulf region.[21] India also became the second largest supplier of manpower to the region, after Pakistan.

CRISES IN IRAN AND AFGHANISTAN

India's economic diplomacy in the Persian Gulf, however, lacked the underpinning of political clout, in the absence of which economic relations seldom flourish. Relations with Saudi Arabia remained poor; those with Kuwait, Bahrain, and the UAE stagnant at a level of lukewarm friendliness. Relations were the warmest with Iraq, but here too the Iraqi version of Baath socialism failed to attract Indians' intellectual or emotional attention. On the other hand, efforts to work out a framework of economic cooperation with Egypt and Yugoslavia fell flat, exposing once again the hollowness of nonaligned collectivism in a complex, multipolar world.[22]

It is in this context that the strategic understanding that grew between India and Iran in the mid-1970s has to be seen. India's diplomatic success in Iran was all the more remarkable because it was scored in spite of Tehran's long-standing treaty relationship with Pakistan. In India's perception, the shah's aspiration to make Iran the dominant regional power in the Persian Gulf did not entirely jell with America's strategic and economic interests in that region. The shah had reacted with studied chilliness to a hypothetical American takeover of Persian Gulf oil installations in an extreme emergency situation. Indians saw certain similarities between Iran and India as an emerging and an emergent regional power in the interlinked geostrategic regions of Southwest and South Asia:

> Indeed certain common features are discernible in Iran's and India's security scenarios and in their behaviour as dominant regional powers. Both attach the greatest possible value to the attainment of security autonomy, and both have to live with dependence on external security for a fairly long time. Both are therefore anxious to maintain and assert as much independence and initiative as possible within the framework of their relationship with their respective patron power. What has charged the Indo-Soviet relationship with dynamism is India's initiatives as a major regional power even at the risk of Soviet disapproval, namely, its nuclear explosion and the annexation of Sikkim. In concluding a far-reaching agreement with Iraq with the help of the Algerian president, the Shah was guided by the interests of his own country rather than the preferences of the United States. The Shah, in other words, would seem to be as much interested in reducing Iran's dependence on the US for security as is India in reducing its dependence on the Soviet Union.[23]

This Indian perception of Iran was confirmed by an Iranian journalist with close links with the shah's Ministry of Foreign Affairs:

> Iran is not that afraid of a direct military threat against itself; its defence forces, large population, vast territory and growing economic might ensure that no such threat would make any major impression. But Iran is anxious to prevent the polarisation of the political situation in the region. During the past ten years, Iran has reaped great benefits from correct and mutually profitable relations with both the United States and the USSR. It would thus wish to see the present balanced situation continue for at least another decade during which, as Iranian policymakers assert, Iran would become strong enough to hold its own against all eventualities.[24]

Less than four years after this Iranian wish was so earnestly articulated, the shah's regime was in ruins, he an exile, and Iran in the grip of one of the most fever-hot revolutions of this century. With the shah's fall, the tenuous bridge between Tehran and Delhi was left in limbo, and the Persian Gulf became a critical area of confrontation between the United States and the local and international forces arrayed against it. To the Carter administration, the American loss of Iran was, in itself, a major Soviet gain, even though the Soviets had no clout in an aroused Iran, nor were they responsible for the collapse of the shah's regime. The White House initiated a series of strategic and political measures in 1979 aimed simultaneously at protecting vital U.S. and Western interests in the Gulf-Middle East region, minimizing losses in Iran, and meeting any overt Soviet military move southward toward Iran.

Several of these measures enhanced India's security concerns without generating more than verbal governmental responses. In November–December 1979, Carter ordered the streamlining of the rapid deployment force (RDF) for use in future crises in the Third World; dispatched special aides to Saudi Arabia, Oman, and Kenya to seek access to military, especially naval, bases; and asked Defense Secretary Harold Brown to make his long-awaited trip to Beijing, thus symbolically inaugurating an era of Sino-U.S. military cooperation. Zbigniew K. Brzezinski, sculptor of much of the president's response to the Iranian crisis, observed in mid-December that the RDF "will give us the capability to respond quickly, effectively and perhaps preemptively in those parts of the world where our vital interests might be engaged and where there are no permanently stationed American forces."[25] A report in the *New York Times* made it clear that the RDF was not necessarily meant exclusively to respond to Soviet military expansion. It might be made available to Egypt if Sadat's insecure regime was menaced by Libya, to Saudi Arabia in the event of a military threat from Iraq or Iran, and to Thailand if it were invaded by the Vietnamèse from Kampuchea.[26] Another report said that the Iranian crisis was causing Washington to shed its reluctance to engage in intervention for the protection of American interests in the Third World, with certain congressional elements "prepared in principle to endorse military intervention even in friendly countries if Western interests were threatened."[27]

As Indian strategic planners and analysts watched crisis clouds darken the skies of the Persian Gulf, they drew the conclusion that the United States was getting ready for military intervention in Iran to rescue the hostages or in Saudi Arabia if that oil-and-sand kingdom's pro-American monarchy faced an external or internal threat.

In this critical ambience in the adjacent Gulf, the Soviet Union carried out its stunning military intervention in land-locked Afghanistan in the closing days of 1979. The intervention aimed not so much to secure a wobbling Marxist regime as to preempt a U.S. military intervention in Iran by placing the Soviet military in a position of strategic vantage.[28] Carter linked the Soviet intervention to the general crisis in the Persian Gulf region, for which, too, he held Moscow partially responsible. A Soviet-occupied Afghanistan, Carter declared, threatened both Iran and Pakistan and was "a stepping stone to their possible control over much of the world's oil supplies."[29] Carter's offer of military and economic aid to Pakistan cast that country's military ruler, General Zia ul-Haq, in an important international role and ended his relative isolation, following the hanging of Zulfikar Ali Bhutto.[30] General Zia clutched at his unexpected luck. His perception of the Soviet intervention in Afghanistan mirrored Jimmy Carter's.[31]

Indira Gandhi returned to the helm of Indian affairs after two years in the wilderness within two weeks of the Soviet lurch into Afghanistan. Even before formally taking over, she framed India's response to that traumatic event. She did not support, nor approve of, the Soviet intervention. But she saw the intervention as legitimate, as, in her view, the Soviets had acted on the request of the Afghan government, and she trusted the Soviet assurance that the troops would be withdrawn as soon as Afghanistan so asked. She also backed the Soviet argument that Moscow's intervention was more of a response to a series of provocations from the United States than a calculated challenge flaunted at the United States. Mrs. Gandhi perceived more danger to India's security in the cold-warish reponses of the United States to the Soviet action, particularly in the arming of Pakistan and making that country a staging ground for the strategies to contain Soviet power.[32]

For Mrs. Gandhi and the majority of Indian foreign policy elite, the traditional strategic divide in South Asia—between Pakistan and India—was now meshed with the Soviet-U.S. divide in the Persian Gulf, the Indian Ocean, and indeed in the global arena. They saw an unprecedented threat to India's hard-earned status as South Asia's regional power, dismantling the favorable balance of regional power in South Asia that India had been able to bring about with its victory over Pakistan in the Bangladesh war in 1971, and the South Asian security "regime" erected on that balance. For the whole of 1980, Indian foreign policy was aimed at defusing the superpower confrontation over Afghanistan and blocking the flow of sophisticated weapons like the F-16 fighter from the United States to Pakistan.

The Afghan crisis generated the biggest ever diplomatic enterprise on India's part, bringing as many as 30 foreign dignitaries to the Indian capital in 1980 and involving visits by Indian diplomats to 20 capitals.[33] It brought Pakistan and India face to face not, alas, in a strategic partnership to safeguard the integrity and independence of South Asia, but as deeply estranged neighbors talking furiously at one another in the abrasive language of discord and disputation. For a while India stood forlorn and isolated in the comity of nations. It was severely cut off from the great bulk of Islamic countries, which rallied to the support of Pakistan at successive sessions of the Conference of Islamic Nations.[34] Pakistan stood as a formidable barrier between India and the countries of the Persian Gulf.

None of these countries showed interest in India's diplomatic efforts in 1980 to insulate the subcontinent from superpower rivalries, more specifically to stop the transfer of F-16 aircraft to Pakistan. Indeed, scholars at New Delhi's Institute of Defense Studies and Analyses saw Pakistan cast by the United States in the role of a security provider to the Persian Gulf, a somewhat tarnished replica of Iran before it was seized by the Islamic revolutionary cohorts of the Ayatollah Rohullah Khomeini:

> Pakistan is by far most suited to play the role of a viable proxy power for the U.S. interests in the Gulf. Although the other two, Israel and Egypt, have their own roles, the Pakistanis seem to enjoy a special position in the RDF strategy. A strong plan for U.S. access to Pakistani facilities, particularly the Gwadar port and the Peshawar air base, was voiced by former chairman of the Joint Chiefs of Staff, Admiral Thomas Moorer. . . . Politically, Pakistan is a moderate or a neutral power in the intra-Arab rivalries and therefore is not unacceptable to most Gulf countries. . . .
>
> Moreover, Pakistan has already established extensive political and military linkages with the Gulf regimes, particularly Saudi Arabia. These linkages may prove to be of immense value in times of crisis. Another factor which favours Pakistan in the proxy role is that like Israel, Pakistan too has a vast, extensive, experienced and modern military with enormous scope for its expansion. Lastly, at least for the present, there is a willing military regime in Islamabad which is not answerable to any public scrutiny of its politics.[35]

REACHING OUT TO THE GULF

India's isolation from the Persian Gulf, however, did not last long. A qualitative change in the situation in the Gulf region began to occur in 1981, offering India opportunities to reach out to the Gulf community, individually as well as collectively. The outbreak of the Iraq-Iran war jeopardized for a while India's assured oil supplies from the Gulf, but India did not find it difficult to arrange for alternative sources of import. What hurt more was the forced departure of a large body of Indian workers, skilled and unskilled, from Iran and Iraq and the consequent loss in hard currency remittances. But the war activated the nonaligned peacemaking mechanism and gave India an opportunity to join with other nonaligned countries on repeated peace missions to the two warring capitals.

The Reagan administration offered Pakistan a package of $3.2 billion in military and economic aid in five years, including some 40 F-16 fighters. India mounted a vigorous campaign in Washington against congressional approval of the package and was handsomely assisted by the powerful Israeli lobby. It was beyond India's clout in the United States to block the passage of the aid package, but the fact that powerful Zionist interests sympathized with India's misgivings about the transfer of sophisticated weapons to Pakistan had an impact on the Reagan administration that nudged General Zia ul-Haq to make a positive response to India's long-standing offer to conclude a no-war pact with Pakistan. Long before General Zia ul-Haq acted on American counsel, the Afghan crisis took leave of the front pages of the world press and of television prime time. The Soviets had dug in for a protracted war of attrition with Afghan rebels; they were not to be dislodged from Afghanistan by real or simulated moral outrage of a world not particularly distinguished for steadfast pursuit of moral principles in the conduct of planetary affairs.

Meanwhile, an oil glut and falling prices of petroleum threw a pale cast of thought on the grand affluent designs of the sheikhs and princes of oil-rich Arabia. The strategic consensus sought by the United States in the Persian Gulf region proved to be elusive. The Gulf countries, notably Kuwait and the UAE, had never been seduced by the Carter Doctrine;[36] before 1980 was out, the Saudis started to keep a certain distance from the anti-Soviet strategies of the United States,[37] and in 1981 took the initiative to frame a regional security doctrine. Its basic premise was that security of the Persian Gulf region was basically the concern of the native states; they should keep external powers out of the region as providers of security.[38]

Indian perceptions of the Persian Gulf countries whispered foreign policy opportunities. Indians saw a climate of disenchantment with the United States building up in the Gulf region, especially among the younger, highly educated generation that had entered the policymaking process. Even the reigning sheikhs and monarchs were seen to have begun to realize the shortsightedness of the total dependence on the West for accelerating the development and modernization of their native lands. The oil power that frightened the West in 1973–74 had lost its sharp edges; the oil-rich Gulf countries were now facing problems of selling their crude; oil prices were tumbling down. The Arabs were so divided that they could hardly use their oil or petrodollar clout to usher in a homeland for the Palestinians. Not only had the OPEC countries locked up 84 percent of their investible surplus in the advanced capitalist countries; they had negotiated long-term dependencies for defense and development that would drain their resources even when their oil wealth was reduced to a trickle. The volatile, even convulsive momentum created by extravagant spending on defense and development was tearing at the social fabric of these conservative Arab societies and distorting their economies. The oil sheikhs and their younger sons and nephews had begun to realize that the singular failure of OPEC had been to engineer productive forces in the developing world that might strengthen their own economies in the long run and make oil money a powerful factor in structuring a new international economic order.[39]

In the autumn of 1980 the Indian government announced a liberal policy for foreign investment designed to attract Arab capital. Finance Minister R. Venkataraman visited several Persian Gulf capitals in October to project the new policy to prospective Arab investors. The first spin-off came in the shape of an agreement with the UAE in February 1981, providing for the setting up of a 1.2 million ton oil refinery in Gujarat and a sponge-iron plant in the UAE, projects that had been hanging fire since 1978. The UAE minister of state for foreign affairs, who signed the agreement on his country's behalf, indicated interest in joint ventures in which UAE natural gas and oil could blend with Indian raw materials and technical know-how. A 50 percent increase in trade was also agreed upon for 1981.[40]

In the spring of 1981 Indians discovered Bahrain. A team of Indian journalists visited Bahrain at the invitation of the government and were received by the emir, Sheikh Isa Bin-Sulman al-Khalifah. Their reports woke Indians to the miracle that had happened in the matter of a decade; a knot of 35 desert islands had boomed into one of the world's leading banking and commercial centers, handling $37 billion in business transactions in 1980, which put it ahead of Singapore as a service center. The emir told the Indian reporters that he was interested in seeking Indian help in setting up small industries in Bahrain. The reporters found that Indians constituted 34 percent of Bahrain's total work force and 48 percent of all foreign workers—far in excess of Pakistanis, who formed only 19 percent—and that many Indians were manning top managerial and technical positions. Their reports awakened India to the possibility of getting a slice of Bahrain's $5.5 billion five-year construction plan and the $800 million project to build a 12-mile causeway to the Saudi Arabian mainland.[41]

When the emir visited Delhi in April, he was not only forthcoming economically but also in broad agreement with India's views about the need to limit, if not eliminate, superpower presence and interference in the Indian Ocean and the Persian Gulf. An economic cooperation agreement between India and Bahrain was concluded, and Bahrain's investment in Indian projects discussed. The investment issue was further followed up by the Indian foreign minister, Narasimha Rao, when he visited Bahrain a year later.[42]

The most important visitor from the Gulf was the foreign minister of Saudi Arabia, Prince Faisal, the first ranking member of the Saudi royal family to come to India after the visit of King Faud 25 years ago. Prince Faisal's talks with Indira Gandhi and Narasimha Rao were wide-ranging, covering the strategic-political situation in the Persian Gulf and the Middle East, the role of the superpowers, Israel-Arab relations, the Iran-Iraq war, the role of Pakistan in the U.S. strategic design in the region, and, last but not the least, economic cooperation between India and Saudi Arabia. Faisal refused to yield to Indian pleading that Saudi Arabia should not finance Pakistan's purchase of F-16 fighters from the United States, and his Islamic rigidity narrowed prospects of political understanding with India. But he was interested in initiating economic and trade linkages with India, and as an earnest of this desire agreed to Indian purchase of 1.5 million tons of Saudi crude in 1982, the first ever oil deal between the two countries.[43]

Encouraged by her talks with the prized visitors from the Gulf, Indira Gandhi put cooperative relations with Southwest Asian countries at the top of her foreign policy priority list in 1981. In May 1981, she herself inaugurated the new policy by well-organized visits to the UAE and Kuwait and followed this up with an equally vigorous visit in April 1982 to Saudi Arabia. In both visits she was accompanied by important cabinet ministers and half a dozen officials heading the economic ministries. The minister for external affairs flew in from Baghdad (where he was leading a nonaligned peace mission) to join her in the UAE and Kuwait. Mrs. Gandhi also collected nine Indian ambassadors in the Gulf region for a comprehensive, self-critical assessment of opportunities, stakes, and impediments of Indian diplomacy in the region.

While she conducted political talks with the leaders of the Gulf countries, her aides engaged in nuts-and-bolts conversations and pushed attractive portfolios to prospective Arab investors. During her UAE and Saudi Arabian visits, Mrs. Gandhi also discussed defense and security matters with the Gulf defense ministers and high military personnel. She demonstrated to the sheikhs of the UAE that she attached considerable political, economic, and security importance to them and their kingdoms and did not regard them as mere owners of magic-begotten wealth. The shiekhs were flattered.[44] Mrs. Gandhi's extensive talks with the king and princes of Saudi Arabia covered political, strategic, and security issues.

Communiques issued at the end of both visits stressed the strategic unity of the Persian Gulf and South Asia; peace and amity in one would enhance peace and amity in the other, while conflict and war in one would endanger the security and stability of the other. Mrs. Gandhi, who had already lent her support to the Fahd plan for a comprehensive settlement of the Middle East conflict and welcomed the formation of the Gulf Cooperation Council, found the Persian Gulf leaders in agreement with India that the regional countries must take care of regional stability and that both regions should be insulated from superpower rivalries and interventions.[45]

The visits were welcomed by all Indians and regarded as landmarks in the conceptual and operational reach of Indian foreign policy. Analysts suggested that the prime minister had won the sympathy and support of a strong, more enlightened, section of the Saudi royal family and princely elite:

> Though it still remains the corner stone of the U.S. defence strategy in the Gulf, Saudi Arabia is becoming increasingly aware of its vulnerability to both external pressures and internal dissensions. It is slowly shedding its old image as a bulwark of Islamic orthodoxy and political reaction. . . . The crown prince who has been functioning as the effective head of government, has been aspiring for a middle role of moderation in Arab affairs between the militancy of hotheads like Col. Gadaffi and the defeatism of the late Sadat. The prime minister would like to encourage Prince Fahd and his advisers to carry forward this new element of rationality in Saudi foreign policy to the logical conclusion of establishing mutually beneficial relations and links with India, the most important country in the region, which offers vast possibilities for Saudi investments in its economic development. After the U.S. froze the Iranian assets, Saudi Arabia and other oil-rich Arab countries have been somewhat chary of putting all their petrodollars in the American basket or investing exclusively in the West. They are more inclined now to seek other avenues of investment in countries like India to enhance their regional political influence. Indian diplomacy now aims at strengthening the hands of those in the Saudi establishment who realise the futility of financing the purchase of F-16 planes by Pakistan at a time when the two countries are trying to improve their relations.[46]

India's relations with Iran also moved out of the trough in early 1982. A former Iranian prime minister, Ayatollah Mahadavi Kani, led a four-member team to Delhi to persuade the Indian government to shift the venue of this year's nonaligned summit conference from Baghdad in view of Iraq's aggressive war on Iran.[47] Almost simultaneously, a 14-man Iranian delegation explored possibilities of Indian assistance to complete several unfinished projects in Iran, including the Ahwaz steel plant and power and fertilizer projects. The Ahwaz steel plant is of particular interest to India because to feed it India had built, with generous capital support extended by the late shah, a large iron ore concentrate plant at Kudremukh, South India, which became a white elephant when the revolutionary regime indicated its unwillingness or inability to go ahead with the deal. As a result of the Iranian team's exploratory talks with Indian officials and trade interests, it was decided that a high-level Iranian purchasing mission would visit India later in the year.[48]

The spring brought to Delhi the foreign minister of Iran, Dr. Ali Akbar Velayati, on a five-day visit during which he met with Indira Gandhi and several ministers, including the minister for external affairs and the minister for defense. The entire political-security situation in the Gulf and South Asia was discussed at great length, the focal points being Afghanistan, the war between Iran and Iraq, and superpower rivalries in the Persian Gulf. Iran's impressive successes in the war with Iraq had buoyed up Tehran's diplomacy. Even more important was the apparent success of the revolutionary regime in bringing the domestic situation under control and its readiness to address itself to rebuilding the ravaged economy. Improvement in relations with the Soviet Union mellowed Iran's stance on the Afghan crisis; Tehran was now ready to participate in tripartite talks between Afghanistan, Pakistan, and Iran through the mechanism devised by the special representative of the UN Secretary-General.[49]

Indian officials found the visitor from Tehran broadly in tune with their own perceptions of conflicts and tensions in the Persian Gulf. However, they could hardly assure Velayati of support for his demand to shift the nonaligned summit from Baghdad, and they remained reluctant to take sides in a war toward the ending of which India had contributed in the continuing nonaligned peace effort. Nevertheless, a broad rapport was established between Iran's and India's foreign ministers, and this led to the decision to set up a joint commission to boost bilateral relations in trade, industry, science and technology, and cultural affairs.[50]

PROBLEMS AND PROSPECTS

As noted, necessity and opportunity propelled India to reach out to the Gulf countries in 1981–82. The initial results of an unusually vigorous and well-planned diplomatic offensive proved to be handsome. However, formidable difficulties remain to be overcome before India can plant itself firmly in the sands of Arabia as a true friend of its princes and peoples and as a viable source of collaboration in their massive development drives.

The problems are complex and of a fairly old vintage, having mingled with the fluids of religious beliefs and loyalties, cultural processes, and political-strategic alignments. As noted, India's relations with Iraq have been the best in the Gulf region. With Kuwait, India has done much better than with the UAE and Bahrain.[51] The problems, then, are mainly with those countries in the Gulf–the UAE, Bahrain, and Saudi Arabia–who follow an orthodox Islamic domestic policy and a pro-Western foreign policy and who are close friends of Pakistan. Indeed, Pakistan remains the hardest barrier between India and these countries, and a great deal of Indian diplomacy continues to be spent in pulling that barrier down.

Mrs. Gandhi realized during her visits to the UAE, Kuwait, and Saudi Arabia that India would continue to lose if it were to compete with Pakistan to dip into the Persian Gulf's petrodollar chests. She found that her rejection in 1981 of the Pakistani proposal for a no-war pact had injured India's image in the Persian Gulf.[52]

In early 1982, she engaged Pakistan in a zigzag process of diplomatic negotiation and scored a propaganda victory by lobbying to the visiting foreign minister of Pakistan a treaty of friendship instead of a no-war pact. While General Zia ul-Haq shrank away from her offer, Mrs. Gandhi hastened to write personal letters to the heads of government of Persian Gulf and Middle Eastern countries informing them of the measures she had taken to improve Indo-Pakistani relations and explaining her objections to the Pakistani acquisition of F-16 aircraft. She also recorded her readiness to conclude a no-war pact with Pakistan if General Zia ul-Haq would assure her that he would not place military bases or facilities at the disposal of the United States in the event of an emergency situation developing in the Persian Gulf.[53]

In 1982, the Gulf regimes were more sympathetic to the Indian perspective of security and stability in Southwest and South Asia than they were in 1980–81. The reason is not far to seek. With the

Afghan issue inching toward a "comprehensive political settlement," the focus in the "arc of crises" shifts back to the Gulf, and here the string of uncertain regimes, in the first winter of their discontent with international oil prices, are in no mood to invite a superpower confrontation. Nevertheless, when Mrs. Gandhi visited Saudi Arabia, she found that the Saudis saw India as hostile to Pakistan, inhospitable to its large Muslim minority, and pro-Soviet. She took extraordinary pains to persuade the Saudis that India had major differences with the Soviet Union over Afghanistan and certainly desired withdrawal of Soviet troops as quickly as possible. Indians realize that a real breakthrough in India-Pakistan relations and India's ability to improve its relations with the United States are two essential preconditions for its success in grasping a large slice of Arab development and investment funds for Indian projects and significant Indian participation in Persian Gulf development.

At present the Indian economic presence in the Gulf region is small and its share of the Arab development funds miniscule. In the last five years, India has received a mere $132 million in direct loans from the Saudi Fund for Arab Economic Development, out of more than $2 billion disbursed. India has done somewhat better with Kuwait and the UAE, having received $472 million in loans from the Arab Development Fund, including $147 million from Kuwait.

Only about 1 percent of the total exports of the Gulf region is bagged by India and 1 percent of construction projects. Yet the Middle East-Persian Gulf region makes 30 percent of India's total imports and takes 20 percent of its total exports. The 70 Indian companies that operate in the region can execute only small or medium-sized projects, although most of these regimes have a fascination—and money—for grand projects. Indian companies have abandoned, for one reason or another, 50 percent of contracts signed for joint ventures.

India's trade performance in the region has been poorer than in Southeast Asia and Africa. One reason is that, unlike in Southeast Asia and Africa, there is no Indian investment in the Persian Gulf. Moreover, the market here demands the best and the most modern items. The Arabs are very strict about delivery schedules and times. India's knowledge about the region as a whole and about individual countries is scanty. There is hardly any data base or documentation center. The Arabs do not see India as an industrial power. India's largest asset is the 500,000 skilled, semiskilled, and unskilled workers employed in the Gulf, who remit $1.5 billion each year. But even these migrant workers create problems in the host countries as well as in India, and, in any case, there seems to be little prospect of an increase in India's manpower export to this region.[54]

Clearly, then, India will have to make most energetic diplomatic and economic efforts to build a noticeable presence in the Persian Gulf. At this time, India has taken the first innovative steps to enter the region "with affection beaming in one eye, and calculation shining out of the other." By 1984–85, India may have to lean heavily on the accumulated petrodollars of the oil-rich Gulf countries to meet the hard currency requirements of its development. This economic compulsion will probably create its own impetus for readjusting India's foreign relations. A major improvement in its relations with Pakistan, normalization of relations with the United States, and a certain measure of distance from thd USSR will help India to gain the required access to Arab petrodollars. Medium and long-term collaboration with Iran should be possible on a widening scale as the revolutionary regime in Tehran picks up the shattered tapestry of economic reconstruction and development.

Superpower rivalries and confrontations in Southwest and South Asia have enhanced the importance of settling regional feuds and conflicts and promoting regional cooperation on the autonomous initiative of the regional countries themselves. It is acknowledged in most countries of the regions that regional differences, tensions, and conflicts allow the superpowers to extend their influence and intervene in regional affairs. Of course, regional feuds and conflicts are not resolved easily. But prospects of amity between India and Pakistan are now better than they have been for many years. If India and Pakistan can conclude a no-war pact or a friendship treaty, its impact on the Persian Gulf will probably be constructive. It is, of course, difficult to see Iran and Iraq working to keep the peace in the Gulf region, but then, who could visualize the accord that was signed between Tehran and Baghdad in March 1975?

The most hopeful development in South and Southwest Asia in the last two years is the realization that continued regional feuds, tensions, and conflicts might lead to more than one war involving the superpowers, spelling disaster for the nations of the region. Both positive and negative forces are at work, making the Gulf and South Asia regions of "half light, half shade." Each uncertain rustling of the diplomacy of regional cooperation sires hope; collapse of each effort spurs despair.

NOTES

1. "Oil is not everything about the Persian Gulf," a French scholar told the writer in Paris in the summer of 1982. "The Soviet Union does not need Arab or Iranian oil, but the Gulf is adjacent to the USSR and the Soviets will remain interested in the Gulf even when oil will no longer gush out of the wells in the region. As for France, we have historical and strategic interests in the Persian Gulf which go beyond oil."

2. James Mellor, ed., *India: An Emerging Middle Power* (Boulder, Colo.: Westview Press, 1978); Stephen Cohen and Richard L. Park, *India: An Emergent Middle Power* (New York: Center for Strategic Studies, New York University, 1978).

3. The Nixon Doctrine implied a shrinking of U.S. security role in regions where there was no vital American interests. The Soviet-U.S. détente also helped India enjoy a benign regional environment for most of the 1970s.

4. Bhabani Sen Gupta, *Soviet-Asian Relations in the 1970s and Beyond: An Interceptional Study* (New York: Praeger, 1976), pp. 170-71.

5. Alan Campbell-Johnson, *Mission with Mountbatten* (London: Hale, 1953), p. 31.

6. K. R. Singh, "India and WANA," in *India's Foreign Policy: Studies in Continuity and Change*, ed. Bimal Prasad (New Delhi: Vikas Publishing House, 1979), p. 249.

7. In Egypt, the Wafd party, led by Nahas Pasha, had left behind a liberal, secular, and democratic tradition, while Nasser severly put down the Ikhwan, or Moslem Brotherhood. In Turkey, the Kemalist movement created a secular tradition that resisted Islamic fundamentalism.

8. Singh, "India and WANA," p. 249; Gurcharan Singh, *The Middle East and Indian Diplomacy* (Pearl River, N.Y.: Alovar Press, 1975), pp. 166–206.

9. Up to a maximum of $30 million. The total cost of the project was estimated at $50 million.

10. Amir Tahiri, "Policies of Iran in the Persian Gulf Region," in *The Persian Gulf and the Indian Ocean in International Politics*, ed. Abbas Amerie (Tehran, 1975), pp. 265–70.

11. Bhabani Sen Gupta, "The View from India," in *The Persian Gulf and the Indian Ocean in International Politics*, ed. Abbas Amerie (Tehran, 1975); *Indian Express*, November 19, 1965. Rajya Sabha, in the upper house of Parliament, expressed its "grave concern"; members suggested that India consult with littoral nations for a common response. The government did not.

12. "It may be a sign of the changing times that so far no furor has occurred in Delhi" over the Anglo-U.S. agreement. *The Statesman*, June 21, 1967. The *Hindustan Times* urged on June 30 a "cautious appraisal" of the development. *The Hindu*, June 8, observed that there was no reason to disbelieve that what was proposed was not a military base but "merely the provision of certain communication facilities." This was the time when India was training two mountain divisions of its army with U.S. assistance, and when Moscow's flirtations with Pakistan caused strong misgivings in India about Soviet policy in South Asia.

A flutter was caused by a paper written by a naval study group of the Defense Services Staff College urging the creation of a strong Indian navy, and, in the meantime, India remaining "nonaligned vis-a-vis both the U.S. and the Soviet Union," for India's objective had to be to free the Indian Ocean from a "Western economic yoke" as well as the "Communist threat of world domination." The paper was published in *Hamla*, a house journal of the navy, without clearance from the Defense Ministry. Its publication was regretted by the minister of external affairs, who asked parliament not to attach any importance to it. *Times of India*, November 11, 1970.

13. These premises were implicit in statements made by the Indian minister for external affairs to parliament in 1970. See Sen Gupta, "The View from India."

14. Ibid.

15. G. K. Reddy, "Power Rivalry in the Indian Ocean," *The Hindu*, November 24, 1980.

16. *Washington Post*, December 31, 1971, and January 10, 1972. According to C. L. Sulzberger in the *New York Times*, the United States and China would have intervened had India carried the war to West Pakistan. "The Soviet Union understood the signal and pressed India for a ceasefire. I know this is true. I have just been in Peking, and Chou En-lai confirmed this to me." *International Herald Tribune*, February 14, 1972.

17. At a national seminar on India security in the 1980s, held in New Delhi in April 1982, the only point on which all participants agreed was the the unilateral U.S. military buildup in the Indian Ocean and the Persian Gulf constituted a threat to India's security and interests as South Asia's regional power.

18. *Times of India*, November 11, 1970.

19. *Economic Survey*, 1981-82, government of India.

20. As a result of deferred payments in the 1970s, India has to pay Iraq and Iran $1 billion during 1980-85. In the 1990s, India will have to pay $200 million every year in addition to normal payments.

21. The Persian Gulf countries where India built significant projects were Kuwait, Dubai, Iraq, UAE, and Saudi Arabia. For a list of India-operated projects abroad, see *Indian Expertise in Projects*, Calcutta, Engineering Export Promotion Council, November 1980.

22. In October 1966, India, Egypt, and Yugoslavia prepared a framework for economic cooperation. A formal agreement was reached on April 1, 1968; it was renewed in 1973 and 1978. The tripartite agreement has been barren of results. In 1975, however, Egypt promised to deliver 500,000 tons of crude for Rs.400 million. A new trade agreement was signed under which India agreed to import oil and rock phosphate from Egypt in return for traditional items as well as engineering goods. Overall, however, the Indian drive to boost trade with the Persian Gulf region has led to a neglect of trade with Egypt and Sudan.

23. Sen Gupta, "The View from India," p. 192.

24. Tahiri, "Policies of Iran in the Persian Gulf Region."

25. *New York Times*, December 16, 1979.

26. Ibid.

27. *New York Times*, December 2, 1979.

28. This is implicitly confirmed by Zbigniew Brzezinski in "The Failed Mission," *New York Times Magazine*, April 18, 1982, in which he indicates that the Soviet military occupation of Afghanistan was one of the reasons Carter rejected a plan that would have cloaked the daring attempt to rescue the American hos-

tages in a larger, punitive military assault on Iran, designed to salvage American national honor in case the rescue operations failed. Also see Bhabani Sen Gupta, *The Afghan Syndrome* (New Delhi: Vikas, 1982), ch. 1.

29. Message to Congress on January 1, 1982.

30. See Sen Gupta, *The Afghan Syndrome*, ch. 7.

31. Ibid.

32. Ibid., ch. 6.

33. Ibid.

34. Ibid., ch. 7.

35. P. K. S. Namboodiri, J. P. Anand, and Sreedhar, *Intervention in the Indian Ocean* (New Delhi: ABC Publishing House, 1982), pp. 196–97.

36. *New York Times*, January 27, 1982.

37. *Indian Express*, February 4, 1982. Several reports in the American press in 1980 suggested that relations between the United States and Saudi Arabia were less than warm. The *New York Times* correspondent in Riyadh reported in March that there were indications that the special relations of 50 years were "gradually cooling." The key question is "Where do Saudi Arabia's long-term securities lie—traditional alliance with the U.S. or with surrounding Arab world and beyond, with the third world and the wider world of Islam? The answer seems to be that Saudi interests are increasingly at odds with the U.S.'s objectives." *New York Times*, March 9, 1980. See also Peter Lubin, "Our Saudi Friends," *New York Times*, December 30, 1979; and David Hirst, "Saudi-U.S. Relations on Collision Path?" *Guardian*, reprinted in *Indian Express*, August 29, 1980.

38. Within two months of the outbreak of the Iran-Iraq war, the six members of the Persian Gulf Cooperation Council, notably Saudi Arabia and Kuwait, initiated discussions on how the council could take charge of regional security. *The Hindu*, November 28, 1980. In January 1981, the six nations discussed a Kuwaiti blueprint for collective regional security, taking time off the Islamic Conference at Taif, Saudi Arabia. *Times of India*, January 30, 1981. In March, the Bahrain foreign minister said that the council intended to keep the superpowers out of the region's security management. *Indian Express*, March 12, 1981. In May, rulers of the six Gulf countries, meeting at Abu Dhabi, called for the departure of military fleets from the Indian Ocean and the closure of all foreign bases in the region. *Times of India*, May 26, 1981.

39. These perceptions are gleaned from Indian analyses of Persian Gulf developments and reporting of events in the region since January 1980.

40. The *Hindustan Times*, in an editorial (December 24, 1980), described the agreement as "a model for expanding economic cooperation with other oil-rich countries." The finance minister also visited Saudi Arabia.

41. D. Sen, "Bahrain to Sign Pact with India," *Hindustan Times*, April 27, 1981; Gautam S. G. Vohra, "Bahrain Keen on Ties with India," *Times of India*, May 12, 1981.

42. *Indian Express*, April 28, 1981; *Times of India*, April 5-6, 1982.

43. *The Hindu*, April 14, 1981. Prince Faisal's pan-Islamic sentiments and Saudi Arabia's strong security support to Pakistan apparently inhibited political relations between India and Saudi Arabia. *The Hindu* report said, "But before India could participate in [Saudi Arabia's] development on any substantial scale,

Saudi Arabia will have to shed its prejudice against non-Muslims and give up its discriminatory attitudes."

The Indian press carried several reports in 1981 about Saudi financial support to Pakistan for the purchase of F-16 aircraft. For example, the Washington correspondent of the *Hindustan Times* reported that Saudi Arabia had agreed to provide $500 million "immediately" to Pakistan for cash purchase of six fighter bombers and other military supplies from the United States for delivery within 12 months. *Hindustan Times*, November 21, 1981.

44. Bhabani Sen Gupta, "Bridging the Gulf," *India Today*, June 1–15, 1981. The Indian press was euphoric in reporting Indira Gandhi's visit to the UAE and Kuwait. See reports in *Times of India*, May 10, 1981 and May 15, 1981; *Indian Express*, May 10 and May 11, 1981; and *The Hindu*, May 12, 1981. Most newspapers wrote editorials highlighting the achievements of the visit. The *Hindustan Times* called it a "triumph," on May 15, 1981. The *Indian Express*, May 16, 1982, said that "India's desire for a higher level of relationship was fully reciprocated" in the Gulf countries.

45. Bhabani Sen Gupta, "The Gulf Narrows," *India Today*, May 15, 1982. As a result of the visit, the decision was taken to set up a joint India-Saudi Arabia commission at the ministerial level to give an impetus to economic and technological cooperation. *Hindustan Times*, April 19, 1982. A long-term contract for Indian import of Saudi Arabian oil is to be negotiated soon. *Indian Express*, April 19, 1982. India and Saudi Arabia were reported to have agreed to work together to "curb bigpower influence" in the Persian Gulf and South Asia. *Indian Express* and *Times of India*, April 20, 1982. For the joint communique, see *Hindustan Times*, April 21, 1982.

Editorial assessment of the visit was very high. The *Indian Express* saw the visit as "quite successful, given the background" (April 21, 1981). The *Hindustan Times* (April 24) said, "The crucial point made by the joint communique was the linking of the security of the Gulf states with that of the Indian subcontinent."

46. *The Hindu*, February 3, 1982.

47. *Hindustan Times*, February 6, 1982.

48. *Times of India*, February 2, 1982; *Indian Express*, February 2, 1982.

49. *Indian Express*, May 2, 1982.

50. *The Hindu*, May 3, 1982, and April 25, 1982.

51. Partly because Kuwait has friendly relations with the Soviet Union.

52. At her news conferences in the Persian Gulf countries, Mrs. Gandhi was repeatedly asked why India remained unfriendly toward Pakistan. In Riyadh, she highlighted India's efforts to build friendly ties with Pakistan.

53. India had proposed a no-war pact to Pakistan as far back as 1949. Successive Pakistani governments turned down the proposal. The Simla agreement of 1972 rules out war as a means of settling the Kashmir dispute but does not cover the entire area of India-Pakistan relations. India suggested a no-war pact to General Zia ul-Haq in the summer of 1980, but the general politely turned it down, saying that the Simla agreement was in effect a no-war pact. In September 1981, however, the Pakistani government suggested that the two countries negotiate a no-war agreement. The U.S. aid package was then up for Senate approval. Mrs. Gandhi took a negative attitude to the Pakistani proposal, which she thought was being made under American pressure with the purpose of blunting the impact

of U.S. arms transfers to Pakistan. Many Indians, however, supported the idea of a no-war pact between the two countries and the concept also received overwhelming popular support in Pakistan.

The first round of talks on the no-war pact between the two countries was held in New Delhi in February 1982, when the then Pakistani foreign minister, Agha Shahi, paid a visit to the Indian capital. Reports said that India asked for an assurance from Pakistan that it would not lend bases or facilities to the United States in any contingencies, an assurance that Pakistan was reluctant to give. When Agha Shahi called on Mrs. Gandhi, she suggested a joint commission of the two countries, which the Pakistani minister accepted. Mrs. Gandhi also offered to sign a friendship treaty with Pakistan. On this the Pakistani mission was noncommittal.

It was agreed that the next round of talks would take place in Islamabad in the spring. However, at the UN Human Rights Commission meeting in Geneva, in March, the Pakistani delegate made some references to Kashmir that led the government of India to postpone the second round of talks indefinitely. Since then, the two governments have been in touch with each other at low key to resume negotiations on the no-war pact. The new Pakistani foreign minister, Shahabzada Yaqub Khan, is reported to have rejected the Indian offer of a peace treaty before a no-war pact could be concluded. Apparently General Zia ul-Haq is not prepared to sign a peace treaty with India as long as the Kashmir question remains unsolved.

54. These points were made at a seminar held at the India International Center, New Delhi, in October 1981, on "India and West Asia."

7

Security with Stability: Can India Provide a Formula?

Aswini K. Ray

Security and stability have been the most obsessive concerns of mankind in the postwar era, and the most elusive goals. The United Nations has sought to institutionalize the global legitimacy of these two concepts by predicating itself on the principle of collective commitment to the preservation of the territorial integrity of the postwar system of nation-states. But ever since its inception, it has been flawed by an inadequate emphasis on the social, economic, and humanitarian content of these two categories of traditional concern. This is not the consequence of any lack of intellectual appreciation of their importance; on the contrary, there is considerable evidence to suggest such an appreciation.[1] But, on the operative level, the United Nations came to be associated almost exclusively with the legal fiction of a collective commitment to the inviolability of the territorial status quo.

I have called this commitment a legal fiction for several reasons. First, it is based on the assumption of the universal legitimacy of the postwar territorial divisions of the world, for which there is little empirical basis, as witness the various secessionist movements in different parts of the world based on religious, linguistic, and ethnic affinities. Second, it does not adequately reckon with the problems created by the collapse of the former global system dominated by the colonial powers and the consequent power vacuum at critical geopolitical centers. Third, it does not take into account the new problems posed by the liberation struggles in many parts of the world and the consequent social and political upheavals. Finally, it ignores the ideological division between the two systems vying on a global scale for the minds of men.

Consequently, since the creation of the UN system, and in spite of it, global security and stability have been sustained by a tenuous "balance of terror" between the two systems, each of them dominated by a superpower with access to the technology of the technotronic revolution. The present international system continues to be an impediment to the nonaligned states' ability, in fact if not in law, to pursue diplomacy by other means, including even the right to wage war. In addition, clearly discernible is a hierarchy of state sovereignty determined by access to technology and raw materials, managerial talent, and the quality of political and economic institutions; and, at the bottom of each of the pyramidal structures of power, policy options at the national level remain heavily skewed against any possibility of vertical mobility. As a result, global security and stability have come to imply a perpetuation of the inequitable hierarchy of power and sovereignty, involving, at the bottom of the two pyramids, the maintenance of illegitimate and unpopular regimes in many countries.

South and Southwest Asia have been historically victimized by the superpowers' operational combination of security and stability, first, because geopolitically this region is the strategic meeting point of the two ideological divides, and, second, because the impact of the postwar collapse of the colonial system has been manifested most sharply in this region. The consequent power vacuum enticed both superpowers to struggle for a foothold in the region and to continue the ideological battle for the minds of peoples entering the postcolonial phase of social and political efforts at nation building, social transformation, and economic development. A third reason is that this has also been a region endowed richly with oil, but with little access to the capital, technology, or managerial talent needed for sustained development. Finally, although historical legacies have largely determined the character of territorial nationalism, various ethnic, tribal, linguistic, and religious loyalties continue to vie with one another for legitimacy and territorial readjustments. Not only have the superpowers used these conflictual situations to introduce their security arrangements into the region but their hegemony has also caused social, economic, and political hardships.

Significantly, nonalignment, with India in the forefront, marked the first challenge to the hegemony of the post–World War II global system. Initially inspired by the urge of postcolonial India to assert its newly won right of national sovereignty in the international arena,[2] nonaligned India has sought to establish the nonaligned movement as a third pole in world politics. This has been manifested in a number of ways: in its refusal to sign the nuclear nonproliferation treaty; in its attempts to build economic and technological self-reliance through a policy of diversified dependence, cutting across the ideological gulf; in its pressure for a New International Economic Order (NIEO); in its attempts to institutionalize the economic complementarity within the Group of Seventy-seven so as to enhance the South's bargaining position vis-a-vis the North; and in its efforts to ensure greater regional autonomy in South Asia through a policy of regional cooperation.

Though never explicitly developed in systematic fashion, India's attempt to change the postwar status quo has been among the dominant underpinnings of India's global diplomacy from the beginning of its independence. In recent times, India has played a leading role in UNCTAD conferences and taken the initiative in hosting a variety of meetings aimed at exploring collective self-reliance.

But, despite such efforts, India's ability to make any dent in the structure of the global system, even in South Asia, has been rather limited, as the Soviet military intervention in Afghanistan suggests. Attempts at promoting regional cooperation have not borne much fruit. Also, judging by the results of the UNCTAD conferences, India's success in advancing NIEO could at best be described as modest.

CHANGING DETERMINANTS

In explaining the inability of Indian diplomacy to foster security in South and Southwest Asia, one has to confront the constraints of limited capability. In the early postwar period, India was opposed by the Western bloc and suspected by the Soviet bloc. Its resistance to the emerging bipolarity was manifest in the option described by Prime Minister Jawaharlal Nehru as "ploughing a lonely furrow," namely, nonalignment. In the 1950s, its efforts assumed greater urgency.[3] But it was constrained by various factors: the USSR's attitude toward India's nonalignment, which only changed from open hostility to lukewarm toleration; a public opinion skeptical of the viability of nonalignment in an era of cold war;[4] and the importance of the Pakistan factor in India's foreign and domestic policies.

India's festering dispute with Pakistan over Kashmir compelled India to adopt a policy of pragmatic adaptation to the global system and to play power politics. This involved tailoring India's perspective on specific issues to obtain needed support. Thus, the need for Soviet backing in the UN Security Council led to some empathy with the Soviet position on various issues. This was magnified out of all proportion by both superpowers. For the Soviet Union, at least, India's nonalignment was preferable to alignment with the West, and Soviet diplomacy showed a degree of sensitivity for India's views that helped to silence Indian domestic critics who continually harped on the danger of India finding itself isolated internationally. For the West, on the other hand, India's policy was, in the words of Secretary of State John Foster Dulles, portrayed as "immoral." As a result, the West magnified the procommunist proclivities of nonalignment, for which there was little empirical basis either from the standpoint of India's foreign policy or its domestic political economy.[5] Given these superpower perspectives, India's ability to instigate global reform was weak.

Yet, even in that phase, India's attempts to break through the constraints of the global system were manifested in its active role in promoting Afro-Asian nationalism[6] and in supporting Arab nationalism, particularly on the Palestinian issue.[7] Paradoxically, at that phase, although unequivocal Soviet support to India helped to widen the social and political base of nonalignment within the country and in many other newly liberated countries of Asia and Africa, the ability of Indian diplomacy to muster support for its perspective was weakened by its partisan image. Being a part of the ongoing global rivalry, and benefiting from it, India could not insulate itself from the logic of its constraints, particularly in the absence of any concrete material base for significant power of its own.

The second phase of India's diplomacy began in the early 1960s, when the superpower rivalry was marked by nuclear stalemate. This military reality was accompanied by the growing political awareness of the need to manage the global system, which was then threatened by China, with greater care. Simultaneously, with the worsening of Sino-Indian relations, leading to the border war of 1962, South Asia became an implicit area of agreement between the superpowers, with India a major beneficiary. While Pakistan was kept on a leash by the United States,[8] the two superpowers courted India. The two rounds of Indo-Pakistani war of 1964 and 1965, followed by the Tashkent agreement of 1966—under the USSR's aegis and with U.S. acquiescence—proved two basic points of relevance to the region: that there was no military solution to the regional conflict in South Asia and that the superpowers accepted this reality, despite their economic and military assistance to the region, which was important to their global rivalry.

By the late 1960s and especially in the early 1970s, however, the growing Sino-Soviet rift and the American debacle in Vietnam contributed to the breakdown of the superpower consensus on China. President Richard Nixon's visit to China in February 1972 and the consequent Shanghai communique, coupled with China's emergence as a nuclear power, contributed to the further loosening of global bipolarity and provided Indian diplomacy with new opportunities at the regional level. India refused to sign the nuclear nonproliferation treaty (NPT), concluded a treaty of friendship with the Soviet Union in August 1971 (as a prelude to a decisive military intervention in the secession of Bangladesh from Pakistan), and defied U.S. pressure, epitomized by the deployment of the aircraft carrier *Enterprise* in the Bay of Bengal during the 1971 Indo-Pakistani war. India also carried out its own nuclear explosion in 1974. These developments led to the Simla agreement of 1975, which was the first decisive attempt by Indian diplomacy to seek international recognition for its preeminence in South Asia.

Developments in neighboring Southwest Asia resulted in a further loosening of the global bipolar system. The emergence of OPEC, the fall of the shah, the eruption of Khomeini's Islamic fundamentalism, and the Iran-Iraq war—all played an important part. The result has been the advent of a period of rare opportunity for India. India has a vast reservoir of skilled, and surplus, manpower, which is already employed throughout the region, now humming with developmental activities of new oil wealth. It has a highly developed infrastructure of intermediate level technology that may be more suitable for the region's economic development than the highly advanced technology of the major industrial powers. These factors, coupled with India's own dependence on Persian Gulf oil and its desire to attract investment capital from the oil-rich producers of the region, have fashioned an inherently sound basis for complementarity.

At the political level, there is now a greater regional recognition of India's nonalignment and leadership role.[9] Even among the superpowers, there is a greater sensitivity to the need for political stability with economic development in India, whose nonalignment no longer evokes the earlier critical responses.[10] In addition, India's current negotiations with China and Pakistan (witness the warm reception accorded General Zia ul-Haq during his visit to India in November 1982) have given its diplomacy greater credibility for seeking to ease regional tensions and flexibility.

It is the present task of Indian diplomacy to take advantage of this historic opportunity to promote security and stability in South and Southwest Asia.

WHAT IS TO BE DONE?

Any plan for regional security and stability must satisfy two basic political criteria: It must conform to the interests of the superpowers, and it must respect the sovereignty of the countries in the region. Moreover, if it is to encompass the social, economic, and humanitarian dimensions of security and stability, then problems (and solutions) have to be formulated in a way acceptable to all parties.

One immediate conceptual problem inheres in classifying South and Southwest Asia in geostrategic terms, with inevitable cold war considerations, whereas such a classification has little relevance to the socioeconomic and psychological challenges faced by the region. This fact has received implicit recognition in the attempt of regional actors to toy with a variety of alternative categorizations, such as nonalignment, Group of Seventy-seven, North-South, Indian Ocean littorals, or Islamic.

The main problems causing insecurity and instability are as follows: economic underdevelopment leading to social tensions and consequent political and institutional instability and a perception of insecurity among the ruling elites; the existence of various forms of authoritarian regimes; the need to moderate the coercive apparatus of the state in the quest for intrasystemic change; relatively large defense budgets in the midst of poverty, malnutrition, and unemployment; and the violation of human rights. All of these contribute in some fashion to the basic sense of insecurity that is shared by ruling elites in the region.

Viewed thusly, the problems of the region may be reduced to clearly identifiable common denominators and traced to their colonial antecedents. But the delimitation of the region is only one aspect of the viability of any regional plan for promoting security and stability. A more important dimension entails ensuring that any plan does not conflict with the vital interests of the superpowers, namely, the security interests of the Soviet Union and the economic interests of the United States and its Western allies, which depend on an ensured flow of oil from the region. Two other considerations are germane: felicitous timing and the credibility of the initiator. For reasons suggested above, the present period offers a rare opportunity for progress. So far as an initiator is concerned, India admirably fills the bill, at least judging by formal criteria.

India should seek endorsement for the establishment of an Afro-Asian planning commission, which would avoid impinging on regional sensitivities over sovereignty. The purpose of such a commission would be to identify the region's main economic problems and their relative order of priority. This could be accomplished by technical experts available within the region. The next stage, the implementation of a regional development plan, would require support from the governments of the region. The most significant difference between the suggested planning agency and existing multilateral and bilateral agencies would be the effort to insulate the former from the power political concerns of the superpowers. Only regional actors would be involved in the process of planning or monitoring operations. Because involvement of one or the other superpower has been a cause of suspicion in the past, the proposed plan might help assuage regional fears and foster cooperation.

A complementary step would be to curtail the freewheeling activities of multinational corporations (MNCs) operating in the region and separate their legitimate economic activities from their political involvement. A code of conduct, drafted by the proposed planning commission, would establish the parameters for activity. This would in no case militate against the philosophy of free enterprise, inasmuch as the competition among such MNCs would be open within the regionally defined priorities for development.

These modest proposals do not affect any vital superpower interest and they may help nurture a greater degree of regional cooperation, for example, beyond that sought by the Gulf Cooperation Council. They may also stimulate the socialist camp to participate more actively in fostering economic development in the region.

Another important problem inheres in the prevalence of authoritarian rulerships or feudal oligarchies, supported by one of the superpowers. Apart from being a fetter on economic development and political stability in any enduring sense, the basic insecurity of such polities compels them to violate human rights. Such regimes cannot provide the basis for any durable system of security and stability, as was vividly demonstrated by the cases of the shah of Iran and Yahya Khan in Pakistan. They may occasionally show some record of growth, judged by quantitative data devoid of social content. But very often even such growth is the incidental by-product of massive foreign aid from a superpower patron, so that the causal factor accounting for growth is not necessarily the authoritarian regime, but foreign aid; indeed, development often proceeds despite such regimes.

Yet, given the reality of international politics, it would be unrealistic to wish these regimes away or to hope for their moral-political transformation. It may be more realistic to explore the possibility of committing them to an irreducible minimum of institutionalized human rights. Cutting across the ideological spectrum, these could include freedom of expression and participation in representative institutions. The enumerated human rights could be culled from the Universal Declaration of Human Rights to which most countries in the region, as members of the United Nations, are already committed; in this way, the commitment to them would not raise any new question pertaining to national sovereignty. But the monitoring of any violation should be kept outside the UN system to insulate it from superpower pressure. This task could be entrusted to a regional human rights commission consisting of representatives from governments and nongovernmental organizations with proven credentials in the region. Its annual report should focus on developments within the region only.

By fostering such initiatives, India could play a significant role in advancing stability and security for itself and its neighbors.

NOTES

1. British Prime Minister Clement Atlee's opening remark at the founding conference of the United Nations in 1945 was "Wars begin in the minds of men, and it is in the minds of men that peace has to be won." The creation of the Economic and Social Council as a principal organ of the United Nations and the need for a Universal Declaration of Human Rights further strengthen this point.

2. Aswini K. Ray, "Nonalignment: Retrospect and Prospect," paper presented at the Indo-Austrian Seminar on Neutrality and Nonalignment, 1982; to be published by the Indian Council of Cultural Relations, New Delhi.

3. For India's reaction to Pakistan's military alliance with the West, see Aswini K. Ray, *Domestic Compulsions and Foreign Policy* (New Delhi: Manas, 1975).

4. Ibid. See also Raman Pillai, *India's Foreign Policy, Basic Issues and Political Attitudes* (Meerut, 1969).

5. Then, as now, the West was India's major supplier of foreign assistance and trading partner. Michael Kidron, *Foreign Investment in India* (London: Oxford University Press, 1965). Despite India's socialist rhetoric, its capitalist course of development has been well documented.

6. G. H. Jansen, *Nonalignment and the Afro-Asian States* (London: Faber and Faber, 1966).

7. India did not deny the right of Israel to exist within its borders, and even permitted Israel to maintain a consulate in Bombay.

8. For a description of U.S. diplomacy during the Sino-Indian war, see John Kenneth Galbraith, *Ambassador's Journal* (Boston: Houghton Mifflin, 1969), ch. 20 and 21.

9. There was unanimous agreement in the fall of 1982, including that of Iran and Iraq, to shift the venue of the next nonaligned summit conference from Baghdad to New Delhi.

10. The visits of Indian Prime Minister Indira Gandhi to the United States in August 1982 and the Soviet Union a month later successfully underscored this point.

Part IV

FUNCTIONALISM

8

The Impact of Arms Transfers on Recipient Countries

Shirin Tahir-Kheli

With the acceleration of arms transfers to the Third World in the past decade and the growing concern over its consequences, much attention has been devoted to the policies of supplier countries. However, perhaps more important, and thus far very much neglected, have been assessments of the effect of arms transfers on the recipients themselves. The aim of this chapter is to examine the effects of arms purchases and transfers on the policies of the key countries of South and Southwest Asia.

Nearly two-thirds of the world's arms exports are to the Third World.[1] The Middle East receives 50 percent of this total. The rapidly accelerating quantity and quality of arms transfers have heightened Western concern regarding the destabilizing consequences of this process. Moreover, efforts by the superpowers to promote arms control in the nuclear and conventional fields cannot be separated from the general phenomenon of expanding levels of arms transfers.[2] Arms exports are substantially higher today than a decade ago.

THE RATIONALE FOR ARMS TRANSFERS: SUPPLIER PERSPECTIVES

The fact that arms transfers have increased significantly is reflective of the changing international environment of the twentieth century. In the past, alliances were predicated on the physical intervention of the stronger partner(s) in support of the weak. The nineteenth-century balance of power in Europe was maintained precisely by the above-mentioned type of intervention, often at considerable cost. The twentieth century brought with it a number of changes. First, the polarization of the world into competing ideologies made the division more fundamental and seemingly more permanent. Second, the growth of nationalism, which accelerated after World War I, became all-encompassing after World War II. A large number of new nations emerged from the territories previously run by colonial powers. As a concomitant of this explosion of nationalism and nation-states, the chances for major power confrontation became worldwide. Third, the discovery and development of nuclear weapons by the United States and the USSR made the cost of a conflagration between the two unacceptably high.

Policymakers faced the dilemma that the rising costs of intervention paralleled the propensity to intervene in defense and pursuit of national interests. Arms transfers offered a way out and became the post-World War II answer to the necessity of being involved, while at the same time reducing the risk of direct superpower confrontation. Such a policy neatly meshed with the growing appetite of the newly emerged less developed countries (LDCs) to mitigate their own sense of threat by arming themselves heavily. It was a policy that offered something to everyone.

From the perspective of the supplier, the substitution of arms transfers for direct intervention offered a number of advantages:

- A presence that could be used in a recipient country to the benefit of the supplier
- A chance to influence the political orientation of nations controlling strategic resources without facing the expense and liability of colonial occupation
- Help to maintain regional balances
- Enhanced capabilities of allies participating in joint defense agreements
- Promotion of deterrence through self-sufficiency
- Enhanced access to governments and elites of regional countries important to the supplier
- Securing of base rights, facilities, and transit privileges
- The opportunity to support both sides simultaneously by arming both parties to a conflict (Soviet assistance to both Iran and Iraq in the current war is a case in point)
- Providing economic advantages and a reduction in per-unit costs of weapons systems, generating budgetary savings, and permitting the supplier to acquire a larger number of weapons
- Enhancing the military capacity of the supplier's industrial base

RECIPIENT PERSPECTIVES

Critics of arms transfers generally view the recipients as if they mindlessly follow superpower dictates. However, LDCs that buy arms are not simply fulfilling the desires of the suppliers. Recipients of arms transfers in South and Southwest Asia are no different from those elsewhere. They fear threats to their security. Their history, often of colonial occupation, teaches them that military weakness is a precursor to external control. Having so recently won independence, they are unwilling to allow challenges to their security to go unanswered. Given these perceptions, recipients see arms transfers as a means for enhancing security, and not, as their critics sometimes allege, as the cause of their insecurity.

A study of defense planning in the region found that in all cases the recipient had its own perception of threat (sometimes at variance with the supplier) and exploited the East-West rivalry to obtain arms, rather than the other way around. For example, the Indo-Pakistani rivalry surfaced within a year of partition of the subcontinent in 1947. The Indian leadership, with its more militantly anticolonial experience, eschewed early contacts with the West in military matters. Recognizing this fact, the Pakistani leadership delved deep into its pro-Western training and found its own exposure to the West not totally uncomfortable. When India refused to align itself with the Northern Tier defense scheme of U.S. Secretary of State John Foster Dulles, Pakistan acted to acquire the United States as an ally.

The subsequent arming of India by Soviet, European, and U.S. sources and the arming of Pakistan by the United States, China, and European nations reflect the decentralized and anarchic nature of the arms trade. Whether this trade (particularly after the termination of U.S. concessional aid and grants in the mid-1970s) is multidirectional or unidirectional has depended on the recipient's experience with the supplier.

Given the availability of several sources for the acquisition of arms, neither India nor Pakistan had to rely on a single supplier. In the case of Pakistan, given its unhappy experience with the United States, it sought to diversify after 1965. In a more general vein, less developed countries have become adept at exploiting the East-West rivalry in order to avoid becoming dependent on a single supplier. The countries of South and Southwest Asia have acquired weapons from a variety of sources. They have been willing to forgo the logistical-military advantages of interoperability for assured sources of supply—a tendency that some Western analysts decry as "irrational."

The countries of Southwest Asia were particularly well placed to pick and choose between supplies and suppliers, because their purchasing power (Iraq, Saudi Arabia, and Iran) multiplied manyfold after 1973. In fact, it can be argued that the rapid acceleration of the European share of the world's arms market has been a direct consequence of expanded arms transfers to Southwest Asia. From the viewpoint of the recipients, diversification offered not only assured supplies but also the availability of a wider spectrum of arms than any single source could or would offer.

Recipients have bought arms for several reasons: to enhance security;[4] to play a major role within their region—witness the desire of the shah to play the role of "policeman" in the Gulf; to ensure that the absence of advanced weaponry did not encourage others to jeopardize their vital interests in the region (the Saudis have felt strongly about just such a rationale for their policy of arms acquisition); to practice deterrence through a policy of maintaining an equilibrium of arms; the exploit the competition between the superpowers; to play off one supplier against another in order to obtain advanced weaponry; to achieve a level of military power commensurate with the economic stake they seek to safeguard, as in the case of Saudi Arabia;[5] to generate modernization and greater economic development (according to one analyst, India has decided to pursue such a strategy in the 1980s, and its military expenditures will rise to 5 percent of gross national product[6]); and to demonstrate their independence, particularly when arms acquisitions are fully paid for by the recipient.

IMPACT OF ARMS TRANSFERS ON RECIPIENTS

Before assessing the effects of arms transfers on the countries of South and Southwest Asia, it may be useful to review some widely accepted assumptions that dominate the literature on arms transfers. These assumptions will then be examined against three specific case studies of conflict—the Indo-Pakistani war of 1965, the Indo-Pakistani war of 1971, and the Iran-Iraq war since 1980—in order to determine how arms transfers actually affected the conflicts, the stability of the domestic systems, and individual attitudes toward the involvement of the superpowers.

Some of the most widely accepted assumptions concerning the effects of arms transfers on recipients hold that the transfer of state-of-the-art, highly sophisticated weapons to the Third World fosters a propensity toward military solutions for regional tensions; the "lower the arms level, the lower the likelihood of war;"[7] arms transfers are a major factor in the emergence of regional powers; major arms sales and military modernization are unnecessary for genuine security or the economic needs of the recipient country; arms transfers "feed local arms races, create or enhance regional instabilities;"[8] transfers of sophisticated weapons destroy all hopes for restraint and "make any war that occurs more violent or destructive;"[9] arms transfers increase the "tendency for outside powers to be drawn in" to regional conflicts;[10] arms transfers create a "white-collar mercenary phenomenon;"[11] and arms transfers threaten the stability of domestic systems and are no insurance against internal instability.

CASE STUDIES

> One characteristic of the South Asian sub-system is that relations between its major states are highly militarized. Cause and effect are intertwined, and one cannot say for sure whether the Cold War led to this development or that it was simply an outgrowth of purely regional hostilities.[12]

This statement is representative of the state of affairs prevailing in the subcontinent. Scholars who lament that external assistance, in particular U.S. arms transfers to Pakistan, are responsible for the Indo-Pakistani hostility have taken on burdens that are not really theirs. Their mea culpa attitude stems perhaps from the feeling that a superpower does (and must always do) something. If it does not achieve anything "positive," then surely it must take responsibility for the "negative" results.

Arms transfers to South Asia were undoubtedly important to the recipients. In fact, their enormity reflects the importance the superpowers attached to South Asia. Thus, between 1954 and 1965, the United States supplied Pakistan with more than $630 million in its grant-military assistance program (MAP), $619 million in defense support assistance, and $55 million in concessional and cash sales. India was supplied $90 million through MAP and purchased $50 million in arms from the United States during the same period; but it bought and received a great deal more from Britain, France, and the Soviet Union.

Pakistan depended on the United States for about 80 percent of its arms in 1965 (a percentage that declined to 30 percent by 1974).[13]

Virtually the entire Pakistani air force and the army were equipped with U.S. weapons. Given this extraordinary dependence, it would seem reasonable to extrapolate that all of the worst fears built into the assumptions on the arms transfers were played out in the Indo-Pakistani war of 1965.

There were important changes in the pattern of arms transfers to Pakistan after 1965. The primacy of the United States as supplier ended with the arms embargo. Islamabad's brief flirtation with Moscow resulted in $30 million in arms, but Beijing stepped in to meet the more basic needs.

The 1971 Indo-Pakistani war was the result of India's exploitation of a number of Pakistani miscalculations and grave errors. The Pakistani military government's acquiescence to the political demand for a free and fair election and the failure of the political elite to abide by the results of the ensuing election brought on the war.

On the surface, all of the assumptions regarding the impact of arms transfers seemingly also apply to the participants in the Iran-Iraq war. Iran's imports of arms speeded up after Richard Nixon's visit to Tehran in May 1972, when the U.S. president made "the key (arms) sales decision" of his presidency.[14] In 1973, Iran imported $526 million in arms from the United States. By 1977, the corresponding amount had risen to $5.7 billion. In 1975, Iran imported more than all countries of South and Southwest Asia combined. It rapidly developed a qualitative advantage over its neighbors with the acquisition of American F-4s, F-14s, British Chieftain tanks, Hovercraft, Italian Sea Killer Mk2 ship-to-ship missiles, and other equipment. Iraq, too, intensified its acquisitions after 1974. By 1978, Iran's total armed forces equaled 413,000 armed with 1,870 tanks and 459 combat aircraft. Comparable figures for Iraq were 212,000 men, 1,900 tanks, and 339 combat aircraft. The goal of Iran and Iraq, as they proceeded to arm themselves, heavily overlapped with the security of interests supplying states.[15]

In order to gauge the actual effect of arms transfers on the policies of recipient countries and to demonstrate the fallacy of some widely held assumptions, let us examine the assumptions individually.

Assumption 1: The transfer of state-of-the-art, highly sophisticated weapons fosters a propensity toward military solutions for regional tensions.

Two points have to be made at the outset regarding the Indo-Pakistani war of 1965. First, India and Pakistan also fought their first war, in 1948, over Kashmir, prior to the commencement of any arms transfers. Second, although in the late 1950s–early 1960s there was a limited transfer of relatively modern U.S. weapons to Pakistan, for example, Patton tanks and light attack jet bombers, it can hardly be said that Pakistan initiated the 1965 war (by moving its infiltrators across the cease-fire line into India-controlled Kashmir) because it possessed a preponderance of highly sophisticated arms. A careful reading of the Pakistani record shows that President Ayub-Khan moved against India not because he had acquired sophisticated weapons but because he feared that the United States was becoming less interested in Pakistani security and was preparing to downgrade the quality and the quantity of future arms transfers.[16] Thus, in the Indo-Pakistani war of 1965, we can say the recipient's key perception was that the supplier would no longer sustain the balance of power equilibrium (the existence of a 5:1 balance in India's favor in 1965 constituted the equilibrium) that had deterred/prevented a war from 1948 to 1965.

The disparity between Indian and Pakistani military capability and readiness was even greater in 1971. The Indians had received huge quantities of war matériel from the USSR just prior to their move into East Pakistan. Yet this weaponry was not the cause of the conflict, it merely provided overwhelming force to an already preponderantly powerful Indian military machine. Overlapping interests between the Soviets and the Indians led to the Indo-Soviet treaty of August 1971. The temptation to "teach Pakistan a lesson" and the desire to put a crimp in the fledgling Sino-American rapprochement were the real root causes from the Indian side, and not arms transfers.

The cruelty of Pakistan's military government against its people in East Pakistan, not the prevalence of sophisticated arms, was also a critical factor in the onset of war. It triggered a massive response by a defiant population to inhumane treatment at the hands of its own government, which India exploited, and the result was the secession of East Pakistan and its recasting into Bangladesh.

Arms transfers to Iran are generally assumed to have initiated the shah's propensity for aggressive behavior toward the countries of the Gulf. Yet a look at the specific facts proves otherwise. As early as 1963, the shah undertook the development of Kharg Island as the major outlet for Iranian oil export in recognition of the vulnerability of Abadan. In 1971, Iranian forces occupied two strategically important islands located at the entrance of the Persian Gulf—the Tunbs and Abu Musa. Military muscle was accompanied by diplomatic dexterity, so that by 1972 the shah had acquired the reputation of being the region's policeman. The catalyst for this development was the announced withdrawal of Britain from the Gulf; this preceded Iran's massive arms buildup, which came after 1973. In other words, the policy launched by the shah was firmly in place by the time enormously increased oil revenues enabled the Iranian monarch to pay for major purchases of new weapons. The vast and sophisticated arsenal subsequently accumulated by Iran strengthened a policy already on track and did not create it.

The Algiers accord of March 1975 seemingly settled the old dispute between Iran and Iraq over the Shatt-al-Arab boundary. But Iraq smarted under the shah's success in establishing the Thalweg principle and bided its time to undo a compromise that it had accepted in return for Iran's termination of support for the Kurds seeking autonomy from it. So long as the shah maintained control and Iranian military strength was substantial, Baghdad did not move against Iran. However, with the onset of the Iranian revolution, the fall of the shah, the chaos of Iran's domestic scene, and the purge of the Iranian army, Iraq seized the opportunity to settle old scores. But Baghdad miscalculated, believing that Iran's isolation from its chief source of sophisticated arms, the United States, meant a vastly weakened military, making the moment propitious for controlling the entire Shatt-al-Arab.

Assumption 2: The lower the arms level, the lower the likelihood of war.

It can as easily be argued that in the case of India and Pakistan, initial fears presaged the growth in arms levels, and not the other way round. Since partition in 1947, the record of suspicion and hostility is manifest in pronouncements of the elite. Each perceived the other as its principal threat. Pakistan, the smaller, more disorganized, and less well-equipped nation, feared Indian supremacy. Its search for arms was merely an expression of its insecurity and of its effort to deter a feared attack by India.

If anything, Iraq's attack on Iran in September 1980 is not an example of conflict arising from higher level of arms. On the contrary, and more likely, it was a consequence of Iraqi perceptions of a lowered level of Iranian military capability resulting from the chaos following the Iranian revolution of the preceding year.

Assumption 3: Arms transfers are a major factor in the emergence of regional powers.

On the surface, the above seems to be a reasonable assumption. However, on closer scrutiny, a number of problems emerge. First, although the existence of a relatively large, modern, and well-equipped military establishment constitutes an element of national power, it cannot be argued conclusively that it alone accounts for a country emerging as a regional power. Other factors–for example, economic assets, population, and system cohesiveness (national integration)–also contribute to the actual and potential power base of a nation and to its status within a region. Second, in a world where arms transfers carry a large and mostly nonconcessional price tag, the purchasing power of a nation determines the quantity and quality of arms transfers. In the absence of a nation's ability to pay (that is, a low economic base), its ability to acquire arms in quantities large and sophisticated enough to buttress its regional position is invariably circumscribed. Third, is it not plausible to postulate that the recipients of major arms transfers are those countries that already have the necessary political clout and thus are already perceived to be regional influentials, for example, India even before 1965? On the other hand, Pakistan, though able to receive arms because of its strategic location and importance to the United States, never enjoyed the status within the region that India did, not even during the heyday (1954-65) of U.S. arms transfers to it. Therefore, relatively speaking, India was always considered *the* regional power in South Asia, and this, incidentally, gave it easier access to the arsenals of the world.

Diplomatically, the shah had begun to play an important role in the Gulf before the 1973 oil embargo resulting from the Arab-Israeli war gave him extraordinary economic clout. The vacuum left by the receding British presence offered the shah a chance to dominate events in the Gulf region. Arms transfers merely supplemented a policy that became increasingly viable after 1969.

Assumption 4: Major arms sales and military modernization are unnecessary for genuine security or the economic needs of the recipient country.

The UN charter recognizes the right of states to self-defense. Insecurities stemming from perceptions of threat impel Third World states to arm, much the same as developed countries do. It is indeed true that the poorer nations of the world cannot afford the burden of military expenditures, but those with antagonistic neighbors and a history of conflict feel they cannot afford not to spend on arms.

If the yardstick of relevance of weapons systems is applied to the need for genuine security argument, the Indo-Pakistani wars demonstrate that the acquisition policies of the belligerents were well suited to their strategy. That is, given the predominantly land-based strategy of war, each side quickly moved to acquire control over the other's territory in order to prevent warfare from spreading to its own territory.

War is obviously a diversion of scarce economic resources. Few nations can really afford to go to war, and it is indeed costly business. Yet war remains a recurring phenomenon in international relations because in the larger interests of states (here a chance to detach Kashmir from India) the price is worth paying. There are other and more specific considerations that impinge on Pakistan as the initiator of the 1965 war. From the outset, the Pakistani military leadership had made it clear to the United States that arms aid would have to be accompanied by economic assistance, not only indirectly through defense support assistance but directly through the five-year economic development plans. Thus it can be postulated that Washington's interest in Pakistan's security led to arms transfers and also resulted in U.S. support for Pakistan's economic welfare. Consequently, Pakistan was made more secure economically than would otherwise have been the case.

The Iranian experience demonstrates the difficulty of testing this assumption, because Iran was in the peculiar position of being able to afford both guns and butter.

The shah wanted to make Iran a major power in a variety of ways, not the least of which was economic. The assumption that economic resources were wasted and economic development was arrested by arms purchases cannot account for the demise of the Pahlavis. Perhaps the shah fell precisely because he put too much emphasis on economic development and wanted it too rapidly. The result was a major dislocation of traditional values and lifestyles. Massive investment in economic development increased corruption and heightened resentment against a regime in which seemingly everyone was on the take. The trickle-down theory of economic improvement ran up against a powerful religious establishment reluctant to move Iran beyond the nineteenth century. It was one man's vision against another's. Arms did not heighten the confrontation, and proof is found in the fact that the shah did not let loose his military machine against his opponents.

Assumption 5: Arms transfers fuel local arms races and create or aggravate regional instabilities.

Arms transfers are the symptom of local rivalries, not the creators. As has already been argued, it was the continued existence of Indo-Pakistani rivalry and the prospect of future conflict that led India and Pakistan to seek arms. In addition, Indian perceptions of a larger role required a respectable military posture. After all, the subcontinent cannot be really that different from the Western world of which it was so long an appendage. There is no better proof that

Assumption 5 has little salience to the 1965 war than the fact that Indo-Pakistani rivalry continued despite arms embargoes by the superpowers. Even in the case of Pakistan, which was particularly hard hit by the U.S. arms embargo, the rivalry did not dissipate. Instead, it was played out in different ways. As one analyst noted:

> The virtual termination of American arms assistance since 1965 has not meant a freeze or even a pause in the arms race between India and Pakistan; both have been able to find other patrons and arms donors, or—as in the Indian case—have also undertaken a program of self-sufficiency in weaponry.[17]

Arguments for the competitive nature of the Indo-Pakistani relationship made earlier are also applicable to the 1971 war. In relative terms, the 1966–71 period was one of reduced levels of arms transfers as compared with the 1954-65 or 1972-80 period. Therefore, if we place the blame for regional instability on the transfer of arms, the 1966–71 period should have been the most quiescent. Indeed, this was not the case. Despite the "spirit of Tashkent," which normalized Indo-Pakistani relations after the 1965 war, regional instability remained. The demise of the Ayub regime resulted, in part, from the discrediting of Pakistan's pro-U.S. policy of which Ayub was the chief architect. The rationale that such a policy was desirable because it provided access to arms was wiped out by the imposition of the American embargo on arms transfers to Pakistan. Hence, to a certain extent, the fall of Ayub, which was a precursor to regional instability leading up to the 1971 war, was a consequence of considerably diminished U.S. transfers of arms.

On the Indian side, the death of Lal Bahadur Shastri at Tashkent in January 1966 brought Indira Gandhi to power. Thereafter, New Delhi reacted to the deteriorating situation in East Pakistan according to the proclivities of Mrs. Gandhi. After all, she was not bound by her predecessor's commitment to the Tashkent agreement. When a target of opportunity for dismembering Pakistan presented itself, she moved swiftly. Thus, the rivalry between India and Pakistan, which characterized the tenure of the first Nehru and preceded arms transfers to the region, once again played itself out in war.

In the case of Iran, and for quite a few countries in South and Southwest Asia, the growth in Iran's stature offered a measure of protection. The shah helped the sultan of Oman defeat the Dhofari rebellion. He also helped President Daud of Afghanistan move to settle his differences with Pakistan, offering the lure of a $2.5 billion economic package toward Afghan development. Today, despite the fact that Iran no longer receives arms transfers of any significance, its policies exacerbate regional instability.

Assumption 6: Transfers of sophisticated weapons end all hopes for restraint and make any war that occurs more violent or destructive.

Applied to the 1965 war, Assumption 6 does not hold true. This statement reflects a tendency on the part of Westerners to assume that non-Westerners have been nurtured in a more violent milieu and therefore do not understand the notion of restraint.

India and Pakistan fought extensively in 1965, but the rules of engagement under which each operated precluded indiscriminate use of force. For example, despite the proximity of population centers to the front, both sides refrained from bombing civilian targets. Such destruction, when it occurred, was more a result of poorly judged distance or mistaken targets than of deliberate excess. Additionally, it can be argued that arms transfers actually reduced the duration and scope of the 1965 conflict by controlling the sophistication of weapons and withholding resupply.[18]

The full force of the rather extensive arsenals of India and Pakistan was not brought to bear in the 1971 war. Once again, civilian targets in both countries were largely spared. The level of escalation was kept reasonably controlled, and the 1971 war was not nearly as nasty and destructive as the capability of the belligerents might have suggested.

This assumption has thus far also not proven to be correct in the conduct of the Iran-Iraq war. Arms transfers in and of themselves do not make the final difference. Leadership, training, and morale are critically important to any war effort. According to an analyst of the war, to "train, expand and modernize simultaneously is difficult for even the most advanced armies to manage; it is an almost impossible task for most developing nations."[19] Neither side has made indiscriminate use of its war resources; indeed, both belligerents have carefully husbanded them.

Iraq, as the initiator of the conflict could have been expected to move with the best of its ground and air equipment to defeat the Iranians quickly and conclusively. But despite gains at al-Ahvaz, Dezful, Khorram-Shahr, Mehran, and Qasr-e-Shirin, the Iraqi thrust slowed down in the face of unexpected Iranian resistance and a conscious decision by the Baath leadership to withhold its best equipment, keep its most modern aircraft away from the war (often seeking sanctuary in third countries), and avoid battle in the cities in order to keep casualties low.[20] The war on the ground was fought at levels of intensity well below the capability of available equipment, some of it as a result of ineptness and much (especially on the Iraqi side, which was not handicapped in trained manpower) because of a conscious decision. Consequently

> Neither country was able to bring its sophisticated ground attack weapons up to maximum effectiveness. For example, Iraq used the Frog-7 and Scud-B surface-to-surface missile on two occasions, both in the vicinity of Dezful. The TOW and Dragon antitank missiles in Iran's inventory saw little action, not even in Khuzistan where the line of sight visibility required by these weapons was excellent.[21]

Neither Iraq nor Iran used its aircraft to carry the war into enemy territory in order to inflict heavy damage, confining attacks primarily to cratering airfield runways. Low priority was assigned by both sides to using their air force in support of ground operations. Violent damage did not occur (despite arms transfers), even though the failure of early warning and command and control mechanisms made airspace violations easy and both sides had difficulty operating their air defense gun systems. In addition, "the surface-to-air missile systems of Iraq (SA-2, SA-3, and SA-7) and of Iran (Hawk, Rapier, Tigercat) were uniformly noneffective."[22]

The conduct of the Iran-Iraq war indicates a level of violence and destruction far below what a comparison of their arsenals suggest is possible. The correlation between arms and violence is weak in the Iran-Iraq war for the following reasons: First, a conscious decision was made by both parties to limit indiscriminate use of force to avoid full-scale bombing of civilian targets, and Iraq's decision to avoid battles in cities. Second, there was an inability on both sides to "design and conduct an interdiction or rational strategic bombing campaign."[23] Their inability to operate sophisticated equipment limited the actual level of violence, although the potential for destruction based on weapon system capability was high. And third, much of the war effort on ground, at sea, and in the air revolved around the problem of resupply.

Assumption 7: Arms transfers increase the tendency for outside powers to be drawn into regional conflicts.

Although arms transfers create a stake in the recipient for the supplier, the effect is not always detrimental. In the 1965 Indo-Pakistani war, it worked to shorten the conflict through the institution of an arms embargo. The United States, which as an ally could have been expected to get drawn in directly, was not. U.S. Secretary of State Dean Rusk (when asked by Pakistan to provide more tangible support to the war effort) said that Washington would not get involved, because "it was being asked to be in on the crash landing when it was not in on the take-off" (a reference to Ayub's initiation of infiltration into Kashmir).

The involvement of the Soviet Union in the 1965 conflict came in January 1966, when, for the first time in a Third World conflict, Moscow committed its prestige to a mediation effort and brought the belligerents to the negotiating table at Tashkent. Thus, whether or not outside powers get involved depends on their perceptions of gain or loss, and not on the extent of arms transfers. Involvement results from a variety of factors and is not simply a consequence of arms transfers.

The phenomenon of arms transfers is usually indicative of a larger interest by the supplier in the recipient. When concessionality is involved, it signifies commitment and recognition of the recipient's importance to the supplier. In other words, it is the commitment that draws in the outside power or powers. Arms transfers then become an important tool, but only one of a variety of existing tools in the interaction between states.

The assumption under examination does not hold true for the 1971 war either. The three major arms suppliers were the People's Republic of China, the USSR, and the United States. For China, arms transfers became a convenient substitute for participation. In 1965, Beijing gave less in the way of war matériel because the American-oriented Pakistani military establishment could only utilize limited types of Chinese hardware. Therefore, in the absence of arms transfers, China had to find other ways of demonstrating its commitment to Pakistan. One way was to become more openly drawn into the Indo-Pakistani conflict. China went so far as to threaten direct military involvement against India on their common frontier, opening up the possibility of a second front for New Delhi. By 1971, the situation had changed. The Sino-Soviet dispute precluded direct risk taking. Hence, China joined the other powers who regularly substituted arms transfers for alliance or even direct intervention. Bruised feelings in Islamabad were placated with accelerated shipments of small arms and spare parts. By 1971, China had enough of a stake in arms supply in Pakistan that it could substitute arms transfers usefully for intervention and still maintain Pakistani goodwill.

Moscow's stake in the Indian armament was even more crucial and substantial in 1971. Demonstrably, arms were a critical component in Indo-Soviet relations in the weeks preceding the war. Once India moved into East Pakistan, the Soviets continued to pour in supplies far in excess of Indian needs against the poorly equipped Pakistan army in the eastern province. Given overwhelming Indian preponderance, enhanced by fresh infusions of arms transfers from the USSR, there was no need for Moscow to intervene directly. In fact, the transfer of arms kept Moscow out because it prevented China from intervening in support of Pakistan by signaling the extent of Moscow's commitment to the Indian cause. Chinese intervention was risky and carried the threat of a Soviet move against China.

The much touted example of U.S. involvement in the 1971 war is highly overrated. The sailing of the U.S.S. *Enterprise* into the Bay of Bengal in the closing days of the conflict carried only limited risk of U.S. intervention. It mostly signaled concern over the possibility of the demise of an ally. The possibility of U.S. arms transfers to Pakistan was moot in 1971 because of the intensity of anti-Pakistan feeling in the U.S. Congress and in the media. Because arms transfers are perceived as signaling a tangible and visible commitment in the subcontinent, the unavailability of this important tool led President Nixon personally to order one of the few alternatives open to him, namely, the move of the U.S. navy task force into the Bay of Bengal.

At the outset of the Iran-Iraq war, fears were voiced in the region and by the United States that the war would create conditions that could be exploited by the Soviet Union. The USSR's treaty with Iraq, the disintegrating situation within Iran, and Iranian isolation–all aroused concern over a major Soviet thrust. Yet the stubborn refusal of the Khomeini regime to seek direct outside assistance, along with its dogged determination to fight on, limited opportunities for direct intervention. Both parties to the war found their own peculiar set of supporters, for example, Saudi Arabia and Kuwait assisted Iraq with funds, and Moscow and Israel offered their hand to Tehran. Iran's war machine put up a reasonable fight. Along with the Pasadran, the revolutionary guard militia, Iran put up a sufficient fight on its own with outside assistance confined to supply of some critically needed spare parts and medical supplies. The final disintegration of Iran, which seemed a distinct possibility in September 1980, did not take place, thus limiting chances of external power intervention.

Assumption 8: Arms transfers create a "white-collar" mercenary phenomenon.

In 1965 and 1971, India and Pakistan possessed a substantial military establishment. The U.S. presence in Pakistan was mostly confined to MAAC, and it essentially ended with the imposition of the 1965 arms embargo. Similarly, although Indian purchases and other acquisitions from the East and the West meant that foreign training and advisory teams were necessary, it was hardly a "white-collar mercenary" phenomenon.

Iran, on the other hand, imported large numbers of foreign advisers and trainers in the country. The purchase of huge quantities of sophisticated weapons beyond Iran's capacity to operate ensured continued need for foreign training programs. Yet, as the war with Iraq demonstrated, dependence on foreign personnel to operate the most lethal weapons systems turned out to be a blessing. Inability to operate sophisticated weapons to their maximum capability limited the capacity of Iran and even Iraq to inflict heavy and crippling damage on each other had they desired to do so. Once foreign advisers were withdrawn, the level of expert advice, training, and maintenance dropped off even more sharply. Thus, by supplying weapons far beyond the absorption capacity of oil-rich recipients, the suppliers not only made huge sums of money but, in the final analysis, retained control over performance.[24]

Assumption 9: Arms transfers threaten the stability of domestic systems and are no insurance against internal instability.

The question of stability goes beyond the discussion of the 1965 war. Assumption 9 has greater applicability for Pakistan, as the immediate stability of the political system is less of a problem for India.

Opponents of arms transfers use system instability as an index of political dissatisfactions resulting from uneven development between the military and civilian realms. Pakistan is cited as a state where the military is unrepresentative in its composition. It is also preponderantly powerful vis-a-vis the political system.

A close look at the evolution of Pakistan and the course it followed after independence reveals a much more complicated picture. The declining credibility of the political elite affected its performance long before any arms transfer tilted the balance in favor of the military. The death of Mohammad Ali Jinnah, the founder of Pakistan, shortly after partition, and the assassination of the first prime minister, Liaquat Ali Khan, started a scramble for power that lasted until the first military coup in 1958. Unlike neighboring India, the absence of sensible and sustained political leadership made Pakistan a very unstable political system. Under such circumstances, arms transfers were not the catalyst but only a contributing factor leading to the supremacy of the military. In a system where the notion is that of "security above all else" because of hostile neighbors, it is futile to go around breast-beating and decrying the fact that "defense expenditures in Pakistan increased rather than decreased because of U.S.

assistance."[25] There is little proof that such increases might not have occurred anyway. In fact, a case can be made that Pakistan's military versus economic and political development may have been even more lopsided without U.S. assistance, leading to even greater instability.

Arguments blaming all the follies of a nation on arms transfers are simplistic and unrealistic. Faux pas were committed long before arms transfers became an international phenomenon and are likely to continue even if strict controls against transfers are implemented internationally. Events in Pakistan throughout 1971 are classic examples of mistakes and miscalculations of a regime that, like the Bourbons of France, "learnt nothing and forgot nothing."

War became a fait accompli once the Yahya regime moved brutally against the East Pakistani population. Details of how all of this occurred are not to be dwelt on here,[26] but the fact remains that the threat to Pakistan's internal stability was a function of the inability of its West Pakistani political elite to work out an acceptable blueprint for the sharing of power with the East Pakistani leadership.

Apart from arguments already advanced regarding Assumption 9, one can state that the arms transfers that enabled Iran to fight off the Iraqi attack made Iran more stable. The war helped the faltering Iranian regime arrest its declining control as it sidetracked the Iranian populace from the economic dislocations of the revolution. It also set aside the ethnic divisions emerging within Iran by focusing on Iranian nationalism. That wars often enhance political fortunes of regimes in power and create national unity is not a phenomenon confined solely to the Third World.

DO ARMS TRANSFERS MAKE A DIFFERENCE TO THE POLICIES OF THE RECIPIENTS?

The following generalizations emerge from the three conflicts examined in this chapter:

1. Recipients of major arms transfers occupy regions of major conflict.
2. Volatility leads to arms transfers, and not vice versa.
3. Arms transfers preclude the need for direct supplier intervention in conflicts and also give a semblance of independence to recipients who are sensitive toward superpower involvement.
4. Recipients buy arms for reasons of prestige plus performance. State-of-the-art weapons are perceived as offering the ultimate protection.

5. Advanced weapons function best as a deterrent. In actual war, they are not used directly or fully, thereby limiting the level and intensity of conflict.

6. Nontechnological recipients cannot end reliance on suppliers unless they master the training, maintenance, and spare-parts cycle.

7. The impact of arms transfers on the risk-taking propensity of recipients is limited unless preceded by other (political, economic, diplomatic) developments and opportunities. When applicable, the propensity for risk taking follows decline (actual or anticipated) in arms transfers.

8. The stability of South and Southwest Asia will largely depend on the resolution of the domestic political and economic difficulties of the various countries. However, arms transfers will continue to be made so long as supplier competition makes controls difficult to impose and recipient fears make controls impossible to negotiate.

IMPLICATIONS FOR SUPPLIERS

This chapter suggests that the arguments against arms transfers by opponents are not convincing. In fact, those who voice concern over arms sales may be focusing on the wrong problems of the recipient. The study of the arms policies of Iran, India, and Pakistan, major arms recipients, suggests the following:

First, suppliers must not generalize about the motivations of all recipient countries. The impact of arms transfers is not uniformly the same on all countries.

Second, suppliers will have to acknowledge that recipients may have certain legitimate security concerns. Thus, as suppliers press to convince recipients that their eventual security depends on a successful resolution of internal political power sharing and economic problems, concomitantly the suppliers must be prepared to share the burden of maintaining external security. Failing that responsibility, recipients will have no choice but to go on putting undue emphasis on arms transfers.

Third, agreement on restraint must be shared by all suppliers. Unilateral arms control policies are unlikely to succeed.

Finally, if the desire for arms control is to result in reducing arms transfers to the Third World, major suppliers must begin to offer regional solutions to security problems. For example, arms transfers to either India or Pakistan cannot be divorced from the overall security issues dealing with the entire subcontinent. In the absence of peaceful relationships between key neighbors, it is unrealistic to expect success in achieving significant arms control.

NOTES

1. Leslie H. Gelb, "Arms Sales," *Foreign Policy*, no. 25 (Winter 1976–77): 5.

2. For example, Andrew Pierre, *The Global Politics of Arms Sales* (Princeton, N.J.: Princeton University Press, 1982); and Philip Farley, Stephen Kaplan, and William Lewis, *Arms Across the Sea* (Washington, D.C.: Brookings Institution, 1978).

3. Stephanie Neuman, ed., *Defense Planning in Less Industrialized States* (Lexington, Mass.: D. C. Heath, forthcoming). The countries studied are Egypt, Israel, Turkey, Saudi Arabia, Iraq, Pakistan, and India.

4. For a discussion of some of the paternalism inherent in Western attitudes toward arms transfers to the Third World, see Richard K. Betts, "The Tragicomedy of Arms Trade Control," *International Security* 5, no. 1 (Summer 1980): 80–110.

5. Ibid., p. 93.

6. Raju Thomas, "Defense Planning in India," in Neuman, op. cit.

7. Anne Hessing Cahn and Joseph K. Kruzel, "Arms Trade in the 1980's," in *Controlling the Conventional Arms Trade*, ed. Cahn, Kruzel et al. (New York: McGraw-Hill, 1977), p. 39.

8. Pierre, op. cit., pp. 3–4.

9. Ibid.

10. Ibid.

11. Gelb, op. cit., p. 17.

12. Stephen P. Cohen, "U.S. Weapons and South Asia: A Policy Analysis," *Pacific Affairs* 49, no. 1 (Spring 1976): 68.

13. Ibid., p. 52.

14. Quoted from an NSC staff member in Pierre, op. cit., p. 145.

15. Discussed in Shahram Chubin, *Security in the Persian Gulf: The Role of Outside Powers* (Montclair, N.J.: Allanheld, Osmun, 1982).

16. From Ayub's perspective, the decline of U.S. interest (which had started after the arming of India in 1962) was reflected in several actions, including the postponement of the aid-to-Pakistan consortium meeting and the cancellation by President Johnson of Ayub's impending visit to Washington. For details, see Shirin Tahir-Kheli, *The United States and Pakistan: The Evolution of an Influence Relationship* (New York: Praeger, 1982).

17. Cohen, op. cit., p. 56.

18. For a detailed discussion of the politics of resupply, see Robert E. Harkavy, "Arms Resupply During Conflict: A Framework for Analysis" (forthcoming).

19. William O. Staudenmaier, "A Strategic Analysis of the Gulf War," in *The Iran-Iraq War: Old Conflicts, New Weapons*, ed. Shirin Tahir-Kheli and Shaheen Ayubi (New York: Praeger, 1983).

20. Ibid.
21. Ibid.
22. Ibid.
23. Ibid.
24. Recognized by a key official in the Pentagon in the following way: "Like the Iranians, (the Saudis) have gorgeous facilities, fully stocked . . . but let's face it, they'll be run by contractors forever." Leslie Gelb, "The Mideast Arms Race: New Weapons, Old Fears," *New York Times*, January 24, 1982.
25. Cohen, op. cit., p. 54.
26. Details given in Tahir-Kheli, op. cit.

Part V

LOOKING AHEAD

9

Toward a U.S. Military Strategy for Southwest Asia

Keith A. Dunn

It is an understatement to say that a revolution in U.S. thinking about Southwest Asia has occurred since 1978-79. Less than a decade ago no one within the government really believed that U.S. vital interests were involved in the region. Other than periodic naval deployments to the Indian Ocean, U.S. forces were not extensively engaged in the area. Hardly anyone could imagine how or why the United States would ever commit its military forces in combat to defend American interests and objectives in the region. Similarly, in the academic community, very little attention or thoughtful writing concentrated upon Southwest Asia. To some extent, those who were involved in thoughtful research on the area were criticized by their colleagues as concentrating on an area of only marginal importance.

The collapse of the Pahlavi dynasty and the Soviet invasion of Afghanistan ended the U.S. decades-old policy of benign neglect. These two "catastrophies" have focused American attention more sharply on the politically unstable region of Southwest Asia than at any other time in the past. They have made it clear that the United States must do things differently if it is to counter the political and military vacuum that has developed in the region since 1978. However, there is still no consensus within the United States, among

---

The views, opinions, and/or findings contained in this report are those of the author and should not be construed as an official Department of the Army position, policy, or decision, unless so designated by other official documentation.

U.S. allies, or within the region on what exactly should occur. Particularly, no agreement exists on what U.S. strategy for Southwest Asia should be.

Part of the problem in developing a military strategy is that few people seem to understand its purpose or how one goes about developing a military strategy. Often, it seems, some observers see a military strategy as an opportunity to advocate the use of military force. This is not a strategist's primary purpose. Rather, his job is to understand U.S. interests and objectives, to interpret decisionmakers' political guidance, and to construct a viable military program (strategy and forces) that will allow a political decisionmaker to accomplish his stated objectives within the parameters of the given political guidance. Equally important, but often forgotten, it is a military strategist's responsibility to be the bearer of bad tidings and to inform policymakers when it is not feasible or practical to develop a military strategy that achieves objectives within available or projected resources.

This chapter will focus on developing a military strategy for Southwest Asia. First, it will address U.S. interests and objectives toward the region. Second, the broad principles (best interpreted as enduring statements of political guidance) that have shaped U.S. policy in its post–World War II global competition with the Soviet Union will be discussed. These principles are particularly important because they establish the larger framework of global U.S. interests that a military strategist must consider as he develops a regional military strategy. A military strategy that may achieve all U.S. interests and objectives in a particular region but contradicts global interests or makes it impossible to achieve objectives in other more important regions may be self-defeating. It is a fact of life that interests are often in conflict with one another. A military strategist, however, must ensure that his proposed military strategy does not needlessly exacerbate the inevitable friction that exists and, if possible, resolves or relieves the friction. Third, some of the current military strategies for dealing with U.S. military deficiencies in Southwest Asia will be examined and critiqued. Finally, the chapter ends with a discussion of some strategic guidelines that, if followed, will lead to the development of a military strategy for Southwest Asia that, I believe, is credible, realistic, distributional, and supportable by regional nations and the American public.

Aspects of the Soviet military threat will be considered throughout, but they will not be analyzed in great detail for two reasons: Several good military assessments have recently been completed emphasizing Soviet opportunities and capabilities, as well as the severe military constraints that Soviet forces face in the region.[1] Also, the existing and projected military threat is an important input into the development of military strategy (as are technology, opportunity, constraints, etc.), because without a military threat there would be very little need for a military strategy. Nevertheless, the threat alone should not determine a military strategy. A military strategy must be based upon the interaction among interests, objectives, and threats. A major problem in American history, however, is that too often this interaction does not occur. As John Lewis Gaddis has argued so correctly, "threats . . . [have] been allowed to determine interests, rather than the other way around."[2] If a strategist allows only the threat to drive his military strategy, he becomes the prisoner of his adversary's actions. Policy becomes reactive rather than deliberate because the military strategist has no independent standards to measure U.S. security and threats to security against other than the presence or nonpresence of an adversary's forces in a particular area. Therefore, in this discussion, U.S. interests and objectives will be the framework that guides the development of a military strategy for Southwest Asia. The threat, including Soviet capabilities and limitations, will be developed as required to show how the strategy needs to be operationalized in terms of forces and their deployment.

U.S. INTERESTS AND OBJECTIVES

The fundamental building blocks of strategy are the concepts of national interests and specific objectives to support the attainment of national interests. Essentially there are four fundamental national interests common to all nations: survival, protection of territorial integrity, maintenance or enhancement of economic well being, and promotion of a favorable world order. In order of priority, survival and protection of territorial integrity are the most vital national interests, and actions that jeopardize those interests should not be initiated lightly or occur haphazardly.

In most instances there is very little disagreement about national interests. They are stated at such a high level of abstraction that anyone can agree with them. However, one must avoid the temptation to eliminate a step in the strategy process by overlooking the broad national interests and to jump immediately to a discussion of regional objectives that policy and strategy are supposed to obtain. If a strategist fails to maintain a broad perspective—that is, an awareness of

U.S. national interests even if they are stated in a vague and often less than satisfactory manner in secretary of defense posture statements, secretary of state announcements, or even presidential State of the Union messages–he will often miss how the pursuit of a specific objective or a combination of regional objectives may conflict with broader national interests, making the defense of certain regional objectives not worth the risk.

America's primary objective, not only in Southwest Asia but also worldwide, is deterrence of Soviet or Soviet-sponsored aggression. Deterrence is the essential objective because military conflict, involving U.S., Soviet, or their primary allies' forces, will threaten the achievement of other U.S. objectives in the region. When forces are engaged in conflict, it is difficult, if not impossible, to achieve stability and peaceful solutions to problems and to ensure the flow of oil. Moreover, a nuclear escalation is a significant risk if deterrence fails in Southwest Asia.

Traditionally, U.S. interests are best served by an international order of stability. As a result, a second major U.S. objective in Southwest Asia has been the promotion of peaceful solutions to the myriad historical, cultural, religious, ethnic, ideological, and economic differences that make the region endemically unstable. The pursuit of this objective serves two specific purposes. First, it can help the United States avoid the unwanted situation where it might have to choose between parties in conflict and adversely affect other interests and objectives. In Southwest Asia, the classic situation that Washington wants to avoid is another Arab-Israeli war. Such an event is a no-win situation for the United States. Support of either side will have an adverse impact on other important objectives in the region. Second, peaceful solutions to regional problems limit Moscow's opportunities to expand its access. The Soviet political system offers few attractive features for the Arab nations of the region. The Southwest Asian regimes are predominantly monarchical, authoritarian, and Islamic; and they have few long-term commonalities with communism or the Soviet Union. As a result, Moscow's primary means of access to the region is its military power, particularly arms sales. To the extent that the United States can successfully pursue peaceful solutions to the regional problems confronting Southwest Asia, it supports the process of evolutionary versus revolutionary political change, limits the need of regional states to resort to violence, curtails Soviet access and influence, and forces Moscow to compete in areas (such as political and economic support) where it has few strong cards to play.

A third increasingly important objective is to ensure that Middle East-Persian Gulf oil will be available to the United States and, particularly, its allies. Following the Soviet invasion of Afghanistan, President Jimmy Carter stated that the United States would use "any means necessary, including military force" to secure its and its allies' interests in the oil-rich Persian Gulf region.[3] A change of administrations has led to no lessening of importance of this objective. If anything, the Reagan administration is committed to creating the military teeth that will allow the Carter Doctrine rhetoric to be operationalized.[4]

As we evaluate the importance of maintaining the flow of oil, one important caveat is important to keep in mind. It is hard to imagine, as some have suggested, that by the end of the century the United States may no longer require Persian Gulf oil.[5] However, even if this did occur, continued access to oil will remain an indirect vital interest of the United States.[6] If the flow of Persian Gulf oil ceased or the price became prohibitive, the United States would be affected, but, more significantly, this could totally disrupt the economies of Western Europe and Japan, given their energy dependence upon Persian Gulf oil. An economic collapse within Europe and Japan would make it virtually impossible to achieve U.S. national interests of maintaining or enhancing the U.S. economic well being. A major economic disintegration in either Western Europe or Japan also could have political repercussions on U.S. world-order interests. However, America's most vital interests—protection of territorial integrity and survival—would not be affected by a cutoff or even a reduction of the flow of Middle Eastern oil. This is an important distinction to keep in mind when we later examine alternative military strategies for Southwest Asia and propose a military strategy to obtain U.S. interests and objectives.

Fourth, since the end of World War II, containment of communism has been a U.S. objective. In Southwest Asia the primary concern has always been the Soviet Union, given its proximity to the region. The United States is specifically interested in keeping the USSR physically out of the region. Washington has used a variety of political, economic, and military instruments over the years to limit the expansion of Soviet political and military influence in the region and to ensure that U.S. allies and other friendly states in the region can resist Soviet coercive efforts.

Fifth, the United States is committed to the political survival and security of Israel. This objective more than any other demonstrates how the pursuit of one regional objective can conflict with the achievement of others. In addition, it indicates why a strategist cannot become too myopic and think of only one geographic area in developing a military strategy. For the purist, Israel is in the Middle East, not Southwest Asia. However, there is no doubt that the Arab nations of Southwest Asia perceive U.S. support for Israel as out of proportion to America's "true interests" in Southwest Asia (access to oil, survival of moderate Arab governments, and containment of Soviet expansion). A primary challenge for a military strategist is the requirement to develop a strategy that balances the objectives of maintaining Israel's security while still maintaining good political relations with the Arab states and access to oil.

NATIONAL STRATEGY

Once interests and objectives have been determined, the next step in the strategic process is to develop a national strategy: a plan for how to employ a nation's military, economic, political, and psychological tools to achieve its interests and objectives. In a perfect world, the president or someone acting for him, possibly the National Security Council, would provide rather specific policy guidance for how much emphasis each one of the tools of national power should receive. Also, those charged with developing specific military, political, economic, and psychological strategies as inputs to the national strategy would be told, before developing their strategies, what sorts of risks the national command authority would be willing to accept to achieve U.S. interests and objectives.

Unfortunately, all strategists must deal with an imperfect world. In the specific case of developing a military strategy, traditionally in the United States, the military strategist does not receive the specific policy guidance that he wants so badly and in fact needs until there is a crisis or a real possibility that U.S. forces may need to be deployed.[7] The reasons for this disconnect are numerous, but General Maxwell D. Taylor has succinctly summarized some of the most important causes:

> For one thing, busy senior officials capable of providing it are usually so engrossed in day-to-day tasks that they have little leisure for serious thought about the future beyond the next federal budget. Also, it is a risky business for a senior politician to put on public record an estimate of future events which, if wide of the mark, would provide ammunition to his adversaries. Similarly, a president who announces specific policy

> goals affords the public a measure of his failure if he falls short of his hopes. Hence it is common practice for officials to define foreign policy goals in the broad generalities of peace, prosperity, cooperation, and good will—unimpeachable as ideals but of little use in determining the specific objectives we are likely to pursue and the time, place, and intensity of our efforts.[8]

This writer accepts Taylor's observations as an inevitable, but lamentable, situation with which a military strategist must deal. This does not mean, however, that a military strategist has no concepts of political guidance upon which to build a strategy. Several enduring principles have guided U.S. policy in the post-World War II period: avoidance of superpower conflict, forward defense, security based on alliances and coalitions, a desire to contain conflicts at the lowest level of violence as is possible, and primacy of domestic issues. Until these principles are specifically rejected, they must be used as the basis for the development of military strategies in peacetime.

Because of the risk of nuclear escalation, the most enduring strategic principle that has guided not only American but also Soviet thinking and actions in the post-World War II period is avoidance of superpower conflict. Both nations have acted with extreme caution when it appeared that their forces might come into direct military contact. The inability to predict with any degree of accuracy what might occur if American and Soviet forces confronted each other has been sobering for Soviet and American policymakers alike. It should continue to affect and constrain U.S. and USSR actions for the foreseeable future.

Forward defense and security based upon alliances are two other principles that have guided U.S. policy in the postwar period. Over the years, the need for stationing U.S. troops overseas has been questioned (for example, the 1970s Mansfield amendments; the Carter decision to withdraw U.S. forces from Korea, which was ultimately reversed; and currently the revival of interest to examine the need for U.S. forces in Europe). This debate over forward deployment (as opposed to forward defense) will continue to be raised, particularly during years of domestic economic hardship. However, the idea of forward defense—facing an enemy somewhere else and not on U.S. territory—should continue to be a major element of U.S. strategic thinking.

Any future debate over forward defense will essentially occur over how the United States can best carry it out. Should the U.S. political and military strategy be based primarily on an alliance strategy, or should the emphasis be on going it alone to the best of U.S. abilities? Obviously, a unilateralist strategy places fewer restrictions upon the United States and makes a strategist's job easier. In an alliance all participants sacrifice a degree of sovereignty and independence of action because of the need to compromise and the requirement of the allies to agree that each one's interests are affected to the same degree before they are willing to commit forces to combat.

In the final analysis, the United States has few viable options but to continue an alliance strategy. The financial cost of trying to go it alone would be prohibitive. Moreover, it is impossible to return to a bygone era of fortress America. The United States can no longer, if it ever could, feel safe and secure in a world in which everyone is hostile or even neutral toward it. World order, economic well being, and even territorial integrity and survival interests would be threatened if Americans had to face a hostile world alone. Through alliance the United States is not only defending allies' interests, it is also defending its vital interests and objectives. Also, effective alliance structures are force multipliers enabling the United States militarily to balance Soviet military power. The United States needs allies' political support to achieve its military objectives.

A military strategist's recognition of the importance of alliances to achieve U.S. interests and objectives, however, must be balanced by an awareness that domestic, not foreign or security, issues are of primary importance to the American public. Except on rare occasions, presidents are elected because of their domestic programs. Incumbents may be defeated or, as in the case of Lyndon Johnson, forced to withdraw from running for office becasue their foreign policy or security programs have an adverse impact on domestic issues. But domestic issues, interests, and policies are the most critical concerns of the American public. Therefore, a strategist must recognize how his proposed military strategy may affect domestic issues and impact on political decision makers' willingness to support his military strategy.

As Amos Jordan and William J. Taylor have recently argued, Americans are generally an impatient lot and are irritated by complex issues and solutions:

> Americans believe that, with a little common sense and know-how, things can be done in a hurry. Neither protracted, limited war nor costly, sustained programs for military preparedness fit this temper of American mind. The initial public reaction to the necessity for the occupation of Germany following World War II was disillusionment;

> after all, the war was over. Stalemate at Korea's 38th parallel brought a similar public reaction in the 1950's.
>
> Impatience, as one of several variables of mood, combined with the aversion to violence, is highly likely to produce public outcry for cessation of American involvement in a prolonged conflict demanding self-sacrifice unrelated to any clear vision of overriding national interest.[9]

The strategist who asks a political policymaker to overlook these American tendencies does not serve his country well, but equally important he probably ensures that his military strategy will ultimately fail.

Finally, as was noted earlier, the primary U.S. objective is deterrence, from limited conflicts through strategic nuclear war. In pursuit of this objective, a primary principle, which traditionally has guided U.S. security policy, is the desire to limit the scope, intensity, and duration of conflicts when they occur. Particularly, U.S. policymakers have been interested in rapidly containing and terminating conflicts that involve Soviet or its allies' forces. Escalation—either vertically toward nuclear weapons or horizontally by geographic expansion of a conflict—is always a risk when Soviet forces are involved. Traditionally this is a risk that American policymakers have wanted to avoid.

There are some indications that the Reagan administration is not inclined to limit the geographic focus of conflicts when the USSR is involved. The merits and demerits of this approach will be examined in succeeding sections.

ALTERNATIVE MILITARY STRATEGIES

There have been a variety of nonmilitary proposals suggested for dealing with U.S. political-military deficiencies in Southwest Asia, such as stockpiling oil in order to reduce dependency and seeking political solutions to regional problems, thus limiting Soviet opportunities to meddle in Southwest Asian domestic politics. Few military strategists would argue against pursuing nonmilitary solutions to achieve U.S. interests and objectives. In fact, the military community is generally one of the strongest supporters of stockpiling oil.

The military strategist may very well encourage a decisionmaker to use whatever nonmilitary instruments that are available to achieve U.S. interests and objectives. However, in the final analysis, a military strategist's job is to develop a strategy and the forces that militarily will deter an aggressor and encourage adversaries to compete with the United States through political and economic means. He also is charged with the responsibility to develop a program to secure U.S. interests by force when other means fail. Although the military strategist can agree with those who see that direct Soviet military actions are the least likely threats and that the most pressing problems within Southwest Asia are internal threats to authority, ethnic clashes, endemic regional problems, etc., which beg for political and economic solutions, he cannot stop there if he is to do his job properly. Ultimately, the military strategist must answer two questions, and these are what separate him from the diplomat and the academic. The first is more long-term and a force development question: What strategy, types of forces, and deployment will deter the Soviet Union from using military force to threaten U.S. interests and objectives? The second is a more short-term operational question: If deterrence fails, how does the United States achieve its interests and objectives then?[10] This responsibility to look beyond deterrence is why the various economic and political solutions will not be addressed. Rather, we will now examine and critique four major military strategies for Southwest Asia that have been proposed since the fall of the shah and the invasion of Afghanistan: nuclear escalation in the theater, conventional tripwire, conventional defense, and geographic escalation outside the theater.

Nuclear Option

In physics there is a principle that for every action there is an equal reaction. A comparison between physics and security affairs is not the best of analogies, but given bureaucratic inertia that can impede change within organizations, there is still a tendency among nations and individuals to overreact when the status quo is altered radically. Before balance returns to policy or perceptions become more in tune with reality, the pendulum quite often swings between extremes.

In the case of Southwest Asia, one initial reaction to the collapse of the "two-pillar" strategy was a nuclear option. A Department of Defense study written to describe U.S. military options in the region after the fall of the shah and before the invasion of Afghanistan, which was leaked to the press, suggested as one option that "we might have to threaten or make use of tactical nuclear weapons" to stop a major Soviet invasion of Iran. According to press reports, the idea was to use nuclear weapons in the mountainous regions along the Soviet border and, if that failed, in the Zagros Mountains farther to the south of Iran in an attempt to block the advance of Soviet conventional forces.[11]

The primary assumption that pushed the Department of Defense study team to consider the use of tactical nuclear weapons was a belief that the USSR could get forces into the area much faster than could the United States. Faced with this belief, and with the political situation in Iran in near total chaos during 1979, the nuclear threat option appeared to be one way to fulfill Carter Doctrine pledges and maintain deterrence.

Conventional Tripwire

Conventional tripwire is an attempt to avoid the obvious bad connotations associated with early use of nuclear weapons and crossing the nuclear threshold. A conventional tripwire force essentially proposes to raise the stakes and risks for Soviet aggression by getting U.S. forces to an area rapidly and placing the escalation burden upon Moscow. It would not be able to defeat Soviet ground force divisions moving out of the Transcaucasus, North Caucasus, and Turkistan military districts. Rather, its objective would be to deter Moscow from giving the march order by creating a force that makes an attacker "believe that the attacked *may* retaliate. That is enough to deter."[12]

In an attempt to develop a strategy for the rapid deployment joint task force that would guide force development planning, Kenneth Waltz has articulated one of the better conventional tripwire philosophies. Waltz advocates the creation of an "asset-seizing, deterrent force" in contrast to a "war-fighting, defensive force" because a force designed for deterrence would be smaller, more mobile, less dependent upon allies, and thus better able to deploy rapidly. According to Waltz, in deterrence, getting there first is more important than having the ability to defeat a determined foe:

> Some depreciate the RDF by saying that "it will get there first with the least." But only that is required in order to implement a deterrent strategy against the Soviet Union. The effectiveness of a deterrent strategy depends on the credibility of theater and not on the ability to defend a position by force. Thus, the 4,500 American troops in West Berlin cannot defend the city; they are there for the sake of deterrence.[13]

Moreover, with a deterrent force and a strategy with deterrence as its primary objective, Waltz claims that the United States can avoid the problem of needing allies to fulfill U.S. objectives and interests, except for limited requirements. Collective action, he recognizes, contributes to deterrence by raising the risk for an aggressor. However, achieving unanimity within alliances is very complicated because allies seldom view threats in the same manner. When allies do not act together, this may adversely affect deterrence by reducing the credibility of the threat or the deterrent response. As a result, Waltz favors a strategy that would require little direct participation of allies in military operations.

Finally, Waltz argues that an "asset-seizing, deterrent force" or conventional tripwire would also deter the United States from proposing military options to solve essentially economic and political problems. Lacking strong enough forces to defeat the USSR, the U.S. military would not be tempted "to counsel preventive war" when it has a temporary military advantage. This constraint, Waltz believes, is an extremely important reason to choose a deterrent rather than a defensive force. If the military community has the capability to respond at will to Soviet threats, Waltz fears that the military's institutional bias will result in more rather than fewer military options being presented to the president.[14]

Conventional Defense

A third alternative is what Wohlstetter has called "meeting a conventional threat on its own terms."[15] This concept is essentially the opposite of Waltz's deterrence approach. It calls for defending U.S. interests and objectives in the region by having adequate forces available to defeat a Soviet aggression.

Two major proponents of this approach, Jeffrey Record and Albert Wohlstetter, differ widely on how to carry out a conventional defense. Record emphasizes a naval/maritime orientation with an emphasis upon maneuver warfare rather than a "firepower/attrition approach":

> What is needed is a small, agile force, based at and supplied entirely from the sea. The model must be Sir John Moore's (and later Wellington's) sea-based strike force hovering off the Iberian peninsula, not Westmoreland's sprawling military bureaucracy in Vietnam.[16]

Wohlstetter favors the increase of naval presence in the Indian Ocean.

However, he does not believe that a total naval/maritime orientation would be balanced or adequate. He proposes essentially a firepower/attrition strategy that would rely heavily upon the air force to interdict Soviet troop movements.[17]

Wohlstetter and Record also differ on the importance of allies to any U.S. military strategy in Southwest Asia. After making the obligatory bows toward the importance of allies, Record essentially adopts a unilateral intervention approach because, as he argues, "to stake the success or failure of an intervention force on the momentary political whims of local regimes in the Gulf serves the security interests of neither the United States nor the Western world as a whole."[18] On the other hand, allied support—particularly an ability for American planes to stage from air bases in Turkey—is critical to Wohlstetter's conventional defense proposal.

Despite these important differences, the advocates of a conventional defense agree on four major issues. First, keeping the oil flowing is significant, but keeping the Soviet Union out of the region is more important. Second, to "prevent the region from becoming forcibly dominated by a single power, be that power the Soviet Union, Iraq, or some other Gulf state," requires a forcible entry capability and a force strong enough to defeat and repel an aggressor.[19] Third, they want to defeat an aggressor in Southwest Asia, but at the same time be prepared to respond in other theaters if the conflict should escalate. Fourth, strong conventional defenses will keep the nuclear threshold high.

Geographic Escalation

The final alternative that has been proposed in recent years is geographic escalation, or war-widening. This idea initially appeared in the later stages of the Carter administration when it was searching for a way to execute the Carter Doctrine, but it has become most identified with the Reagan administration's defense policies.

A strategy of geographic escalation, or war-widening, essentially is based upon five major premises. First, the loss of strategic nuclear superiority has removed a major deterrent to Soviet aggressive behavior. As a result, the USSR is viewed as more brazen and willing to initiate military actions to threaten U.S. interests at any other time. Also, the loss of nuclear superiority is supposed to suggest that the United States has lost escalation dominance, meaning that the threat of nuclear conflict may no longer be perceived as a real threat by

Moscow.[20] Second, the points of most likely conflict with the USSR in the coming decade—the period when U.S. conventional and strategic nuclear vulnerability is supposed to be greatest—are in areas that are nearer to the Soviet Union than the United States. Here, the most often cited example is Southwest Asia. Third, many observers believe that any conflict with the USSR, particularly a naval conflict, will automatically escalate to global warfare.[21] Thus, the United States must begin with an assumption of global warfare and plan how to fight such a conflict. As Fred Ikle wrote just before he joined the Reagan administration, the Soviets need to be faced with the possibility that "the first campaign does not guarantee a successful ending for a global war."[22] Fourth, because the USSR is primarily a continental power, the best way to execute a war-widening strategy is through the use of U.S. naval power and exploitation of U.S. naval technological superiority over the Soviet Union. Fifth, given the buildup of Soviet conventional capabilities over the last 20 to 25 years and the decline in the American nuclear deterrent, the United States can no longer automatically assume that U.S. forces, even in conjunction with its allies, will be able to defeat the USSR at the primary point of tension.

Geographic escalation's appeal rests on its promise to increase U.S. options and deal with the issue of allies being reluctant to support U.S. initiatives in times of crisis. With geographic escalation, U.S. policymakers are no longer supposed to be tied to responding to the event and place of Soviet aggression. Rather than reacting, advocates of war-widening see the strategic initiative being returned to the United States. For example, some advocates of geographic escalation have suggested that, if the Soviet Union moved toward Persian Gulf oil, the United States could seize important Soviet outposts, such as Angola or Cuba. Others have suggested that the United States might want to consider carrying the battle to Soviet territory to blockade the Kola Peninsula or Vladivostok if the USSR should initiate further aggressive actions in Southwest Asia and the United States lacked the military power to stop Soviet forces at the initial place of aggression.

According to one school of thought, war-widening with a naval emphasis is supposed to handle reluctant allies by manipulating or forcing allies to accept U.S. positions and military strategy. This approach was best described in an article that Francis J. West, Jr., wrote before he joined the Reagan administration as the assistant secretary of defense for international security affairs. According to West, the defense of NATO and the Persian Gulf are intimately intertwined. The problem is that "NATO Europe as an alliance persists in ignoring this linkage."[23] NATO refuses to consider expanding its operational boundaries beyond the Tropic of Cancer. It continues to view the world through defensive, reactive eyes that focus on the Central Region to the exclusion of the rest of the world, when, in West's opinion, the most immediate threats to European security exist outside NATO, particularly in the Persian Gulf.

West suggests that adopting a maritime strategy—particularly one with a geographic escalation focus—will create a set of circumstances where NATO will be required to participate in a global war against the United States if Moscow should initiate direct military actions in the Persian Gulf. A strategy that links the Persian Gulf and NATO would demand that the United States be ready not only to fight in Southwest Asia to protect oil but also to reinforce Europe in the event of deterrence failure in the Persian Gulf. Because Europeans have a major role to play in European SLOC protection, it is inevitable, in West's view, that "NATO would be drawn into the naval combat."[24] This would cause NATO military to act outside its traditional boundaries of responsibility. This is why West believes that

> [The] US response to Soviet action in the Gulf should be one of horizontal escalation. In the global balance, the Soviet gain in the Gulf is overshadowed by the mobilization of the West and by the naval campaign. NATO reinforcement require movement at sea. Unlike land and tacair forces, the oceans are a medium without boundaries for separating antagonists. NATO agreement to reinforcement is an agreement to naval combat. NATO cannot stay out of a US-Soviet war because the naval threads are too intertwined.[25]

PRINCIPLES TO GUIDE SOUTHWEST ASIAN MILITARY STRATEGY

Any proposed military strategy, to have a reasonable chance of success, must satisfy four important criteria. It must be credible, realistic, distributional, and supportable, not only in military terms but also by allies and the American public. The four alternatives just discussed accomplish some of these criteria, but not all. In this section, we will critique the existing alternatives, suggesting where they fall short and propose initiatives that would make U.S. military strategy for Southwest Asia credible, realistic, distributional, and supportable.

Credibility

Credibility is the capacity to be believed, to suggest actions, proposals, strategies, etc., that others (friend and foe) will accept as plausible. Contrary to the arguments posed by Waltz, the naval unilateralists, and conventional defense advocates, such as Record, there are four major reasons why a credible strategy for Southwest Asia must begin with the basic principle that U.S. actions must be part of a collective response. First, as was noted earlier, alliances can adversely impact on deterrence by reducing the assurance of action. However, U.S. policy in the post-World War II period has been based on a coalition or alliance approach to security problems. In fact, one of the strongest cards that the United States has always claimed that it held in its competition with the Soviet Union was that its allies were assets, whereas Soviet allies have traditionally been political, economic, and military drains upon the Soviet Union. What the United States loses in flexibility by approaching problems in a collective manner is more than offset by the political, economic, and military contributions that allies make.

Second, although Americans generally find it hard to believe, there is a strongly held belief among some oil-producing states that the primary purpose of the rapid deployment joint task force is not to protect them but to seize oil in a crisis. A policy of collective response will not eliminate these concerns, but, as Dov Zakheim has argued, it "would mitigate some of the political sensitivities that the deployment of American forces in the Indian Ocean arouses among littoral states."[26]

Third, a commitment to collective response offers to create geographic escalation in ways that would be more credible to a Soviet defense planner than would the threat that the United States would seize Angola or Cuba or attack critical vulnerabilities if Soviet forces moved toward oil facilities. With French forces in Djibouti and British and Australian naval forces in the Indian Ocean, Moscow already faces the risk that any military actions in the region could not be localized. Whether or not it wants to, any Soviet military actions could draw extraregional nations other than the United States into a military conflict to protect forces already in the area. Expansion of existing combined military exercises among U.S., British, and Australian forces in the Indian Ocean, particularly if augmented by the formal participation of French forces, not only would enhance "the prospect of coordinated crisis response by the states involved" but also would complicate Soviet risk and military-balance assessments, thereby contributing to deterrence.[27]

Fourth, contrary to the claims made by naval unilateralists and geographic escalationists, even a war-widening strategy would require support from other nations. There is no doubt that the Soviet Union faces a variety of significant military vulnerabilities that can and should be exploited in the event of deterrence failure. One of the more often cited Soviet naval vulnerabilities is the lack of uninhibited access to the open seas, which makes the Soviet navy susceptible to choke-point interdiction. Each of the USSR's four fleets must transit critical international straits; if those straits were closed, the Soviet naval threat not only in Southwest Asia but worldwide would be virtually nonexistent, except for a brief war at sea. The problem is that now and in the future the United States requires not just allied military support but, more importantly, it needs allied political support if it has any hope of sealing the critical straits. Even if the United States had clear naval superiority over the Soviets, could fight simultaneously in multiple theaters, and would not need allies' military assistance as it does now to close various straits, without allied political consent those capabilities could not be executed in time of crisis. If Greenland, Iceland, and the United Kingdom refused to allow U.S. forces to use facilities and air and naval vessels to base out of their countries, it is hard to imagine how the United States would close the gap. Likewise, if Japan would not allow U.S. forces based in Japan to participate in operations to seal the Sea of Japan, how could the United States effectively deny Soviet access to the Pacific? The United States would need similar positive political decisions from Turkey and Sweden and Denmark before it could attempt militarily to close the Dardanelles or the Kattegat and Skagerrak areas.

Realistic Assumptions

A viable military strategy must be built on realistic assumptions. In the case of Southwest Asia one of the most important assumptions that will affect the development of a strategy and the forces to support it is the issue of strategic warning. If the assumption is that little or no strategic warning will exist, then the strategist is driven toward having sufficient forces in the region deployed well forward to defend until reinforcements arrive. On the other hand, an assumption that warning will exist makes it less of an imperative to have ground forces in place because time (how much, admittedly, is an issue of debate) to bring forces into a region, both to signal commitment as well as to defend objectives, should exist. Also, an assumption that sufficient strategic warning will exist to deploy forces into a region reduces the necessity to threaten nuclear escalation.

In the case of Southwest Asia, U.S. military strategy should be driven by an assumption that strategic warning will exist. Planning for strategic warning is a political necessity. In most states of the region, a U.S. ground force presence or even a large support presence to build the infrastructure for air bases or ground force staging areas would cause domestic political problems for the host nation, contribute to regional instability, and invite exactly the types of Soviet political and military meddlesome behavior that the United States wants to avoid. On the other hand, planning for strategic warning is a militarily realistic assumption. Soviet ground and naval forces in the region are not structured or postured for a "no-notice attack" or a "bolt from the blue" scenario.[28]

The low readiness status of the 25 Soviet ground force divisions in the Caucasus, Transcaucasus, and Turkestan military districts means that Soviet defense planners would have to augment those divisions with significant numbers of personnel and trucks from the civilian economy to make them combat ready. More than 60 percent of those divisions are Category III in readiness status. If one assumes that on any given day Category III divisions are manned between 25 and 33 percent, the Soviets would have to mobilize approximately 200,000 reservists to bring all divisions up to strength. This is no easy task, despite the claims of some advocates of Soviet short-warning attack scenarios, as Soviet record keeping on reservists is apparently not as good as we have assumed in the past.[29] Bringing divisions up to strength and "marrying" personnel with equipment in storage and trucks from the civilian economy take time. Moreover, personnel and equipment do not make an effective military unit. To do the latter requires some training to create unit cohesion. This is probably why on each of the recent occasions that the USSR has used its military forces as a blunt instrument to attain its interests and objectives—Czechoslovakia and Afghanistan—the Kremlin has taken months to build and prepare its forces before they were used.

Similarly, Soviet naval deployments in the Indian Ocean suggest that Moscow believes that a sufficient period of preconflict crisis would allow it to realign its naval forces and create a more favorable naval war-fighting capability in the region. At first glance, the normal peacetime deployment of 20 Soviet ships in the Indian Ocean is impressive. However, normally only four to five of the ships are surface combatants. In addition, the Indian Ocean squadron has very little offensive capability, power projection, or staying power. The squadron normally spends most of its time at anchor off the coast of Socotra Island performing surveillance and intelligence functions. As Bruce Watson has said in a recent book on the Soviet navy, the Indian Ocean squadron's "mission is primarily political."[30]

If the USSR would have any hope of neutralizing U.S. carrier task groups that have traditionally been deployed to the Indian Ocean when some regional crisis erupts to threaten U.S. interests and objectives, the squadron would have to be reinforced, and, as in the case of ground forces, this takes time. Assuming a cruising speed of 18 knots, it would take the Soviet navy 18 days to deploy ships from the Pacific Fleet. Submarines would take even longer. Deployments from the Northern Fleet via the Atlantic and Cape of Good Hope, a distance of 14,000 miles, would take more than 35 days. It would require nearly 30 days to reinforce the Indian Ocean squadron from the Mediterranean or Black Sea Fleet via a route through the Strait of Gibraltar and around the Cape of Good Hope. Moscow could reduce the deployment times from the Mediterranean or Black Sea if it used the Suez Canal. In a crisis, however, the latter route would be an extremely risky venture, given the narrow confines of the canal, the large French presence at Djibouti, and the poor political-military relations that currently exist among Moscow, Egypt, and Saudi Arabia.

All of this suggests that the United States will have some strategic warning. How much time, and, if the United States or regional nations will react to the warning, are the critical, unanswerable questions. However, if the political will does exist, for the United States to react effectively it must have the capability to deploy forces–ground as well as naval and air–once deterrence fails. In the case of naval strategic mobility forces (which are most important to the army), funds for building modern logistic support ships appear in the "out" years of the Reagan proposed five-year defense budget.[31] Unfortunately, the history of such programs actually being funded when it comes time to request the money is not all that good. Conversely, requests for two nuclear aircraft carriers appear in the FY 1983 budget. A 600-ship navy with 15 carrier battle groups would provide the United States with a capability to deploy an attack carrier in the Indian Ocean without drawing down forces from other theaters, as now must occur. This is an admirable goal. However, in a resource-constrained environment when defense budgets and particularly the survivability of large carriers are being questioned not only in Congress but also by serious students of naval strategy, it might be more practical to reexamine the priority of some U.S. defense programs before we invest $12 to $15 billion per carrier task group. Specifically, in the case of Southwest Asia more attention should be given to sea and air mobility assets. Logistics and strategic mobility questions are not high-visibility projects in comparison to $3.5 billion for aircraft carriers, $12 to $15 billion for carrier task groups, $30 to $40 billion for the B-1 program, or $35 to $50 billion for the MX program. However, in the long run, the ability to get divisions from the east coast of the United States to the Persian Gulf within two weeks and be able to sustain them may contribute more to deterrence than any of the above programs because it presents the USSR with the possibility that it would face U.S. forces on the ground and those forces would not be a weak tripwire.[32]

Distribution

The idea of distribution is a close corollary to establishing realistic assumptions. A perfect military strategy, even if that were possible to obtain, cannot achieve all U.S. interests and objectives in Southwest Asia. To have a reasonable chance of success, a strategy for the region—or any region, for that matter—must depend upon a whole host of political, economic, and military instruments available to the United States. Moreover, the strategist must decide which instrument or instruments should be given the most emphasis in order to achieve U.S. goals. This is particularly true in the case of Southwest Asia. As a number of analysts have pointed out, domestic coups, insurrections, instability within authoritarian and monarchical regimes, civil disturbances, political succession problems, revivals of indigenous military rivalries, and domestic instability associated with too rapid economic modernization that clashes with traditional Islamic values are all more likely threats to Southwest Asian security than a direct Soviet military invasion. United States political and economic instruments can better deal with these "more likely" threats. A military strategist accepts this situation, but at the same time realizes that the United States must have the capability to respond to the worst-case situations because an inability to respond in effect increases the likelihood that they may occur. Deciding how much emphasis to place upon political, economic, and military instruments in a particular situation or region is the most difficult, and often most misunderstood, part of a strategist's job.

The idea of distribution also applies specifically to the development of a military strategy. As used here, distribution does not imply that the defense budget necessarily should be divided equally among the three uniformed services in an effort to achieve some sort of artificial balance or that each service should be represented equally in a military operation. Rather, the concept of distribution suggests that assets should be systematically—not randomly or equally—apportioned in an attempt to achieve some end. In other words, the military strategist must decide and then recommend to political decision makers the proper proportion or mix among the services that would provide the best opportunity to achieve U.S. interests and objectives. The mix and which service should have primary responsibility for a particular contingency should vary, depending on the theater of operation, threat, and objectives to be obtained. For example, the U.S. Army and the Air Force have the primary responsibility in Europe because, in the event of conflict in that theater, they would play the dominant role with the navy supporting them. The opposite is true in the Pacific, and, as a result, the U.S. Navy is the dominant service there.

In Southwest Asia, naval forces will constitute a major part of the forces necessary to achieve U.S. objectives. However, contrary to the arguments made by naval unilateralists, one can still advocate the need for a strong navy and believe that carrier task forces are important, but, at the same time, believe that U.S. military strategy for Southwest Asia must be based on more than a maritime strategy. Naval forces in the region can do many things, but they cannot accomplish all U.S. objectives.

Naval forces, particularly "over the horizon" forces, which can be rapidly reinforced to establish superiority in the Indian Ocean, will help achieve deterrence. Critics argue that naval forces do not demonstrate a strong commitment because they can be withdrawn just as rapidly as they can be deployed. This is true. Nevertheless, "over the horizon" forces would have to be considered by a prudent Soviet planner. To the extent that they convince the Soviets that the American commitment to Southwest Asia is real and the risk of challenging that commitment cannot be calculated or possibly controlled, deterrence will be enhanced.

Naval forces in Southwest Asia will also contribute significantly to U.S. war-fighting capabilities. The ability to obtain naval superiority in the region would help to keep the sea lines of communication open and facilitate the arrival of other reinforcements (air, marine, army, and navy). Naval air could fly some interdiction. However, distance factors cut both ways and adversely impact on U.S. capabilities as they do on the Soviet Union. I have argued elsewhere that range limitations of Soviet frontal aviation aircraft, when studied in conjunction with the distances that the Soviets would have to operate over in Iran, create serious military constraints for the USSR.[33] However, similar problems would affect U.S. capabilities. The primary attack plane of U.S. aircraft carriers is currently the A-6, the Intruder. It has an unrefueled range of only 700 miles and a refueled range of 950 miles. This does not reach very far into the Persian Gulf.[34] The range considerations are even more significant when one realizes that naval officers will be unwilling to risk high-value platforms like aircraft carriers by sailing them into the Persian Gulf when air superiority is in doubt and they may be vulnerable to land-based missiles. In other words, naval forces, including naval air, would be hard pressed by themselves to confront invading Soviet land forces in Southwest Asia.

To some degree, the naval forces' inability to keep Soviet ground forces out of Southwest Asia may be an unjustified criticism, because maritime strategy supporters and horizontal escalationists are not really arguing that naval forces will face aggression at its point of inception. Rather, they propose to punish the USSR so badly at some other point on the globe that the Soviets will stop their aggression and withdraw. As a declaratory peacetime strategy, these suggestions may have some merit in contributing to deterrence. However, as a war-fighting strategy, too heavy a dependence upon a naval-oriented horizontal escalation approach suffers from three glaring problems.

First, such a strategy implies an escalation of objectives from a limited objective to stop Soviet aggression at some point on the globe to the "ultimate" military defeat of the USSR. Rather than working to limit the scale and scope of conflict, the risk is that by increasing the points of friction between the superpowers the possibility of nuclear escalation will increase. Second, how, where, and when do the superpowers stop fighting if a strategy of horizontal escalation is executed and it is successful? Suppose an attack on Soviet naval bases on the Kola Peninsula or the Far East maritime provinces engages enough Soviet forces to stabilize a Southwest Asian conflict, making it possible to defend the region's oil facilities. Could the United States or the Soviet Union negotiate a settlement when U.S. and USSR military forces are engaged in an area of vital Soviet interest, or must the USSR also be defeated on the original secondary front? Third, if American objectives in the region are to keep oil flowing over the long term and to ensure that the region does not fall under the dominance of hostile outside powers, then it is extremely difficult to justify a strategic equation that argues American objectives would be served by taking some area that is important to the USSR, such as Angola or Cuba. This might serve American political needs for retribution, but a military strategy is supposed to facilitate the achievement of U.S. interests and objectives. Retribution should not be the goal of a strategist.

A naval-oriented strategy for Southwest Asia can accomplish some objectives, but it cannot accomplish everything. Ultimately, to defend not only the oil fields but also the more vulnerable pumping stations and loading facilities from an external attack requires ground forces and a viable air defense system forward of what one intends to defend. In the pursuit of a balanced military strategy, it is not an issue of naval power versus air and land power. As Robert Komer, former undersecretary of defense for policy, has said, they "are not viable alternatives but indispensable corollaries. We need both."[35]

If the strategist functioned in an unlimited resource environment, he would recommend building all the divisions, planes, and ships, as well as strategic mobility assets, that were required. This is unrealistic, however, because resources are constrained. Therefore, in the development of forces for Southwest Asia, when inevitable tradeoffs among programs must occur, the strategist should look toward creating a balance in U.S. capabilities. This means increasing strategic mobility assets because of current shortfalls in those areas. In every crisis in Southwest Asia during the last 14 years, the United States has been able to bring enough naval forces into the area to establish naval superiority.[36] The major limitations on Soviet naval power in the Indian Ocean (a lack of staying power, little offensive punch in the fleet, and limited power projection capabilities because of too few modern logistic ships) will not be significantly improved by the end of the 1980s or probably the mid-1990s.[37] Therefore, the United States in crisis periods will probably be able to continue to establish naval superiority for limited periods by drawing down forces from other theaters. The same cannot be said with assurance for land forces if strategic mobility assets are lacking. For this reason, in the pursuit of a wise distribution of assets and forces to achieve U.S. military strategy, when hard choices about expensive, high-visibility hardware programs must be made (CVNs, B-1, MX, M-1, AH-65, etc.), those programs ipso facto should not be given precedence over less glamorous strategic mobility assets. If the United States is unable to support and sustain its forces in Southwest Asia, it will be driven toward options like nuclear or geographic escalation, and the risks of such options have been discussed above. Moreover, no one has ever done well in predicting where the next crisis will occur (prior to 1978, how many people predicted that Southwest Asia would dominate U.S. defense planning in the 1980s?). Strategic mobility assets can be used anywhere.

Supportable

Finally, a military strategy must be supportable not only in logistical terms, as has been mentioned, but also in a domestic political context. If the American public is unwilling to support a military strategy, the forces to bolster the strategy will probably not be procured in congressional budgetary debates and the strategy will lack the political will to be executed in a crisis. Earlier it was argued that a credible military strategy for Southwest Asia requires an alliance approach. It is equally important that a supportable military strategy for the region have an alliance backing.

The reason that alliance cohesion is necessary is rather simple. As was noted at the beginning of this chapter, ensuring the flow of Persian Gulf oil is an indirect vital U.S. interest, but it is critical for U.S. allies' economic survival. As a global nation and the most militarily powerful adversary of the USSR, the United States has a responsibility as well as a need not to think in myopic, ethnocentric terms. Nevertheless, if some time in the future the United States is required to use military force in the region to defend objectives that in the short run are more important to its allies but in the process puts at risk American survival interests, it may not be too much to ask that before undertaking such steps our allies support such a venture.

It probably would serve no useful purpose in noncrisis periods to threaten allies with the ultimatum that, if they refuse politically to support American approaches, they must go it alone. That would not serve either U.S. or its allies' interests. Besides, many of the issues that appear to divide America from its allies both in and outside Southwest Asia are differences of opinion over means, not ends. In a crisis many of the perceived differences could evaporate. However, in the final analysis, the United States needs to avoid a repeat of the 1973 Middle East war when some European allies not only refused to support U.S. actions but also actively worked to undermine U.S. policies. If it is concluded that allies would not politically (or hopefully militarily) support the use of U.S. military force in a Southwest Asian crisis, then the military strategist may have no other realistic choice but to advise U.S. policymakers not to use military force. To do otherwise would be to suggest high-risk military alternatives that ultimately would falter because the American public would lack the political will to see them through.

CONCLUSION

By way of a conclusion, it seems worthwhile to reiterate some basic points in order to highlight important issues and to avoid misinterpretations. First, U.S. interests and objectives for Southwest Asia, or for that matter any geographic region, should guide the creation of a military strategy. The threat is an important input for the development of a military strategy, but it should not be the sole determinant of a military strategy. Also, the strategist must guard against suggesting alternatives and proposals that may achieve objectives in the region, but in the process put at risk more fundamental national interests such as survival or create unnecessary friction among other global or regional objectives that are equally important. In Southwest Asia, deterrence is the primary objective. This must be the objective, not only because of the severe military problems that the United States would face if it had to fight a major conflict in the region but also because obtaining a major U.S. objective of maintaining the flow of oil depends on deterrence. To fight to defend oil inherently means not only will disruption occur but also it will be some time before the flow of oil can be resumed. The oil facilities, particularly pumping stations and storage areas, are extremely vulnerable to military operations.

Second, the process of developing a military strategy and the forces to support it is not an attempt to reject other alternatives and to advocate the use of military force to achieve U.S. interests and objectives. Most analysts of Southwest Asia recognize that the immediate problems in the area are political and economic in nature. Their solutions depend upon political and economic options, and military strategists can and do support these nonmilitary initiatives. However, a military strategist is charged with additional responsibilities and does not do the decisionmaker justice if he does not look beyond economic and political solutions. It is his job to suggest to political decisionmakers a military strategy (or strategies) within realistic force levels that will deter the USSR and other nations from using military force to threaten U.S. interests and objectives and that will create an environment in which political and economic options can be pursued. Additionally, if deterrence fails, the military strategist has the responsibility to advise decisionmakers how military force can or cannot be used effectively to defend U.S. interests and objectives and reestablish deterrence. In other words, the process involved is not an either/or situation with choices only between political or economic solutions versus military options. To be successful in Southwest Asia and the world at large, U.S. economic, political, and military strategies must be integrated and mutually supportive.

Finally, for a military strategy to have a reasonable chance of success, it must be credible, realistic, distributional, and supportable. Since the fall of the shah and the invasion of Afghanistan, four major military strategies for dealing with U.S. military deficiencies in Southwest Asia have been suggested: nuclear, conventional tripwire, conventional defense, and geographic escalation. Although each proposal has fulfilled some of these principles, none adequately addresses all of them. Except for the Wohlstetter version of a conventional defense option, all the others suffer from the same major strategic vulnerability: They are either unilateral, nonalliance attempts to deal with Southwest Asia or, according to one school of thought among geographic escalationists, attempts to manipulate and leave allies with no options but to support U.S. actions.

Some critics will argue that too much emphasis has been placed on allies, alliance backing, and collective action in the development of a military strategy for the region. They will claim that there is no guarantee that in a crisis allies will support U.S. policy. There is some merit to those criticisms, for no strategy is risk-free. However, there is equally no guarantee that the American public will or should bear the financial burden required if the United States tries to build a military capability for unilateral action in Southwest Asia. Even if we could financially afford it, I would still place more emphasis upon collective rather than unilateral action. An alliance approach threatens to create geographic escalation in ways that are believable to the Soviets. Rather than geographic escalation occurring because of U.S. military weakness at the point of primary friction, other nations would expand the conflict because Soviet actions threatened their forces in the region or their interests and objectives. Besides, in the long run, the United States is defending objectives that are more crucial to its allies. Under these conditions, an alliance approach has a better chance of being acceptable to an American public that traditionally has been more interested in domestic than in foreign affairs issues.

NOTES

1. See, for example, Joshua M. Epstein, "Soviet Vulnerabilities in Iran and the RDF Deterrent," *International Security* 6, no. 2 (Fall 1981): 126–58; Keith A. Dunn, "Constraints in the USSR in Southwest Asia: A Military Analysis," *Orbis* 25, no. 3 (Fall 1981): 607–29; *Challenges for U.S. National Security: Assessing the Balance–Defense Spending and Conventional Forces*, a preliminary, Pt. II, prepared by Carnegie Panel on U.S. Security and the Future of Arms Control (Washington, D.C.: Carnegie Endowment for International Peace, 1981), pp. 149–94; and Thomas L. McNaugher, "The Military Threat to the Gulf: The Operational Dimension," paper presented at the Biennial Conference of the Section on Military Studies, International Studies Association, University of New Hampshire, Durham, November 5–7, 1981.

2. John Lewis Gaddis, *Strategies of Containment: A Critical Appraisal of Postwar American National Security Policy* (New York: Oxford University Press, 1982), p. 285.

3. *New York Times*, January 24, 1980, p. A12.

4. For a few statements of Reagan administration commitment, see Department of State, "Middle East Regional Security," Current Policy no. 270 (Washington, D.C.: Bureau of Public Affairs, March 23, 1981); Department of State, "U.S. Strategy in the Middle East," Current Policy no. 312 (Washington, D.C.: Bureau of Public Affairs, September 17, 1981); Department of State, "Pursuing Peace and Security in the Middle East," Current Policy no. 332 (Washington, D.C.: Bureau of Public Affairs, October 21, 1981); and Caspar W. Weinberger, "Requirements of Our Defense Policy," *Department of State Bulletin* 81, no. 2052 (July 1981): 46–48.

5. Christopher Van Hollen, "Has the Persian Gulf Passed Its Prime?" *Washington Post*, December 27, 1981, p. D7.

6. For more information on the concept of direct and indirect vital interests, see William O. Staudenmaier, *Strategic Concepts for the 1980's*, Special Report (Carlisle Barracks, Pa.: Strategic Studies Institute, U.S. Army War College, May 1, 1981), pp. 4–6.

7. Even in a crisis, it is not clear that strategists will receive political guidance. For more on this point and the disconnect between strategy and policy in general, see William O. Staudenmaier, "The Strategic Process: Considerations for Policy and Strategy in Southwest Asia," in *U.S. Strategic Interests in Southwest Asia*, ed. Shirin Tahir-Kheli (New York: Praeger, 1982), pp. 16–20.

8. Maxwell D. Taylor, *Precarious Security* (New York: Norton, 1976), p. 17.

9. Amos A. Jordan and William J. Taylor, Jr., *American National Security: Policy and Process* (Baltimore: Johns Hopkins University Press, 1981), p. 54.

10. For more on the difference between operational planning and force development planning, see Staudenmaier, "The Strategic Process," pp. 20–24.

11. The 1979 Department of Defense study–also referred to as the Wolfowitz Report–is summarized in Richard Burt, "Study Says a Soviet Move in Iran Might Require U.S. Atomic Arms," *New York Times*, February 2, 1980, pp. A1, A4. See also Kenneth N. Waltz, "A Strategy for the Rapid Deployment Force," *International Security* 5, no. 4 (Spring 1981): 49–73, which refers to the Wolfowitz Report extensively.

12. Waltz, "Strategy for the Rapid Deployment Force," p. 66 [emphasis in original].

13. Ibid., p. 67.

14. Ibid., pp. 49–50, 71–73.

15. Albert Wohlstetter, "Meeting the Threat in the Persian Gulf," *Survey* 25, no. 2 (Spring 1980): 165.

16. Jeffrey Record, *The Rapid Deployment Force and U.S. Military Intervention in the Persian Gulf* (Cambridge, Mass.: Institute for Foreign Policy Analysis, 1981), p. 3.

17. Wohlstetter, "Meeting the Threat in the Persian Gulf," pp. 170–83.

18. Record, *Rapid Deployment Force*, p. 64.

19. Ibid., pp. 2–3.

20. For a good articulation of this position, see Francis J. West, Jr., "Conventional Forces Beyond NATO," in *National Security in the 1980s: From Weakness to Strength*, ed. W. Scott Thompson (San Francisco: Institute for Contemporary Studies, 1980), p. 324.

21. See Richard Halloran, "Reagan Selling Naval Budget as Heart of Military Mission," *New York Times*, April 11, 1982, p. A24, where Secretary of the Navy John Lehman is reported to have stated that planning for a regionally limited naval war with the USSR is impossible: "It will be instantaneously a global naval conflict."

22. Fred Charles Ikle, "NATO's First Nuclear Use: A Deepening Trap?" *Strategic Review* 8, no. 1 (Winter 1980): 23.

23. Francis J. West, Jr., "NATO II: Common Boundaries for Common Interests," *Naval War College Review* 34, no. 1 (January–February 1981): 61.

24. Ibid., p. 63.

25. Ibid.

26. Dov S. Zakheim, "Towards a Western Approach to the Indian Ocean," *Survival* 22, no. 1 (January/February 1980): 13.

27. Ibid., p. 14.

28. For more detailed analyses to support the arguments about Soviet military constraints, see Dunn, "Constraints on the USSR in Southwest Asia," pp. 607–29; and Keith A. Dunn, "Power Projection or Influence: Soviet Capabilities for the 1980s," *Naval War College Review* 32, no. 5 (September-October 1980): 31–48.

29. Keith A. Dunn, "Do Any 'Mysteries' About the USSR Still Exist?" *Orbis* 26, no. 2 (Summer 1982): 374–76.

30. Bruce W. Watson, *Red Navy at Sea: Soviet Naval Operations on the High Seas, 1956-1980* (Boulder, Colo.: Westview Press, 1982), p. 148.

31. See Herschel Kinter, "The Reagan Defense Program: Can It Hold Up?" *Strategic Review* 10, no. 2 (Spring 1982): 26–29; William R. VanCleave, "Strategy and the Navy's 1983-1987 Program: Skepticism Is Warranted!" *Armed Forces Journal International*, April 1982, pp. 49–51; and *Report of Secretary of Defense Caspar W. Weinberger to the Congress on the FY 1983 Budget, FY 84 Authorization Request and FY 1983-87 Defense Programs* (Washington, D.C.: U.S. Government Printing Office, 1982), p. III-36.

32. When the SL-7 container ship is converted to a roll-on, roll-off (Ro-Ro) configuration, it will be able to carry 122 tanks of the M-1 type and a mixed variety of 183 helicopters. Alternatively, a converted SL-7 will be able to carry

a maximum of 183 tanks or a mix of 332 helicopters. If loaded at time of crisis, a ship can deploy to the Persian Gulf via the Suez Canal in 11½ to 12 days or 15 to 17 days if the canal is closed. It would take approximately 20 hours to load a ship and 16 to 18 hours to unload at a port. If the environment is not benign, it could take as much as two and a half to three days to offload. Given the distances involved, these are rather impressive statistics. However, the United States has bought and is in the process of converting only eight SL-7s at this time. Conversion should be completed by the end of 1983. U.S. Congress, Senate, Armed Services Committee, *Department of Defense Authorization for Appropriations for FY 1982*, Hearings, 97th Congress, 1st Session, Pt. IV, Sea Power and Force Projection (Washington, D.C.: U.S. Government Printing Office, 1981), pp. 1823-24.

33. Dunn, "Constraints on the USSR in Southwest Asia," pp. 614-16, 619-25.

34. Thomas L. McNaugher, "A U.S. Military Posture for the Gulf," paper presented at the International Studies Association, Cincinnati, Ohio, March 24-27, 1982, p. 15.

35. Robert W. Komer, "Security Challenges of the 80's," *Armed Forces Journal International*, November 1981, p. 69. See also Robert Komer, "Maritime Strategy versus Coalition Defense," *Foreign Affairs* 60, no. 5 (Summer 1982): 1124-44.

36. Watson, *Red Navy at Sea*, pp. 150-51.

37. Dunn, "Power Projection or Influence," pp. 31-45.

10

Regional Security as a Policy Objective: The Case of South and Southwest Asia

Barry Buzan

The preceding chapters in this book have examined aspects of the security problem in South and Southwest Asia. Their emphasis has been empirical, and they have all, in their various ways, been based on the assumption that regional security policy is a feasible objective. Indeed, this assumption is built into the title of the project that gave rise to this book: Security and Stability in South and Southwest Asia. In this chapter I will try to draw together some of the threads of argument developed by the regional experts to see whether they lead to any coherent conclusions about regional security as a policy objective. I will begin on a rather abstract plane by looking first at the problem of defining "region" as a meaningful unit of analysis and then at the meaning of security as a policy objective. From there, I will go on to develop the idea of security complexes as an analytical framework for thinking about regional security policy, and I will apply this framework to the case of South and Southwest Asia. Finally, some observations will be made about the nature of the regional security policy problem for this area.

DEFINING "REGION"

Defining "region" is not such a trivial problem as it might, at first glance, appear to be. Whatever criteria we use, by focusing on "region" we are trying either to demarcate or to create a meaningful unit of policy analysis. We must somehow differentiate the regional unit from the seamless web of relationships that connects all of the states in the international system. No region forms a perfectly isolated subsystem, and some reason could be found for grouping together almost any collection of countries. Between these two extremes are various groupings that display enough cohesion to warrant designation as a subsystem. They are not so completely detached from the rest of the system as to constitute a single, sovereign actor, but the affairs of their members are significantly more dominated by relationships among them than they are by relationships with states in other parts of the system. Our problem is to find the groupings that best serve the purposes of regional security analysis.

There are two advantages to the regional unit of analysis. First, it enables us to concentrate our attention on a manageable entity that is larger than a single state but much smaller than the international system as a whole. Second, the area we designate as a region should, by reason of the factors that make it cohere, constitute a significant entity within the definition of the policy problem. In other words, the first advantage can be achieved by picking any set of countries that is less than the whole, but the second advantage requires more sophistication and can only be achieved if we can identify the primary patterns of linkage that define security regions. Is Asia a meaningful unit, as has been argued by some,[1] or should one look for broader units like Afro-Asia, or narrower ones like the Gulf or the subcontinent?

The main danger in pursuing a regional unit is of imposing artificial boundaries on events. Any definition will involve questionable inclusions and exclusions. For example, is Turkey part of the Middle East or part of Europe? Fixing a region as a unit of analysis naturally focuses attention on events within the region, while discounting the influence of events outside it. Because no region is perfectly isolated, there is a risk of distortion in analysis. This risk escalates rapidly if the region is poorly defined, so that the analytical framework excludes factors that are of crucial importance to events within it. An extreme example would be a definition of the Middle East that excluded Egypt on the grounds that it is part of Africa. One has to guard against the designation of an area as a region leading to excessive assumptions about either its degree of detachment from surrounding actors or its degree of internal cohesion.

Regions have traditionally been defined in a fairly casual manner, which, I will argue, provides a suboptimal approach to security analysis. Four kinds of approach have dominated. The first uses general geopolitical criteria and gives rise to regions like South America, Africa, Asia, and the Middle East. The second is similar, but gives more weight to cultural and ethnic factors. These give rise to regions like Latin America, the Arab world, Africa south of the Sahara, the Far East, and the Indian subcontinent. As a rule, both of these approaches are too broad to capture entities useful in security analysis, and the criteria used to define them are not central to the dynamics of security. That said, however, it must be acknowledged that ethnic factors may well be relevant to the definition of regional security entities, as seems to be the case in both South Asia and the Middle East. The third approach reflects a policy sphere defined by the interests of some particular state. Thus, Japan created its Greater East Asia Co-Prosperity Sphere, the United States declared its Monroe Doctrine, and the Soviet Union has its empire. Although useful for security analysis, this approach creates a highly ethnocentric perspective on security dynamics.[2] The fourth approach is the one that underlies this book—the definition of a region according to the dimensions of a particular security policy crisis. South and Southwest Asia get defined as a region because they encompass the domain of an unresolved confrontation between the United States and the Soviet Union that centers on the tension between Western interests in access to Gulf oil and the unknown, but ominous, significance of the Soviet occupation of Afghanistan. The hazard of this approach is that it emphasizes the security dynamics of the superpowers at the expense of the dynamics generated by the states within the region. Do these local dynamics fit into the same pattern as the present superpower crisis? We will return to this crucial question in a later section.

At this point, we need to consider the meaning of security as a policy objective. Because we are trying to find a way of defining regions appropriate to security policy analysis, the obvious course is to use the concept of security as a basis for defining regions.

SECURITY AS A POLICY OBJECTIVE

Security is a notoriously difficult concept to pin down. Arnold Wolfers labeled it an "ambiguous symbol" and argued that it "may not have any precise meaning at all."[3] This ambiguity identifies it as what W. B. Gallie has called an "essentially contested concept."[4] Such concepts as justice and power elude tight definitions. They define areas of concern more than they define absolute conditions. Definitions can only approach precision within the context of a particular case study, and even then, as demonstrated often in discussions about security, there is much room for disagreement. Security is a universal concept, but it has no universal rules of application: We know what it is about, but we cannot say precisely what it is. As a general idea, it contains rather than resolves contradictions, and for this reason it is difficult to translate it into agreed terms of policy. Contradictions exist inter alia between individual security and national security, between national security and international security, and between violent means and peaceful ends. These contradictions bedevil both the definition and the making of security policy, and only by taking a broad view of the concept can we have any hope of coming to terms with them.[5]

This broad view is relevant to our attempt to use the idea of security to define regions, and we need to explore a few of its dimensions before we proceed to that task. Two questions guide our enquiry: Which sectors of the security problem are we interested in, and to which referent objects of security do we wish to give priority? The answers to these questions are usually interrelated.

The concept of security applies to many sectors. Political security makes just as much sense as military security, and neither is unrelated to security in the economic and social sectors. Sometimes we can discuss a security problem largely within the confines of a single sector, be it military or social, but the evidence in the case of South and Southwest Asia indicates a need to incorporate all four sectors. Social security arises as a problem because of the clash between traditional and modern cultures and the stresses of development. The very structure of society is unstable and transforming in most of the area. This social tension partly underlies a pervasive political insecurity that arises from weakly founded governments fearful of both internal opposition and external meddling and subversion. The purely political impact of the Iranian revolution on the conservative governments of the other Gulf states indicates the salience of the political dimension to security in this area. Economic security has many aspects worthy of note, especially in South Asia, but its main feature for our purposes is the dependence of the West on continued supplies of oil from the Gulf.

Military security is a pervasive problem in the area at several levels. It is a problem within the local states as their armies apply force to segments of their own population, as in Pakistan, Oman, Iraq, Iran, Syria, Israel, Afghanistan, and others. It is a problem among the local states as they juggle military threats against each other and all too frequently resort to war. Since the 1950s at least seven major wars have been fought within the area, and minor conflicts and threatening troop deployments have been too numerous to catalog.[6] And it is a problem because of the increasingly military flavor of superpower rivalry in the area: Within the last few years the superpowers have extended their direct military presence in the region from its former focus in the eastern Mediterranean to include the large area around the Gulf. In addition to the arms supply and advisers that have traditionally been part of their policy toward the local states, the Soviet Union now occupies Afghanistan and has a significant military presence in South Yemen and Ethiopia, and the United States has greatly increased its naval strength in the Indian Ocean and has established several adjacent bases. The area is fast becoming, as Gary Sick observes elsewhere in this volume, a third front in the cold war.

As is abundantly evident from the preceding chapters, the security factors in these four sectors are inseparably entangled with each other. Social tensions feed political instability and invite intervention by neighbors. Domestic and local conflicts encourage military responses that not only generate their own dynamic of power struggles and security dilemmas but also stimulate the competitive involvement of larger external powers. This involvement feeds back into the social and political instabilities by way of both economic and military impacts that the external powers make on local affairs, as well as by way of their direct ideological impact on the local struggles over the form of political economy to be adopted. In other words, the security problem in this area cannot be comprehended unless all four sectors are included in its definition. Neither the security problem as seen by the local states nor the security problem as defined by the superpowers can be separated from this pervasive interplay of factors across the sectors.

The complex entanglement of sectors raises the second question about the referent objects of security. The concept of security makes no sense unless we have an answer to the question: The security of what? In discussing sectors we have already identified two possible answers: the local states and the superpowers. It is by no means self-evident that these two objectives are either consistent within themselves or with each other, and if they are not consistent, then we are going to have trouble finding a meaning for the term "regional security." Before we can apply the concept of security to the definition of region, we need to clarify some of the policy problems attaching to the choice of referent object.

The problem of identifying a referent object of security can be posed in terms of a spectrum. At one end of the spectrum we find individuals, and a zealous reductionist might argue that all security problems can ultimately be collapsed down to this level.[7] At the other end we find the international system as a whole, and an equally zealous holist might argue that no part of the system can be made secure until all of it is so blessed. Between these extremes lie a host of possible referent objects ranging from towns and counties declaring themselves nuclear-free zones, through groups like the Kurds and the Basques that find themselves trapped within or between states, to multistate groupings like alliances or regions. Prime among these intermediate options is the state, which carries most of the official responsibility for security. Even by concentrating on the state, however, we do not eliminate the referent object problem.

Taking a single state would clarify matters considerably, but sits uneasily against both our objective of regional security policy and our conclusion about the linkages arising from interplay among the sectors. The single state as a referent object is a substantial aid to narrowing down the range of our concerns to some manageable scope, but it does this only at the cost of serious ethnocentric distortions of perception. In order to address the security problem on a regional scale, we are obliged to consider the interests of many states, both within and outside the area, and to find some way of encompassing the conflicts and contradictions that exist among them. In so doing, we lose the easy association between security and stability as objectives. Although stability may describe the security objective of a single state, it rarely applies across a group of states. Within a group, some states are likely to be revisionist, and for them, stability is the definition of the problem rather than the form of the solution.

The promulgation of stability as a correlate of security identifies a status quo perspective on security. Such a perspective can only be applied to a regional scale on two conditions: that a single-state security perspective is being taken, or that all the states in the area concerned share a status quo outlook. The first condition will tend to lead to polarized, conflict-oriented perceptions of the situation if, as is usually the case, revisionist actors are present in the area. The second condition clearly does not apply to South and Southwest Asia on either the local or the superpower level. All states, whether revisionist or status quo, have the right to security as an objective, and if we are trying to address the security problem at a regional level it does not help our cause to adopt an assumption like stability that goes against the interests of some of the states involved.

Our approach to security on the regional level must therefore incorporate, rather than avoid, the patterns of tension and conflict that exist among the states within the area. It must also incorporate the patterns of tension and conflict generated by states outside the area, but impinging on it. Although we can assume that these patterns are connected, we cannot assume that they constitute an undifferentiated phenomenon. In dealing with regional security, we must accept that many referent objects are in play, and that each of them has its own perspective on the problem that entangles all of them. Regional security will be susceptible to many interpretations, and we must take care to specify at least which level we are giving priority to—whether the local level or the extraregional level—when we are discussing security as an objective.

One further problem arises from treating the state as our prime referent object, and that is the ambiguity that attaches to the state as an entity. The state itself is an essentially contested concept.[8] It is not immediately or self-evidently clear exactly what it is that is to be made secure when we talk about national security. Is it just the machinery of the state, which, as Dyson points out, is not the same as the state itself?[9] Is it the population and the territory? Is it some intangible such as culture, ideology, or legal rights? Is it the vested interest of some ruling group? Or is it some combination of these things? If a narrow choice is made, such as the interests of an elite, then the term "national security" is scarcely necessary, as we can define the referent object in its own terms. If national security involves a range of referent objects, then contradictions in the meaning of the term cannot be avoided. The security of individuals, for example, not infrequently stands in inverse correlation to the security of state institutions.[10] As a military president of Brazil is said to have quipped: "Brazil's doing fine, but the people are doing badly."[11]

This problem of ambiguity in the concept of the state creates serious difficulties for any attempt to apply the idea of national security. These difficulties are mitigated, though by no means removed, if the state in question enjoys political stability based on a broad social consensus. In such a state, like Sweden, the United States, or Japan, violence plays a relatively minor role in domestic politics, and the state as a political entity has sufficient coherence to justify its role as a referent object of security. These states are strong as states. In other words, they have a firm and stable political identity that is important both in terms of lowering their vulnerability to political threats and in terms of establishing them as coherent objects of security. We will call such states strong states, and we will distinguish that usage from the traditional idea of strong powers, which refers more to an actor's command over resources. There is no necessary correlation between strength as state and strength as power, as illustrated by Denmark, which is a weak power but a strong state, and by Pakistan and South Africa, which are both considerable powers, but weak states. The existence of ruthless and authoritarian government, as in Argentina or Iran, does not mark a strong state in the usage adopted here.[12] Indeed, the need for harsh government often indicates a weak state.

Weak states create severe problems for security analysis. What are we to make of states like Chad, Lebanon, or El Salvador as objects of security? When the political coherence of a state is insufficient to provide a basic foundation for order, violence becomes a major feature of its domestic life. Under such conditions, the concept of national security cannot apply to much more than the territorial integrity and legal existence of the state. The contradictions between state and citizen, or between rival groups contesting control of the state, become so great that the idea of national security is sapped of meaning. The contending individuals and groups become more relevant as objects of security than does the hollow shell of the state, and the whole emphasis of the security problem is within rather than around the state. The security of governments becomes the paramount concern, and although the term "national security" may be invoked to legitimize government actions, its use in such a context reflects political expediency and confuses rather than clarifies the issues at stake.

States can be placed along a spectrum ranging from weak states at one end to strong states at the other, with most states falling somewhere between the extremes. The problem with an area like South and Southwest Asia is that it contains a high proportion of states toward the weak end of the spectrum. Because political legitimacy in such states is fragile, they are vulnerable to politically mobilized ethnic, religious, or ideological forces that threaten the authority of the groups currently holding power. This means that any investigation of the security problem must look at relations within states as well as at relations between them. Unfortunately, the domestic insecurities of weak states provide an ideal forum for external meddling and intervention, whether in the political or in the military sector. Consequently, domestic and external security issues become inextricably entangled, and it becomes impossible for external actors to intervene in the regional security dynamic without at the same time intervening in the domestic political affairs of the local states. Regional security thus comes to depend, to a considerable extent, on the domestic stability of states as well as on the character of relations between them. An unstable weak state can explode into revolution, like Iran in 1979, with consequences that endanger the political stability of its neighbors. Even under normal circumstances, all actors will be tempted to play politics in each other's domestic arenas. Because external success can be a factor in internal stability, the local patterns of state relations and the domestic conflicts within the participating states interact to increase insecurity all around.

We can conclude from this discussion of security as a policy objective that the concept requires a broad approach. Both in terms of sectors and in terms of level of referent object, a security perspective produces a complex picture of overlapping relational patterns. The security of any given referent object, be it an individual, a state, or a region, cannot be understood without taking into account the position of other actors. Security and insecurity are not primarily a characteristic of particular actors, but more a product of larger patterns of relations that encompass several sectors and several levels. Our task is to use this broad notion of security as a guide to defining the groupings that best serve the purposes of regional security analysis.

SECURITY COMPLEXES AS A FRAMEWORK FOR ANALYSIS

The broad concept of security that we explored in the previous section invites us to look for sets of actors connected by their interlocking security concerns. We will label such a set a security complex, and define it as a group of actors whose primary security concerns link together sufficiently closely that their security problems cannot realistically be considered apart from one another.[13] Because states are the actors that normally carry most of the responsibility for security, and also command most of the capabilities relevant to it, they constitute the principal membership of security complexes. But a concentration on states does not prevent us from looking at security factors within states as well as those between them. In deciding which states to include and which to exclude from any security complex, our principal guide will be linkages among the primary security concerns of the states involved. We will give particular emphasis to situations where primary security concerns are mutual between states, as they are between the United States and the Soviet Union. The objective is to find sets of states whose security affairs are both sufficiently closely linked together and sufficiently differentiated from the security affairs of states outside the set that they constitute a meaningful unit for regional security analysis.

One problem in this approach is that very powerful states may impinge on a local complex in a largely unidirectional manner. The Soviet Union, for example, has a much greater security impact on the states of the Middle East than they have on it. The solution to this problem is to differentiate security complexes according to the power and reach of the main states within them. Local complexes are composed of states whose influence is mostly confined within the bounds of their own region, whereas the two superpowers form the heart of a complex that encompasses the whole planet. Our approach will be to start by identifying the local complexes and then work upward to see how local complexes fit into the higher level complexes defined by greater powers. This tactic has the advantage of enabling us to differentiate between the dynamics of the local complexes and those of the higher level ones. If we can identify complexes that have significance as entities in their own right, then this layered approach to interaction between lower and higher level complexes should enable us to avoid the classic errors of regional security policy analysis: placing too much emphasis on the role of great powers, or placing too much emphasis on the role of local factors. The approach through security complexes should enable us to identify both levels as important and, to some extent, independent, and to ask how they interact with each other in relation to the security objectives of the actors on both levels.

If we apply the idea of security complexes to the area of South and Southwest Asia, we find two distinct local complexes, which we label the South Asian complex and the Middle Eastern supercomplex.

The South Asian complex centers on the interlocked insecurities of its two major actors, India and Pakistan. Its structure is consequently quite straightforward, and the minor states caught up in it, mostly for reasons of geography—Nepal, Bhutan, Bangladesh, and Sri Lanka—make little impact. Afghanistan and Burma reside on its periphery. The core rivalry between India and Pakistan, which defines the South Asian complex, has existed since both states became independent in 1947. The two states have fought three wars (1947–48, 1965, 1971), and throughout the period each has been at the center of the other's local source of insecurity. Their rivalry has adopted most of the conventions that mark relations between competing states. They have unresolved territorial disputes in Kashmir and in the Rann of Kutch, which give their hostility a tangible and enduring touchstone. Less tangibly, there is a long-standing power struggle between them that reflects Pakistan's unwillingness to allow the naturally greater weight of India to result in de facto Indian hegemony over the subcontinent. This struggle has manifested itself in a continuous arms race between the two that now seems close to spilling over into the great equalizer of nuclear weapons.

The insecurity that India and Pakistan create for each other is exacerbated by domestic insecurities in each that link to their rivalry with each other. Although the two countries do not appear to meddle in each other's politics in any blatant way, their respective political constitutions are locked into a state of tension. Pakistan is organized on the principle of Islamic unity, and India is organized on the principle of secular federalism. Because India contains a large body of Muslims, the principle of Pakistan threatens India with secessionism, and the principle of India threatens Pakistan with dismemberment or absorption. This source of unease is amplified by the territorial disputes between the two countries because the populations at stake represent a defense by each of its organizing principle. Each state also has internal problems of dissent and separatism (in Assam and the south in India, among the Baluchis and the Pathans in Pakistan), though these are more serious in Pakistan, which is much the weaker of the two states as a coherent political entity and has already suffered one partition (the creation of Bangladesh in 1971).[14]

The Middle Eastern supercomplex is a much larger and altogether more difficult entity than the South Asian one. It has no single center, it encompasses two dozen states, and it is bound together by extremely complicated and unstable patterns of alignment and conflict. The term "supercomplex" is necessary, because although distinct poles of conflict exist, no one of them dominates the complex in the way that India and Pakistan dominate the South Asian one. The several poles define subcomplexes within the supercomplex, each having an identifiable dynamic of its own, but being sufficiently strongly tied into the larger patterns to deny its status as a security complex in its own right.

The Middle Eastern supercomplex is primarily, but not completely, an Arab phenomenon, its three principal cores of conflict centering on its three non-Arab members, Israel, Ethiopia, and Iran. Its membership comprises these three plus all the members of the Arab League. Geographically, it extends from the Western Sahara, in the west, to Somalia, Oman, and Iran, in the east, and from Iran, Syria, and Morocco, in the north, to Somalia and Sudan, in the south.

Its three principal subcomplexes center on the Gulf, Israel, and the Horn of Africa, and minor subcomplexes can also be identified centered on the two Yemens and on Algeria and Morocco. The main actors in the Gulf subcomplex are Iran, Iraq, Kuwait, Saudi Arabia, and the small Gulf states. Several territorial disputes exist among them, and a general power rivalry among the three largest states (Iran, Iraq, Saudi Arabia) is reinforced by political differences (radical versus conservative), ethnic differences (Arab versus Persian), and religious differences (Sunni versus Shiite). Political intervention in each other's affairs is quite common, whether it be positive, like Gulf Arab financial support for Iraq's war effort against Iran, or negative, like the encouragement of Kurdish rebels by Iran and Iraq within each other's territory. Relationships among the states are complicated by ethnic and religious minorities with connections across state boundaries, and military tensions within the subcomplex have produced one major war (Iran-Iraq) and several skirmishes (Iraq-Kuwait and Iran and the Gulf Emirates over Iran's seizure of islands).

The Arab-Israeli subcomplex involves almost all of the Arab states to some degree, but the states principally engaged in it are Israel, Egypt, Syria, Jordan, and Lebanon, with Iraq, Libya, and Saudi Arabia also playing important roles. The dispute here is much more focused than that in the Gulf. It centers on the existence of Israel as a general political question, on a number of more particular territorial disputes arising from the expansion of Israel since 1947, and on the fate of the Palestinians. The dispute is sharpened by the ethnic and religious differences between the Arabs and the Israelis and by the political problems created in Arab states by the Palestinian diaspora. Although the prime focus of this subcomplex is Israel, significant disputes exist among and within the Arab states that often impede the logic of a clearly polarized dispute. Syria has major claims against Lebanon, and serious rivalry is as common as serious collaboration in relations between Syria and Egypt and Syria and Jordan. The civil war in Lebanon illustrates both the domestic levels of Arab disunity and the way in which these connect upward to interstate security relations. This subcomplex is heavily militarized and has produced five major wars, a continuing arms race, and numerous minor incidents of violence.

The Horn subcomplex is much less important than either the Gulf or Arab-Israeli ones, and is more peripheral to the affairs of the supercomplex as a whole. It centers on disputes between Ethiopia, on the one hand, and Somalia, Sudan, and secessionist Eritreans, on the other. Ethnic and religious differences intensify the dispute and provide the main lines of linkage to the supercomplex as a whole. This subcomplex has produced one significant war between Ethiopia and Somalia, many military incidents, and a long secessionist war within Ethiopia. Another minor subcomplex centers on the rivalry between Algeria and Morocco. This involves territorial disputes, tension between a conservative and a radical regime, and engagement in a war of succession to determine control over the Western Sahara.[15] Several other patterns of hostility can be found within the supercomplex, including rivalries between Libya and Egypt, between North and South Yemen, and between Syria and Iraq, but these we can subsume within the supercomplex.

The supercomplex is bound together by the extent to which its members involve themselves in each other's affairs, and this involvement is heavily conditioned by the Arab and Islamic factors that nearly all of them share. The combination of Pan-Arabism and Islam creates a regional politics, if not a regional polity, which draws its legitimacy from shared culture and religion, as well as from the more nebulous ideology of Arab unity. This regional politics is expressed in the Arab League and in the various unifying attempts that have marked relations among Arab states, as well as in a much higher degree of mutual involvement and intervention in domestic politics than is normally the case in international relations. To say that a regional politics exists, however, is not to say that it encourages regional unity in any harmonious sense. The members of the supercomplex are much more tied together by the insecurity they create for each other than by any positive links. This involvement in each other's politics is seldom benign, because for the most part it is conditioned by ideological divisions that exist within the larger framework of Pan-Arabism and Islam.

Because Islam is itself a political ideology, in the sense that it is used as a framework for government, the combinations of alignments and hostilities possible with the more conventional political divide between left and right are numerous. Thus, radical regimes make trouble for conservative ones, puritanical Islamic regimes undermine those with secular leanings, and Sunni and Shiite factions become part of the political game. Patterns of alignment can change quickly and drastically when unstable governments fall, as in Libya (1969), Iraq (1958), and Iran (1979), emphasizing the rewards to be gained by playing politics in weak states. Odd coalitions that cross subcomplex boundaries are common, for example, the radical grouping among Libya, Syria, and Iran in 1980,[16] and no one is surprised to find Moroccan security forces working in sympathetic conservative Gulf states.

These habits of regional politics mean that many members of the supercomplex at large will tend to become involved in the affairs of any given subcomplex. The involvement of virtually all of the Arab states in the confrontation with Israel illustrates this tendency clearly. Outlying states like Morocco have sent troops to fight Israel, Libya has supplied much political rhetoric and has played a role in the arms race, and the Gulf Arab states have contributed extensive funding. Most Arab states experience the problem of Israel directly in the form of the Palestinian diaspora, and the Palestinians thus constitute another link that binds the supercomplex together. The fight against Israel is one of the few causes that unites the Arab states more than it divides them, and their behavior cannot be explained by normal balance of power, ideological, or security reasoning. Only those forces that bind together the supercomplex can explain why a far-flung set of states, many of which have serious conflicts among themselves, has united to oppose Israel.

Similar patterns affect the other major subcomplex in the Gulf. Iraq bridges the two subcomplexes because of its geographical position, but Jordan, Syria, Israel, Egypt, and Libya all play significant parts in Gulf affairs. These cross-linkages can lead to bizarre patterns of alignment when combined with the religious and political factionalism outlined above. Syria, for example, is currently at odds with Iraq for political reasons, and so backs Iran against Iraq in their war. This is despite the fact that Syria and Iraq share not only their Arabness but also a common stance against Israel. This current situation has to be seen against a background in which Syria and Iraq not only share, at least in name, the Baathist ideology, and in which moves toward military union between the two were being discussed as recently as 1978, but also in which Syrian domestic politics is both heavily influenced by external affairs and a significant factor in Syria's foreign policy.[17] The Syrian pattern is not unusual, for all the Arab states within the supercomplex find their domestic politics enmeshed with the politics of the region to a considerable extent. Because political relations at both levels are unstable, the insecurity that defines the supercomplex is both widespread and intricately interconnected.

We can conclude from this discussion that the area of South and Southwest Asia contains two distinct local security complexes. Each of these has its own defining security dynamic that no only provides it with a significant measure of internal cohesion but also demarcates it from its neighbors. The internal dynamics of these complexes originates with them and constitutes a prime security concern for the states involved. One immediate consequence of this analysis for our present purpose is that it requires an extended interpretation of what is encompassed by "Southwest Asia." Although we may be able to discount safely the role of the North African states, we cannot hope to understand the security problems of the Gulf states without setting them into the full context of the Middle Eastern supercomplex, including Egypt and the Horn. To attempt a regional security policy analysis on a fragment of a local complex would be to invite serious distortion in understanding the position of the states within the region.

But neither of these complexes functions as an isolated entity, and so we must look at their ties to each other as well as at their position in higher level complexes. On the local level, we can identify a number of security issues that cross the boundaries of local security complexes. Libya, for example, is militarily engaged in the internal affairs of Chad, Morocco has territorial disputes with Spain, Somalia has territorial disputes with Kenya, and until recently, Iran had security agreements with Turkey and Pakistan. All of the African states within the supercomplex are also members of the Organization of African Unity and are thus involved to varying degrees in the political affairs of the continent as a whole.

For our purposes, the most important of these links is that between the Middle Eastern and the South Asian complexes. Pakistan is the focus of this link, and it is the Islamic connection that provides much of the substance of its ties to the Middle Eastern supercomplex. In essence, Pakistan has played its Islamic card in order to cultivate relations with, and gain support from, the Middle Eastern states as part of its general strategy of maintaining a balance against India. Islamabad has cultivated political and economic links with the Gulf states in particular and has taken an active stance in the Islamic Conference. Pakistan had an important security agreement with the shah of Iran and has received arms and finance from the Gulf states in part return for the loan of its own skilled military personnel. Serious speculation also exists about Arab funding for, and participation in, the Pakistan nuclear weapons program.[18] Although these relations are significant, they do not disturb the essential integrity and separateness of the two complexes. The Middle Eastern contributions to Pakistan make only a minor contribution to its relations with India and do not create security tensions between India and the Gulf. Pakistan does not play a significant role in the security dynamics of the Middle East, and there is no discernible interaction between the local security dynamics of the two complexes. Wars between India and Pakistan have few repercussions in the Middle East, and wars in the Middle East make no greater impact on South Asia than they make on any other part of the world that depends on Middle Eastern oil.

There are two higher level security dynamics that impinge on the Middle Eastern and South Asian complexes: that between the United States and the Soviet Union and that between the Soviet Union and China. No consensus exists on whether these should be treated as two separate, but interacting, complexes or as a single, three-sided complex. We will treat them here as separate, referring to the first as the global complex between the superpowers and to the second as the Sino-Soviet complex.

The Sino-Soviet complex is centered on the rivalry between China and the Soviet Union, which became manifest after 1960. Although much of its dynamic occurs directly between the two communist giants, their rivalry has inevitably spilled over into their relations with neighboring Asian states, as well as, to a lesser degree, into their relations with states worldwide. The Soviet Union has pursued something like a containment policy against China in Asia, and China has responded by cultivating its own line of contacts, both with some of its neighbors and with major Western powers to which it was previously opposed.

The Sino-Soviet complex makes little impact on the Middle East but plays a significant role in South Asia. In the Middle East, the global superpower complex dominates, and China plays only a marginal role as an arms supplier to Egypt, North Yemen, and Sudan. Because of the prevalence of Islam, the Middle East is infertile ground for ideological competition between Peking and Moscow, and geographically it lies outside their struggle over containment in Asia. In South Asia, by contrast, substantial ties connect the local complex to its higher level neighbor. India has received major supplies of arms from the Soviet Union since 1962, and the two have been bound by a treaty of friendship since 1971. Pakistan has had a significant security relationship with China since 1963, which although not apparently formalized in a treaty, has involved both supply of arms by China to Pakistan and Chinese support for Pakistan in the 1965 and 1971 wars with India. These cross-linkages are reinforced by the direct border dispute between India and China that led to the brief war between them in 1962 and to the subsequent perception in India of China as a military rival and threat. The patterns of hostility within the two complexes thus amplify each other, the weaker powers supporting each other against the stronger, and vice versa. Given the disproportion in power between the two complexes, however, the impact of the Sino-Soviet complex on South Asia is quite large, whereas the impact of the South Asian complex on Sino-Soviet relations is small. Soviet and Chinese influence in South Asia acts to intensify the rivalry between India and Pakistan, not least by the supply of arms and the assurance of support. But India and Pakistan weigh little in Sino-Soviet affairs, and although India treats China as a major element in its security problem, India is a marginal element in Chinese security concerns. Two distinct security dynamics are at work here, but they coincide within South Asia in such a way as to reinforce the rivalry already existing in the local complex.

The impact of the global complex on South Asia is similar in form to that of the Sino-Soviet complex and is not unconnected to it. South Asia was drawn into the affairs of the global complex during the formative years of the cold war. In the early 1950s, Pakistan seized the opportunity offered by American containment policy and aligned itself with the West against the Soviet Union. This tactic enabled Pakistan to tap extensive supplies of free or low-cost arms that it could apply to its major problem of redressing the balance with India. During this period, India preferred a strictly nonaligned policy, which had the effect of alienating it from the United States. Partly because of the pressure created by the supply of modern arms to Pakistan, and partly because of the conflict with China, India's nonalignment was slowly replaced by security association with the Soviet Union, culminating in the 1971 treaty. Pakistan's relations with the United States have varied considerably in enthusiasm, but the basic alignment has remained stable, despite a low point during the period from the mid-1960s through the 1970s resulting from an American arms embargo, preoccupation in Vietnam, and disapproval of Pakistan's nuclear ambitions.

The two competitive interventions from external complexes into South Asia have tended to reinforce each other by intensifying the same local patterns of alignment. Soviet-Indian relations have been pushed by both higher complexes, and the rapprochement between the United States and China during the early 1970s removed the contradiction for Pakistan of having its two major supporters opposed to each other. Indeed, Pakistan played an important role as go-between in bringing the two together. Through the mechanism of arms supply and political support, the superpower complex, like, and in conjunction with, the Sino-Soviet one, has intensified and rigidified the pattern of insecurity within the South Asian complex. The external powers have not caused the insecurity between India and Pakistan, but they have helped to sustain it, and they have played key roles in its wars. The prospect of Chinese intervention was a significant factor in Indian military calculations during 1965, and all three powers loomed prominently during 1971. The history of the South Asia complex thus cannot be understood without comprehending both its internal dynamic and the impingement on that dynamic of the rivalries from the two higher level complexes.[19]

The impact of the superpower complex on the Middle East is much more complicated than in South Asia, reflecting the more differentiated and mobile structure of the supercomplex. We do not have the space here to review it in detail, but the basic outlines will suffice for our purposes. Both superpowers are heavily engaged in the Middle East, though the pattern of their engagement is less stable than in South Asia, having fallen victim in several places to local developments. The United States has long-standing security relations with Saudi Arabia, Israel, Jordan, Morocco, and Bahrain. It has more recently established relations with Egypt and Oman, and it has lost its relationships with Ethiopia and Iran. The Soviet Union has treaties with Iraq, Syria, Ethiopia, and South Yemen. It has supportive security relations with Algeria, Libya, and the Palestinians, and it has lost treaty relations with Egypt (1971-76) and Somalia (1974-77).[20] The Soviet Union borders directly on the Middle East, as China does on South Asia, and transboundary ethnic patterns underlie insecure boundary relations between it and Iran. Both superpowers have become engaged in the Middle East as a result of their cold war rivalry, and because the area is contiguous to the Soviet Union, it became an arena for containment. The Western powers tried to connect the containment ring of NATO, SEATO, and CENTO across the northern tier of Turkey, Iran, and Pakistan, and the Soviets tried to leapfrog their influence into wherever Arab hostility to the West provided an opening. In addition to the cold war, American and Western interest was also drawn into the region by the huge stakes in oil and by the legacy of colonial relations, including Israel.

As in South Asia, the most obvious impact of the higher complex on the local one has been to intensify local patterns of insecurity through the competitive provision of arms and political support. The superpowers are engaged to some extent in all of the subcomplexes within the region, but they are conspicuously engaged in the Gulf, the Horn, and the Arab-Israeli ones.[21] In the Horn, a revolution in Ethiopia enabled Soviet influence to supplant American, but only in exchange for the loss of Soviet presence in Somalia. The Soviets armed first Somalia, and then Ethiopia, on a considerable scale and have played an important role in the war against secessionist Eritreans. The United States has not taken over the abandoned Soviet position in Somalia on anything like a reciprocal scale, but it has reached agreement on limited base rights with the Somali government.

In the Gulf, the traditional pattern was Soviet support for Iraq, and American support for Iran and Saudi Arabia, but the revolution in Iran and the war between Iran and Iraq have left a disturbed environment in which only American support for the south Gulf Arabs seems firm. Iraq has loosened its ties with the Soviet Union, and Iran has become a center unto itself. The huge quantities of arms supplied mainly by the superpowers have greatly conditioned rivalries within this subcomplex without giving the superpowers much control over local relations. The American attempt to cultivate Iran as both a bastion of containment and a local, pro-Western hegemony collapsed disastrously in 1979, revealing in the process the dangers of trying to turn weak states into strong powers. Both superpowers now seem minded to increase their direct presence in the area, with consequences that remain to be seen both for themselves and for the local states.

In the Arab-Israeli subcomplex the pattern of superpower involvement has been intense and costly, and for the United States, filled with contradictions. The United States has been Israel's principal ally and arms supplier, and American policymakers have had the unenviable task of trying to reconcile this position with their extensive relations with Arab states fiercely opposed to Israel, such as Jordan, Saudi Arabia, and the small Gulf states. American support for Israel does not fit well with either of its other interests in the area (oil and containment) and cannot be subsumed under the unifying umbrella of its general anti-Soviet and anticommunist stance. The Soviet Union has exploited this American dilemma to the utmost, using support against Israel as its main entry into Arab politics. As in the Gulf, both countries have supplied enormous quantities of weapons. The Soviet Union has reequipped Egypt and Syria on several occasions, and the United States has done the same for Israel, and their competitive arms supply to Iraq and Saudi Arabia has also figured in the Arab-Israel military equation. Neither superpower has reaped much control over events in return for its largesse, and both have been victims of turnarounds in local attitudes.[22] The nature of their own competition forces them to continue their rivalry in the area, and the input of resources that this involves serves once again to amplify the patterns of insecurity generated by the local complex. The extent and nature of superpower involvement also reinforce the justification for treating the supercomplex as a unit. Neither superpower can disentangle itself from the numerous strands that connect the Gulf and Arab-Israel subcomplexes, and both are locked into a rivalry that spans the whole region and feeds back into the turbulent universe of Arab politics.

What can we conclude from this application to South and Southwest Asia of security complexes as a framework for analysis? The framework has enabled us to identify two distinct local complexes and to outline the way in which these interact with each other and with the higher level complexes that penetrate them. Both the local and the higher level complexes can be seen to have their own core security dynamics, and the regional security problem results from the interaction of these dynamics rather than from any one of them singly. The local and the higher level security perspectives are equally important as components of the regional security problem, but the two levels seem seldom to harmonize beyond a superficial level. A few deep harmonies of interest can be found in connections between higher and lower level complexes–for example, shared Soviet and Indian concerns about China, and, in the days of the shah, shared Iranian and American concerns about the Soviet Union. But frequently the partnerships between members of higher and lower level complexes appear to be based on expediency, with each pursuing security objectives defined by its own complex and paying little attention to the concerns of the other. Thus, Pakistan has been much more concerned about the threat from India than from the Soviet Union, and the United States has been much more concerned about the Soviet Union than about relations between Pakistan and India. Similarly, the Soviet Union has frequently found its associates in the Middle East to be more interested in fighting each other than in uniting in any larger cause, as was the case between Syria and Iraq, between Libya and Egypt, and between Somalia and Ethiopia.

This clash of interests and perceptions between the local and higher levels forms a major part of the regional security problem and is usefully highlighted by the approach through security complexes. Regional security is a problem at two different levels, and these levels are not necessarily, or even frequently, in harmony despite the superficial appearance of alignment patterns across the lower and higher level complexes. The intrusion of the higher level complexes into the lower level ones is much facilitated by the patterns of insecurity that exist on the lower level, and for this reason, the typical product of interaction between the two levels is intensification and rigidification of the the local disputes, including disputes within as well as between states. This result frequently does not serve superpower interests, as the Americans discovered in Iran and the Soviets in Egypt and Somalia. The disruptive influence of external powers is amplified by the prevalence of weak states with their fragile governments and unstable relations. It is only marginally offset by elements of control imposed by the powers on the local states. As the number, frequency, and intensity of wars in South and Southwest Asia testify, the external powers have added their own conflicts into this area much more than they have muted the local propensities for strife. After-the-event peace efforts like Camp David, and like the Soviet mediation between India and Pakistan after their 1965 war, cannot be dismissed as insignificant, but they hardly indicate control over the tide of events.

A final conclusion is that the justification for treating South and Southwest Asia as a single region rests almost exclusively on superpower perspectives of the regional security problem. It does not accord with local patterns and perceptions, except possibly in the case of Pakistan, and any analysis of regional security in this context must keep in mind that the local states are, by and large, dancing to a different tune from the superpowers. Afghanistan provides the key to tying the Middle Eastern and South Asian complexes together. It is peripheral to both local complexes, but the Soviet occupation in 1979 created a challenge to containment that threatened American and Western interests directly, more so given the exposed position of Pakistan and the collapse of Western influence in Iran. Only in the grand geostrategic perspective of the global superpower complex, as Gary Sick points out, does this area assume the unity of a "third strategic zone" in the struggle between the United States and the Soviet Union.

REGIONAL SECURITY AS A POLICY OBJECTIVE

The problem of disharmony between security perspectives at the local and global levels constitutes a core dilemma in any attempt to formulate regional security policy. As we have seen, actors at each level are likely to have quite different definitions and priorities in the region. The simultaneous pursuit of objectives by actors at different levels can easily work at cross-purposes, with the result that neither the local states nor the external powers achieve their desired ends. In defining regional security, local states tend to give priority to domestic stability, nation building, and the dynamic of the local complex within which they are situated. Global powers, by contrast, tend to define security in terms of region- and world-spanning criteria like containment, access to strategic areas, sea lines of communication, patterns of ideological alignment, and geostrategic defense considerations. There may easily be very little real correlation of interest between local and external powers that are nominally aligned. Actors at both levels are obliged to have a security policy for the area: the local states, because they are inescapably situated within it; global powers, because they cannot avoid either their own global influence or their competition with each other. Global powers influence events everywhere even if they do nothing. Because actors at both levels must have security policies, it is easy for them to fall into associations of convenience, each seizing on the apparent willingness of the other to be exploited to its own ends. Thus, Pakistan could turn its American-supplied arms against its own minorities and against India, while the United States was counting Pakistan as a vital link in its chain of containment. Similarly, as noted above, the Soviets have often found their allies in the Middle East pointing their guns at each other.

As we have argued, this disharmony of interests between the two levels is a key element in the regional security problem, because it blocks any coherent understanding of comprehensive criteria for regional security. If the local states concentrate on playing out the dynamics of their own complex, they may have little regard for the concerns of the superpowers. And if the superpowers concentrate on playing out the dynamics of their global rivalry, they may have little regard for the concerns of the local states. In such a situation, the local states risk coming out the losers, because they contrive at a game that makes them pawns. In that game, the superpowers can set objectives for themselves that override local interests completely. The United States, for example, needs to keep Saudi Arabia on its side for economic and geostrategic reasons, and that objective places major external constraints on the evolution of Saudi domestic politics. The Soviets faced a similar problem in Afghanistan, and did not hesitate to take over the country completely. Local forces can still disrupt or overwhelm superpower machinations, as in Egypt in 1972 and Iran in 1979, but they cannot free themselves from the continuous pressure of external powers using their area as an arena for their own game. The result of security games being played on different levels at cross-purposes is endemic instability and crisis. The dynamics of the local complex constantly disrupt the superpower game, thereby stimulating fresh rounds of external intervention, while the dynamics of the superpower game pump arms and political support into the local complex and in the process intensify the contradictions and conflicts within and among the local states.

Given this problem of incompatible or uncoordinated objectives at the different levels, can we use the idea of security complexes to clarify regional security as a policy objective?

If the idea of security complexes is taken as a static framework, it cannot tell us much about policy objectives. In the static mode, the principal application of the idea is in identifying appropriate units of analysis at the regional level. Such identification is useful in several respects. It allows us to make structural comparisons among security complexes as durable fixtures in the international system. It enables us to avoid silly or inappropriate assumptions about regional units of analysis like those that underlie the proposal for the Indian Ocean as a zone of peace.[23] It requires us to consider the security dynamics at both the local and the global levels, and so helps avoid the analytical biases of both regional experts and global power analysts, while incorporating the strengths of both perspectives. It also helps to clarify the choices about policy objectives by separating the different dynamics at work, but it does not suggest much about either policy options or priorities.

Security complexes, however, can also be seen as a dynamic framework, and in this mode they suggest more about policy objectives. In the dynamic mode, we view security complexes as evolving structures or subsystems within the international system overall. At any given time, we can freeze-frame the film of history and pick out the then-existing pattern of security complexes. Run the film on, and the pattern changes. Security complexes are durable but not permanent features of the international system, and we can identify a variety of lines along which they can evolve. These lines suggest general molds within which particular policy objectives might be cast, and although they do not immediately offer clear policy prescriptions for decision makers caught in the turmoil of day-to-day events, they do suggest broad objectives within which shorter range options might be assessed.

Over time, a security complex can move in any of four basic directions. First, it can continue in its current form, with the membership and the fundamental pattern of relations that define it remaining unchanged. Considerable shifts of power and alignment might take place within a complex without marking a departure from a basic status quo, as they have done within South Asia and the Middle

East during the previous three decades. Because security complexes represent quite durable patterns, "more of the same" will be a reliable forecast in most instances.

Second, a security complex can move toward an internal resolution of some sort. Two broad alternatives exist for this outcome: the effective victory of one side or the resolution of conflicts and the transformation of the complex into a security community.[24] If one side in a security complex becomes so dominant that the others give up the struggle and accept its hegemony, then the conflict that defines the complex is effectively resolved. This might happen in South Asia if India's internal development made it so powerful that Pakistan could not longer compete. It might happen in a more extreme form in the Middle East if the Arab states defeat Israel, but given the remaining disputes among the Arab states, even the elimination of Israel seems unlikely to resolve the local subcomplex. A happier form of resolution occurs if the conflicts at the heart of the complex are settled by some form of agreement among the members that enables them not to see each other as sources of threat. A security community of states in harmony with each other does not seem a likely outcome in South and Southwest Asia, but it might occur in the Horn as a result of ethnic and territorial adjustments, or in the Gulf by an extension of the Gulf Cooperation Council to include Iran and Iraq.

Third, a security complex might transform itself so radically as to require its redefinition as a unit. This could happen either because one or more of the principal members disintegrates, thereby creating a new configuration of power and sovereignty, or because the local security dynamic expands to incorporate more actors. Disintegration is perhaps easiest to imagine in South Asia. Further partitions of Pakistan could make the complex effectively monopolar, or, less likely, a breakup of India could produce a multipolar complex. Expansion could occur because of new disputes, new alliances, or the increasing power of one or more members. One could imagine, for example, a fusion of the South Asian complex with the Gulf subcomplex in two ways. Either Pakistan could greatly strengthen its ties to the Gulf states in such a way as to create an Islamic alliance against India,[25] or else two expanding and dominant powers like India and Iran could begin to define each other as regional rivals on a larger scale, as briefly appeared possible when Iran was under the shah.

Fourth, a security complex can be overlaid by a major assertion of direct presence in its affairs on the part of larger outside powers. This is most likely to happen if the local area concerned becomes a crucial arena in an intense power struggle within the global superpower complex. The superpowers will try to create boundaries for their own spheres of influence, and the dynamic of their struggle will suppress or freeze that of the local complex. The best examples of this process are in Europe and the Far East. In both places, the superpowers have committed themselves to a heavy direct presence and have established rigid boundaries between their spheres. In Europe, their boundary cuts through the middle of Germany and freezes the local security dynamic almost completely. One effect of it is to create something very like a security community in Western Europe, although the durability of that condition would only be tested in the event of the superpowers' withdrawal from the area. In the Far East, the boundary is easier to handle because it is mostly at sea, but it intersects with the local complex in Korea, where the two dynamics coincide. American attempts to extend this system to Southeast Asia failed.

These four outcomes for a security complex represent ideal types. Because they involve the intersection of two dynamics, the local and the global, they are not necessarily mutually exclusive. An internal victory might lead on to transformation by expansion, or be a result of it, and the overlay option can interrupt the local dynamic at any point. One might argue, for example, that the superpowers overlaid the local complexes in Europe and East Asia to prevent an internal victory by, respectively, Germany and Japan, from leading to expansion.

As ideal types, these four model outcomes offer a useful framework within which to consider the problem of regional security policy objectives in South and Southwest Asia. Once again, the approach through the idea of security complexes forces us to consider the separate dynamics of the local and global levels and how they interact with each other. It seems clear that the basic trend in both local complexes is for a continuation of the status quo. The defining rivalries in both complexes are still very much alive, and neither transformation nor internal resolution appears likely in the foreseeable future. In the Middle East, continuing warfare in several places is evidence of the vitality within the supercomplex. There are no strong signs of major collapses, grounds for conflict resolution, or decisive victories. In South Asia, India looks a more likely candidate for dominance than any country in the Middle East, but the process of nuclear proliferation in both India and Pakistan is sufficiently advanced to ensure that Pakistan will not easily be eliminated as a major player unless it collapses for internal reasons. If left to their own devices, the two local complexes look set to continue in the same patterns that have defined them for the last three decades. Because those patterns are deeply conflictual, we cannot expect significant initiatives toward regional security policy to come from the local states except in the context of their rivalries with each other.

For the superpowers, two levels of choice about regional security policy exist: their policies toward each other and their policies toward the local complexes. It is quite conceivable that the superpowers might not care at all about the local complexes except inasmuch as their dynamic interfered with the larger process of global rivalry. Something along these lines appears to be the case in the Gulf and the Horn, where the behavior of the United States and the Soviet Union reflects an opportunistic playing in local waters to secure objectives defined by self-interest (oil) and superpower rivalry (spheres of influence/containment). It does not appear to be the case as concerns the United States and Israel, where American policy is deeply committed to preventing certain local outcomes (the defeat of Israel) and promoting others (an internal resolution of some sort). Neither does it appear to be the case for the Soviet Union and South Asia. For Moscow, a peaceful resolution of the South Asian complex would have the advantage of freeing India to play a more active role as a balancer against China. An Indian victory might have the same effect, but only at the risk of drawing in the United States, as demonstrated by the *Enterprise* task force incident during the 1971 war.[26] The Soviets have not so far succeeded in cooling down the India-Pakistan rivalry, and it is not clear whether their new position in Afghanistan will help or hinder them in this objective. The attitudes of the Soviet Union to the local affairs of the Arab-Israel subcomplex, and of the United States to those of South Asia, in their own right, are unclear, although both superpowers are engaged in the context of their rivalry with each other.

If we consider regional security in terms of the superpowers' relations with each other, then concerns about the local complexes become secondary. Each superpower will define its desired (or required) sphere of influence, and regional security will depend on the degree of harmony or conflict between them, on the respective priorities they assign to goals in that area, and on their ability and willingness to allocate resources to that sector of their struggle. Because the historical record makes it abundantly clear that the interests of the United States and the Soviet Union conflict in this area, the question of regional security hangs on their respective willingness and ability to allocate resources to it. Their conflict of interest precludes a mutual withdrawal, which leaves them with two major options: Either they play competitively in the local complexes, trying to use the local dynamic to advance their own interest and block that of the other, or they involve themselves much more heavily and directly, by overlaying the local complexes along their own lines.

If the superpowers choose to compete indirectly through the local complexes, then the main result is to perpetuate regional instability and insecurity. By adding their own rivalry to those already present within the local complexes, the superpowers tend, as we have seen, to amplify hostility and conflict. Their own rivalry prevents them from moderating or restraining the local dynamic, and each of them can easily provide sufficient resources to the region to prevent the other from engineering a durable resolution to the local complex that works in its favor. At best, they will end up with a stalemate that follows the divisions in the local complex. Such a stalemate might well be relatively stable in terms of superpower interests, but would mean perpetual insecurity for the local states. For the superpowers, a semipermanent zone of instability may be an acceptable form of boundary: Each side can have confidence that neither can gain the upper hand in the area, provided that both restrain their own direct presence. The cost of such an arrangement is a permanent risk of crises arising from the dynamic of the local complex, and the consequent need to manage the dangers of escalation. A disadvantage of this approach is that it gravely complicates, if not makes impossible, the successful pursuit of policy objectives at the local level by either external power. In the environment created by their own rivalry, neither will be able to help resolve a local complex in the fashion it desires. Soviet support to Arab states can undo American attempts to resolve the Arab-Israeli subcomplex, and American support for Pakistan can offset Soviet attempts to encourage a security community in South Asia. One further problem with this approach is that it assumes a willingness on the part of both external powers to allow the other substantial access into the region. If one seeks to exclude the other completely, as the United States once sought to do, then the prospect of endless gaming with one's rival within the region already counts as a substantial setback. There is also a possibility that a heavy commitment by one superpower to a single party within a complex might significantly prejudice its ability to compete with its superpower rival. American support for Israel has aspects of this problem about it inasmuch as it creates opportunities for the Soviet Union, and restricts possibilities for the United States, within the Middle East supercomplex.

The second option–for the superpowers to overlay the local complexes–requires them to commit much greater resources and, therefore, presumably, to assign a high priority to their affairs within the region. This option has considerable salience for South and Southwest Asia, not only because it parallels what the superpowers have done in Europe and the Far East but also because recent developments imply an increased will on the part of both superpowers to engage their resources directly in the area. The Soviet occupation of Afghanistan, and the buildup of American naval and military forces and facilities in the Indian Ocean both imply dissatisfaction and frustration with the arms-length, indirect competition of the past. Many difficulties confront any major move in this direction, however, because the conditions in South and Southwest Asia provide no parallel with the conditions that allowed the overlay option to occur in Europe and the Far East. Three obvious factors that would impede any attempt to implement an overlay strategy are:

1. The greater unwillingness of the superpowers to confront each other directly given that the risks to both of the nuclear balance between them are much higher and better understood than in the earlier years of the cold war.

2. The absence of a clear geographical boundary between their spheres of influence, which arises from the complexities of their involvement in the Byzantine network of local alignments.

3. The near universal absence of will within the region for any major, sustained, direct presence of either superpower.

The advantage of the overlay option is that it does provide security and stability on a regional scale, whatever the costs to local interests that get trapped on either side of its lines. But the factors militating against it in South and Southwest Asia are very strong. The risk of direct conflict over the establishment of a boundary would be extremely high, and the cost of mounting a dominating local presence in the absence of substantial local backing for it would be enormous. Only the pressures arising from one superpower feeling that its local position was in danger of complete rout by the other, or that its rival's position was so weak that complete rout might be accomplished, would justify direct intervention on the necessary scale, and neither of these conditions seems likely to arise.

We can conclude, then, that the prospects for regional security and stability in South and Southwest Asia are extremely poor. No harmony of objectives exists either among the local states or among the outside states whose power impinges on the region. As a consequence, no consensus exists at either level about the conditions for a regional security regime. Furthermore, local conditions do not favor a paralyzing cold war overlay of the type instituted in Europe and the Far East, which is the only short-term option for security on a regional scale. The conflicts within the local security complexes are active and irrepressible, and they are intensified by their interaction with a major and durable superpower rivalry, which involves, as Gary Sick points out, a third phase in the struggle over containment. In these conditions, the outlook must be more of the same—which is to say, arms races, wars, interventions, coups, revolutions, terrorism, tension, and insecurity. Only if the superpowers could agree to harmonize their interests in the region would any prospect of security and stability for South and Southwest Asia emerge.

NOTES

1. Michael Brecher, "International Relations and Asian Studies: The Subordinate State System of Southern Asia," *World Politics* 15 (1963): 203-35.

2. On the pitfalls of ethnocentrism, see Ken Booth, *Strategy and Ethnocentrism* (London: Croom Helm, 1979).

3. Arnold Wolfers, *Discord and Collaboration* (Baltimore: Johns Hopkins Press, 1962), p. 147.

4. W. B. Gallie, "Essentially Contested Concepts," in *The Importance of Language*, ed. Max Black (Englewood Cliffs, N.J.: Prentice-Hall, 1962), pp. 121-46.

5. For an extensive discussion of this problem, see Barry Buzan, *People, States and Fear: The National Security Problem in International Relations* (Brighton, England: Harvester, 1983).

6. There have been four wars around Israel, two between India and Pakistan, and one between Iran and Iraq. Lesser events include fighting within and between the two Yemens, various Iran-Iraq border incidents, the fighting along the Suez Canal during 1969, various threatening troop movements by Syria, Iraq, and Jordan against each other, and the separatist and interstate wars in the Horn involving Ethiopia and Somalia.

7. Arguments in this direction can be found, for example, in P. A. Reynolds, *An Introduction to International Relations* (London: Longman, 1980), pp. 47-48; and Robert E. Osgood and Robert W. Tucker, *Force, Order and Justice*, Part II (Baltimore: Johns Hopkins Press, 1967).

8. Kenneth H. F. Dyson, *The State Tradition in Western Europe* (Oxford: Martin Robertson, 1980), pp. 205-06; and Buzan, op. cit., ch. 2.

9. Dyson, op. cit., p. 3.

10. See Buzan, op. cit., ch. 1.

11. *Guardian Weekly*, August 15, 1982, p. 14.

12. To confuse strong government with a strong state is a category error that conflates the state and its institutions (see note 9). Some writers do, however, use the term "strong state" to refer to governing institutions; see, for example, Youssef Cohen, B. R. Brown, and A. F. K. Organski, "The Paradoxical Nature of

State-Making: The Violent Creation of Order," *American Political Science Review* 75 (1981): 905-07; and Stephen D. Krasner, *Defending the National Interest: Raw Materials Investments and U.S. Foreign Policy* (Princeton, N.J.: Princeton University Press, 1978).

13. For an extensive discussion of security complexes, and a more detailed study of the South Asian complex, see Buzan, op. cit., ch. 4.

14. On the South Asian complex generally, see B. Sen Gupta, "India's Role as a Regional Power," *Journal of International Affairs* 29 (1975); G. S. Bhargava, "India's Security in the 1980s," Adelphi Paper 125 [London: International Institute for Strategic Studies (IISS), 1976]; R. G. C. Thomas, "Indian Defense Policy," *Pacific Affairs* 53 (1980); Onkar Marwah, "India and Pakistan: Nuclear Rivals," *International Organization* 35 (1981).

15. This involves Algerian backing for the Polariso, rather than direct conflict between Algerian and Moroccan forces.

16. Itamar Rabinovich, "The Foreign Policy of Syria," *Survival*, July/August 1982, p. 179.

17. See ibid. for a discussion of the domestic and foreign linkages affecting Syrian policy.

18. See, for example, Z. Khalizad, "Pakistan and the Bomb," *Survival* 21 (1979): 248; and A. Kapur, "A Nuclearizing Pakistan," *Asian Survey* 20 (1980).

19. On American, Soviet, and Chinese impact on South Asia, see, for example, R. Jackson, "The Great Powers and the Indian Subcontinent," *International Affairs* 49 (1973); J. P. Chiddick, "Indo-Soviet Relations 1966-1971," *Millennium* 3 (1974); G. J. Viksnins, "Indo-Soviet Military Cooperation," *Asian Survey* 19 (1979); Stockholm International Peace Research Institute (SIPRI), *The Arms Trade with the Third World* (Stockholm: Almqvist and Wiksell, 1971), pp. 468-501, 742-58; W. J. Barnds, "India and America at Odds," *International Affairs* 49 (1973).

20. The annual editions of the *Military Balance and Strategic Survey* (London: IISS) provide a useful record of the making and breaking of the numerous security relations within the Middle Eastern supercomplex.

21. In this context, it is interesting to note that the superpowers have conspicuously abstained from close involvement in the Algeria-Morocco dispute over the Western Sahara.

22. For an analysis of the limits to superpower influence on events in the Arab-Israeli subcomplex between 1967 and 1973, see Lawrence L. Whetten, "The Arab-Israel Dispute: Great Power Behavior," Adelphi Paper 128 (London: IISS, 1976-77).

23. See Barry Buzan, "Naval Power, the Law of the Sea, and the Indian Ocean as a Zone of Peace," *Marine Policy* 5 (1981). The attempt to make a meaningful regional security entity out of the Indian Ocean cannot avoid drawing a boundary that cuts through the middle of virtually every security complex except the South Asian one that borders on that ocean. The chance of reaching a significant security agreement under such conditions is vanishingly small. Even the limited attempt by the United States and the Soviet Union to find a basis for naval limitations foundered, among other reasons, because of the difficulty of agreeing on measures for naval presence.

24. On the idea of security communities, see Karl Deutsch et al., *Political Community and the North Atlantic Area* (Princeton, N.J.: Princeton University

Press, 1957); and K. J. Holsti, *International Politics: A Framework for Analysis* (Englewood Cliffs, N.J.: Prentice-Hall, 1967), ch. 16.

25. One possible vehicle for such a development would be if Pakistan became a supplier of nuclear weapons for Islamic states.

26. J. M. McConnell and H. M. Kelley, "Super-power Naval Diplomacy: Lessons of the Indo-Pakistan Crisis 1981," *Survival*, November/December 1973.

11

Observations

Alvin Z. Rubinstein

The preceding chapters emphasize the difficulty of trying to promote security and stability in a region of weak and unstable states. National rivalries, ethnic separatism, religious cleavages, Islamic militancy, political unrest, and socioeconomic disruptiveness stemming from mismanaged modernization are pandemic. These forces, so capriciously destabilizing, mock long-term strategies for managing change, but they are more unpredictable than unmanageable.

Perhaps the most portentous unknown is the effect of Ayatollah Rouhollah Khomeini's stern brand of Islamic fundamentalism on the politics of the Gulf. Having spawned the erratic but successful Iranian revolution, Khomeinism has surmounted various internal challenges and the aggression from Iraq and become a force for both national renewal and regional insecurity. Its shock waves continue to unsettle the domestic politics and international relations of the region and make building stability a highly tentative endeavor. Yet, for all the military prowess that it demonstrated in humbling Iraq, Iran today is much weaker militarily than it was in the heyday of the shah, and its threat to the Arab regimes in the Gulf is less military than ideological.

The Arabs know this. They recognize the unlikelihood of a direct Iranian attack—except on Iraq—fearing rather that Iran's militant theocratic regime might be seen by opponents of modernization and alienated minorities as an alternative to their oligarchic, Western-linked, rule. If so, one way for the West to reassure the oil-rich kingdoms of the Arabian Peninsula would be to make unmistakably clear to Tehran that any military attack would encounter an immediate and appropriate response, that Khomeini will not be permitted to use the sword to spread his revolution abroad. Deterring the aggressive impulses in Khomeinism would serve to strengthen the resolve of the Gulf Arabs to act firmly in the face of subversion and give added pause to radicals who might, out of misjudgment, strike at existing governments in the expectation of armed assistance from Iran. On the other hand, it will be far more difficult, should present efforts to modernize and promote change be rejected or be proven inapplicable, to dispel the belief that Khomeini's proposed theocratic solution for Iran's internal turmoil is a feasible alternative for the Arab states of the Gulf. How to prevent the rivulets of discontent from converging and sweeping away the present system of Arab rule ultimately depends on the political, not military, acumen and actions of the Arab rulers themselves.

There was broad agreement among the conferees, though not unanimity, on the proposition that the Soviet Union is not at present the principal threat to security and stability in the Gulf-Indian Ocean region, despite the Soviet occupation of Afghanistan. This point was made forcefully by one Indian analyst: "India has lived with a U.S. presence in Iran for 30 years; and it could live with a Soviet presence (in Iran and Afghanistan) as well." The view that Moscow would be willing to hazard a military takeover in the Gulf was, given the West's dependence on the region's oil and the likely reaction of the United States, not considered convincing.

Just as heightened nervousness in the region is more often than not a function of the fear of subversion and disruptive domestic forces and not of a Soviet invasion, so Washington's attempt to establish a permanent military presence in the Gulf is seen as more potentially destabilizing to the regimes the United States seeks to strengthen than anything the Soviet Union can or is apt to do in the region. The Gulf Arabs' reaction is to counter Washington's constant chatter about a Soviet threat with hyperbole on the centrality of the Arab-Israeli dispute and the danger to them of U.S. support of Israel and the Camp David accords. They want a U.S. presence in the region, but a discreet one. The conferees believed that Arab-Western interests would be better served if the United States maintained an over-the-horizon presence that could be brought to bear very quickly in the event of need, rather than on-the-ground bases. The discussions, however, revealed that there were quite differing views on the nature and hierarchy of threats to pro-Western leaderships in the region, as well as the preferred ways to cope with them.

There was agreement that the potential role of middle powers in helping to promote security in the region was a neglected subject. Given the inability of the United States and the Soviet Union to control events, and the prevalence of regional fragmentation, it was believed that the countries of Western Europe and India–the middle powers considered most suitable prospects for a greater role–might be able to contribute to the twin processes of nation building and building security in the Gulf-Indian Ocean region.

It was suggested that to be effective a Western European role should be cast within a multilateral framework; it should focus on efforts at institution building between the European Community and, for example, the Gulf Cooperation Council. Unilateral and bilateral initiatives, although useful, have a stop-gap, temporal character; they need to be supplemented by longer term ties between regions. There was agreement that these and similar views, though highly tentative, merit further exploration. Furthermore, if the Western Europeans want to play a more active role in the Gulf, they may have to rethink the hard questions about military expenditures and the kinds of conventional forces they should maintain, first, to enhance their credibility as a security alternative to the superpowers and, second, to improve their ability to influence U.S. policy.

India, seemingly a likely candidate to play a part in promoting stability and security in the Gulf, has so far done little. Preoccupied with Pakistan, China, and the Soviet Union, New Delhi has viewed the region and its problems with Indocentric detachment. Economic relations, though potentially significant and growing somewhat, remain of marginal importance to both India and the Gulf countries. For the time being, India prefers to stress its involvement in the nonaligned movement, despite the problems inherent in being a nonaligned country surrounded by unfriendly nonaligned states. A more active Indian role in the Gulf is unlikely also because the Indian leadership does not perceive a threat to India from anywhere in Southwest Asia, including even the Soviet military presence in Afghanistan. Moreover, New Delhi is realistic enough to know that better relations with the Arab governments of the Gulf, and even with Iran, cannot be secured without first effecting a reconciliation with Pakistan. Peace with Pakistan is prerequisite for any active Indian engagement in the Gulf. There are occasional glimmers of greater Indian interest in the Gulf, but nothing sustained or substantive. In the foreseeable future, as in the recent past, India is likely to be a marginal actor in the Persian Gulf region.

Security and stability both entail not just a military dimension, but political, economic, cultural, and social dimensions as well. Though interrelated conditions, they are independent, and the assumption is unwarranted that one cannot be had without the other. Indeed, any notion of security that overlooks how inherently unstable and fragile are most of the states in South and Southwest Asia runs the risk of defining the term so narrowly as to be counterproductive. What we are left with is agreement that no one analytical model for building security and stability will suffice; that perceptions of level of analysis (that is, nation-state, regional, global) all have something useful to contribute; that in the current situation of complexity and uncertainty, the superpowers alone cannot ensure either security or stability; and that piecemeal approaches need to be developed and continually adapted to the restlessly changing reality in the Third World.

Index

About The Contributors

BARRY BUZAN is lecturer in the Department of International Studies, University of Warwick (United Kingdom). He received his Ph.D. from the London School of Economics and spent two years as a postdoctoral research fellow at the Institute of International Relations of the University of British Columbia. His publications include *People, States and Fear: The National Security Problem in International Relations* (forthcoming); and *Change and the Study of International Relations* (co-editor).

SHAHRAM CHUBIN is director of research of the Program for Strategic and International Security Studies at the Graduate Institute of International Studies in Geneva and a fellow of the International Institute for Strategic Studies in London. He has written widely on Middle Eastern affairs and regional security. His publications include *Iran's Foreign Relations; Soviet Policy Toward Iran and the Gulf;* and articles in *Survival, International Security, Problems of Communism,* and *Foreign Policy.*

ADEED DAWISHA is deputy director of studies at the Royal Institute of International Affairs, London. In addition to numerous articles, he is the author of *Egypt in the Arab World: The Elements of Foreign Policy; Saudi Arabia's Search for Security;* and *Syria and the Lebanese Crisis.* His most recent work is *The Soviet Union in the Middle East: Policies and Perspectives* (co-editor).

KEITH A. DUNN is a strategy analyst at the Strategic Studies Institute, U.S. Army War College. He has contributed chapters to several books on Soviet foreign and defense policy. His articles have appeared in various journals, including *Orbis, World Affairs, Naval War College Review, Parameters, Journal of the Royal United Services Institute for Defense Studies,* and *Military Review.*

ASWINI K. RAY is associate professor of political studies at the Jawaharlal Nehru University in New Delhi. He received his Ph.D. from the University of Heidelberg and was a research fellow at the university's South Asia Institute from 1969 to 1973. His publications include *Domestic Compulsions and Foreign Policy: Pakistan in Indo-Soviet Relations* and articles in various scholarly journals.

ALVIN Z. RUBINSTEIN is professor of political science at the University of Pennsylvania and senior fellow of the Foreign Policy Research Institute. He is the recipient of a number of awards, including fellowships from the Ford, Rockefeller, Guggenheim, and Earhart foundations. Among his publications are *Soviet Policy Toward Turkey, Iran, and Afghanistan; Soviet Foreign Policy Since World War II: Imperial and Global;* and *Red Star on the Nile: The Soviet-Egyptian Influence Relationship Since the June War.*

BHABANI SEN GUPTA is research professor at the Centre for Policy Research in New Delhi. The recipient of a number of awards, including a Rockefeller Foundation Fellowship, he received his Ph.D. from the City University of New York and was a senior fellow of the Research Institute on Communist Affairs of Columbia University. His publications include *Soviet-Asian Relations in the 1970s and Beyond: An Interperceptual Study; Communism in Indian Politics;* and *Fulcrum of Asia: Relations Among China, India, Pakistan, and the Soviet Union.*

GARY G. SICK, who retired as a captain in the U.S. Navy in 1981, served in the office of the secretary of defense and on the National Security Council during the Ford and Carter administrations. His responsibilities focused on the Middle East, with particular emphasis on U.S. policy in the Persian Gulf and Indian Ocean. Dr. Sick spent the 1981–82 academic year as a research associate at Columbia University writing a book on U.S. policy toward Iran. He joined the Ford Foundation in the fall of 1982.

MICHAEL STERNER was a career American diplomat for 25 years, with the bulk of his experience in Middle East affairs. He was ambassador to the United Arab Emirates in 1974–76. From 1977 to 1981, he was deputy assistant secretary of state with special responsibility for Arab-Israeli peace negotiations. He is now a consultant based in Washington, D.C.

SHIRIN TAHIR-KHELI is currently a member of the Policy Planning Staff of the U.S. Department of State, on leave from Temple University, where she is associate professor of political science. She is a fellow of the Foreign Policy Research Institute, and spent the 1980–82 period as a senior analyst at the Strategic Studies Institute, U.S. Army War College. Her publications include *The United States and Pakistan: The Evolution of an Influence Relationship; U.S. Strategic Interests in Southwest Asia* (editor); and *The Iran-Iraq War: Old Conflicts, New Weapons* (co-editor).

Additional Conference Participants

Dr. Karen Dawisha, Center for International Studies, London School of Economics

Pierre Lellouche, Institut Francais des Relations Internationales, Paris

Dr. Giacomo Luciani, Istituto Affari Internazionali, Rome

Jagat Mehta, Foreign Secretary (Retired), Ministry of External Affairs, Government of India

Dr. James Piscatori, Royal Institute of International Affairs, London

Dr. M. M. Puri, Panjab University, Chandigarh, India

Dr. Udo Steinbach, Deutsches Orient-Institut, Hamburg, West Germany

Mrs. Frankie R. Rubinstein, Conference Secretary